The COMPLETE ILLUSTRATED *Guide to*

Shaping Wood

LONNIE BIRD

The Taunton Press

The Taunton Press
Inspiration for hands-on living®

The Taunton Press, Inc., 63 South Main Street, PO Box 5506, Newtown, CT 06470-5506
e-mail: tp@taunton.com

DESIGN: Lori Wendin

LAYOUT: Suzi Yannes

ILLUSTRATOR: Mario Ferro

PHOTOGRAPHER: Lonnie Bird

LIBRARY OF CONGRESS CATALOGING-IN-PUBLICATION DATA:
Bird, Lonnie.
   The complete illustrated guide to shaping wood / Lonnie Bird.
      p. cm.
   Includes index.
   ISBN: 978-1-56158-400-0 hardcover
   ISBN: 978-1-62710-766-2 paperback
   1. Woodwork. I. Title.

TT180 .B57 2001
684'.08--dc21   2001027430

Printed in the United States of America
10 9 8 7 6 5 4 3 2 1

To Linda and our beautiful daughters, Rebecca and Sarah.

Acknowledgments

WRITING A BOOK IS A TEAM EFFORT that requires the ideas, support, and work of many people. Through this work, new friendships are often forged and old friendships are deepened. With this in mind, I want to say thanks to the many people who helped me with this project:

Mike Foster of Freeborn Tools, for providing custom shaper cutterheads. Brian Boggs, for allowing me to photograph his steam-bending process. Helen Albert and Jennifer Renjilian of The Taunton Press, for their patience and encouragement. Andy Rae, for his ideas and critical feedback. Gary Rogowski, for providing photos. Jason Bennett, woodworker, friend, and patient stand-in, for many of the photos in this book.

Most of all, I want to thank my wife and best friend, Linda. Without her love, patience, and hard work, this book would not have been possible.

Contents

SECTION 1 Tools · 8

SECTION 2 Materials · 27

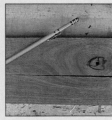

PART TWO Cutting Shapes · 32

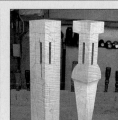

Introduction

SHAPE IS A FUNDAMENTAL ELEMENT of design. All furniture styles, even seemingly simple designs such as Shaker, use shape to enhance, increase function, and define style. For example, the sensuous curve of a chair back adds comfort as well as visual appeal, and the slender taper of a table leg creates lightness without sacrificing strength. Shape is critical to the ultimate success or failure of a piece of furniture. It simply can't be ignored.

Before shapes can be created, they must first be visualized and then drawn. There are tools and templates available for drawing geometric shapes; but organic, freeform curves are often best sketched freehand. Fortunately, the natural movements of the wrist and elbow make it possible for anyone to draw flowing curves with a bit of practice.

As I've illustrated in this book, the choices available for shaping are numerous. And it's not necessary to have access to a shop full of power tools, either. Many woodworkers are rediscovering hand tools along with the pleasure and satisfaction that comes with their use. Planes, saws, chisels, and other edge tools all require patience and a degree of skill; but they yield a handmade look and texture as well as a deep sense of accomplishment.

Learning to tune and effectively use power tools can be satisfying, too. And many power tool techniques, such as template shaping, yield efficiency that is unmatched with hand tools. Machines are also a good choice for many labor-intensive tasks, such as planing and sawing stock to size, providing more time for creating details by hand that machines simply can't duplicate. For example, a bandsaw is an efficient choice for sawing a curve in preparation for refining and sculpting the same curve with a spokeshave and a rasp. As a long-time woodworker who seeks pleasure from the craft, I've learned to enjoy both hand and power tools for what each has to offer.

As you explore the pages of this book, it's my hope that you'll be inspired by the creativity and challenge that comes with adding shapes to your next woodworking project.

How to Use This Book

IRST OF ALL, this book is meant to be used, not put on a shelf to gather dust. It's meant to be pulled out and opened on your bench when you need to do a new or unfamiliar technique. So the first way to use this book is to make sure it's near where you do woodworking.

In the pages that follow you'll find a wide variety of methods that cover the important processes of this area of woodworking. Just as in many other practical areas, in woodworking there are often many ways to get to the same result. Why you choose one method over another depends on several factors:

Time. Are you in a hurry or do you have the leisure to enjoy the quiet that comes with hand tools?

Your tooling. Do you have the kind of shop that's the envy of every woodworker or a modest collection of the usual hand and power tools?

Your skill level. Do you prefer simpler methods because you're starting out or are you always looking to challenge yourself and expand your skills?

The project. Is the piece you're making utilitarian or an opportunity to show off your best work?

In this book, we've included a wide variety of techniques to fit these needs.

To find your way around the book, you first need to ask yourself two questions: What result am I trying to achieve? What tools do I want to use to accomplish it?

In some cases, there are many ways and many tools that will accomplish the same result. In others, there are only one or two sensible ways to do it. In all cases, however, we've taken a practical approach; so you may not find your favorite exotic method for doing a particular process. We have included every reasonable method and then a few just to flex your woodworking muscles.

To organize the material, we've broken the subject down to two levels. "Parts" are major divisions of this class of techniques. "Sections" contain related techniques. Within sections, techniques and procedures that create a similar result are grouped together, usually organized from the most common way to do it to methods requiring specialized tools or a larger degree of skill. In some cases, the progression starts with the method requiring the most basic technology and then moves on to alternative methods using other common shop tools and finally to specialized tools.

The first thing you'll see in a part is a group of photos keyed to a page number. Think of this as an illustrated table of contents. Here you'll see a photo representing each section in that part, along with the page on which each section starts.

Each section begins with a similar "visual map," with photos that represent major groupings of techniques or individual techniques. Under each grouping is a list of the step-by-step essays that explain how to do the methods, including the pages on which they can be found.

Sections begin with an "overview," or brief introduction, to the methods described

therein. Here's where you'll find important general information on this group of techniques, including any safety issues. You'll also read about specific tools needed for the operations that follow and how to build jigs or fixtures needed for them.

The step-by-step essays are the heart of this book. Here a group of photos represents the key steps in the process. The accompanying text describes the process and guides you through it, referring you back to the photos. Depending on how you learn best, either read the text first or look at the photos and drawings; but remember, they are meant to work together. In cases where there is an

The "VISUAL MAP" tells you where to locate the essay that details the operation you wish to do.

A "SECTION" groups related processes together.

The "OVERVIEW" gives you important general information about the group of techniques, tells you how to build jigs and fixtures, and provides advice on tooling and safety.

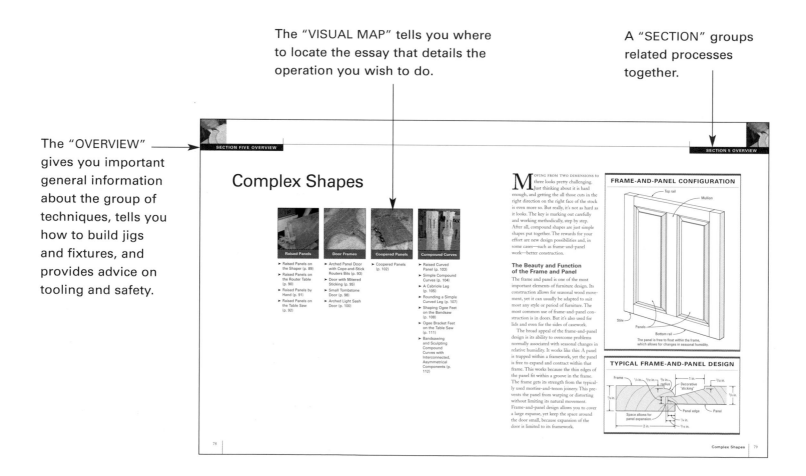

SECTION FIVE OVERVIEW

SECTION 5 OVERVIEW

Complex Shapes

Raised Panels

► Raised Panels on the Shaper (p. 89)
► Raised Panels on the Router Table (p. 90)
► Raised Panels by Hand (p. 91)
► Raised Panels on the Table Saw (p. 92)

Door Frames

► Arched Panel Door with Cope-and-Stick Routers Bits (p. 93)
► Door with Mitered Sticking (p. 95)
► Small Tombstone Door (p. 98)
► Arched Light Sash Door (p. 100)

Coopered Panels

► Coopered Panels (p. 102)

Compound Curves

► Raised Curved Panel (p. 103)
► Simple Compound Curves (p. 104)
► A Cabriole Leg (p. 105)
► Rounding a Simple Curved Leg (p. 107)
► Shaping Ogee Feet on the Bandsaw (p. 108)
► Ogee Bracket Feet on the Table Saw (p. 111)
► Bandsawing and Sculpting Compound Curves with Interconnected, Asymmetrical Components (p. 112)

MOVING FROM TWO DIMENSIONS to three looks pretty challenging. Just thinking about it is hard enough, and getting the all those cuts in the right direction on the right face of the stock is even more so. But really, it's not as hard as it looks. The key is marking out carefully and working methodically, step by step. After all, compound shapes are just simple shapes put together. The rewards for your effort are new design possibilities and, in some cases—such as frame-and-panel work—better construction.

The Beauty and Function of the Frame and Panel

The frame and panel is one of the most important elements of furniture design. Its construction allows for seasonal wood movement, yet it can usually be adapted to suit most any style or period of furniture. The most common use of frame-and-panel construction is in doors. But it's also used for lids and even for the sides of casework.

The broad appeal of the frame-and-panel design is its ability to overcome problems normally associated with seasonal changes in relative humidity. It works like this: A panel is trapped within a framework, yet the panel is free to expand and contract within that frame. This works because the thin edges of the panel fit within a groove in the frame. The frame gets its strength from the typically used mortise-and-tenon joinery. This prevents the panel from warping or distorting without limiting its natural movement. Frame-and-panel design allows you to cover a large expanse, yet keep the space around the door small, because expansion of the door is limited to its framework.

FRAME-AND-PANEL CONFIGURATION

Top rail

Mullion

Stile

Panels

Bottom rail

The panel is free to float within the frame, which allows for changes in seasonal humidity.

TYPICAL FRAME-AND-PANEL DESIGN

Frame

Decorative "sticking"

Space allows for panel expansion

Panel edge

Panel

alternative step, it's called out in the text and the visual material as a "variation."

For efficiency, we've cross-referenced redundant processes or steps described in another related process. You'll see yellow "cross-references" called out frequently in the overviews and step-by-step essays.

When you see this symbol, ⚠ make sure you read what follows. The importance of these safety warnings cannot be overemphasized. Always work safely and use safety devices, including eye and hearing protection. If you feel uncomfortable with a technique, don't do it, try another way.

At the back of the book is an index to help you find what you're looking for in a pinch. There's also list of further reading to help you brush up on how to use tools and keep them sharp, as well as some general references on design.

Finally, remember to use this book whenever you need to refresh your memory or to learn something new. It's been designed to be an essential reference to help you become a better woodworker. The only way it can do this is if you make it as familiar a workshop tool as your favorite bench chisels.

—The editors

"STEP-BY-STEP ESSAYS" contain photos, drawings, and instructions on how to do the technique.

"CROSS-REFERENCES" tell you where to find a related process or the detailed description of a process in another essay.

The "TEXT" contains keys to the photos and drawings.

"TIPS" show short-cuts and smart ways to work.

"VARIATIONS" show alternatives for doing a step.

"WARNINGS" tell you specific safety concerns for this process and how to address them.

Tools, page 8

Materials, page 27

PART ONE

Tools and Materials

THIS BOOK WAS DESIGNED to give you many techniques and options for making shapes in wood. By showing several methods to achieve a result, you can choose the technique that works best for you and suits the tooling that you have available. But choosing the right tools for the job is essential to creating shapes, from designing and laying out the shapes to cutting, turning, carving, or bending them. This part introduces the tools for shaping wood and provides advice how best to use them and, more important, how to use them safely.

The shaping techniques discussed here all apply to wood, but all lumber is not the same. The characteristics of the stock can affect the success of shaping operations. Before you take on a project, take the time to understand the type of lumber you need for the kind of operation you have chosen, and select your stock carefully.

Tools

A CRITICAL FIRST STEP BEFORE cutting any shape is to plan the cuts and make a layout. Good layout forms a critical road map to the shaping sequence and direction. It also provides key information such as angle of direction, curve of line, and accurate spacing. To create accurate layout lines, you'll need a few good-quality tools.

Layout Tools

Squares are certainly the most common layout tool and something that no woodworker can be without. Squares have a multitude of uses, including setting machinery, checking squareness of stock, and laying out and transferring perpendicular lines.

It pays to get a quality square; in fact, cheap squares are often not truly 90 degrees. Even if they have a true 90-degree angle, cheap squares are usually not solid enough to withstand the inevitable knocks they'll suffer in an average workshop. You can check a square for accuracy by using it to

Basic layout tools include a steel rule with gradations to 1/64 in. and a reliable combination square.

A combination square excels at transferring dimensions, especially in multiple parts.

Sliding bevels can be used to transfer angles accurately and for joinery layout, such as dovetails.

draw a pair of lines perpendicular to the edge of a board. If the lines are not parallel, the difference represents twice the error of the square.

The combination square is most useful because the sliding head gives it greater versatility than other types. It can be used as an inside and an outside square, a gauge for marking parallel lines, a depth gauge, and a 45-degree square.

The *sliding bevel* is used for laying out and checking angles other than 90 degrees. Bevels consist of a steel blade that pivots and locks within a steel or wood handle. The best bevels have a locking lever that swings out of the way; others use a wing nut, which can sometimes be an obstruction. Years ago, bevels were available in about five sizes, ranging from 6 in. all the way to 14 in. Unfortunately, it's difficult to find more than one or two sizes of bevels today, unless you search local flea markets or tool auctions for the old ones.

Triangles are available wherever drafting supplies are sold. The most common are the

TESTING A SQUARE FOR 90-DEGREE ACCURACY

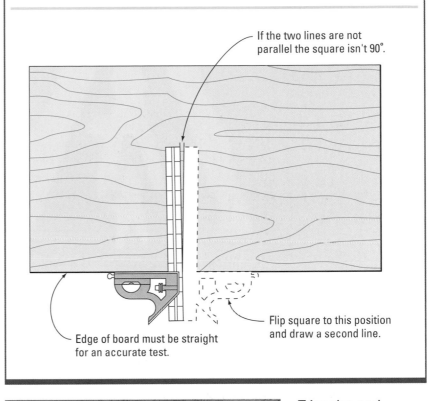

If the two lines are not parallel the square isn't 90°.

Flip square to this position and draw a second line.

Edge of board must be straight for an accurate test.

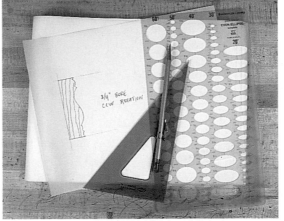

Triangles and templates are invaluable when designing complex shapes such as molding profiles.

45/90 degree and the 30/60/90 degree. Both are available in sizes as small as a few inches to as large as a foot or more. They're useful for drawing and laying out geometric shapes.

You can transfer measurements with a divider or step off divisions of a line or segments of an arc. When one side is fit with a pencil, the tool becomes a compass for drawing circles.

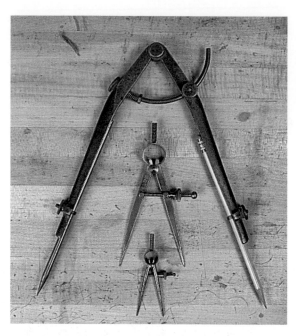

A French curve is an invaluable aid for designing flowing curves.

A trammel is used to draw large circles, beyond the range of a compass.

Like the square, the *rule* is another common and invaluable tool. Most steel tapes and wooden folding rules measure in 16ths of an inch. While this is fine in most cases, it's advantageous to have a steel rule with etched divisions down to $\frac{1}{64}$ in. The etched lines provide a way to position accurately a sharp pencil, scriber, or the legs of a divider.

As their name implies, *dividers* are used for accurately dividing a line into equal segments. Setting dividers is often a process of trial and error. The line is stepped off and the legs are adjusted until the final step lands at the end of the line. Although dividers are useful for stepping off divisions on a straight line, they are equally useful for dividing segments of a curve or a circle. Another use for dividers is checking and transferring measurements on turnings and carvings. Although most woodworking tool catalogs carry only one size of dividers, it's useful to have three or four sizes. For a greater selection, check with a supplier of machinist's tools.

Some dividers are designed with a removable leg that can be replaced with a pencil for use as a compass. The *compass* is used for drawing circles and arcs. Large circles, beyond the range of a compass, are best drawn with a *trammel*. This tool consists of a pair of steel points that clamp to a stick. One of the points can be replaced with a pencil for drawing.

If you have only an occasional need to draw a large circle or arc, a length of stick will work. First, drill a hole in each end at a distance equal to the radius. Next, insert a pencil at one end and a nail at the other. This simple shopmade layout tool is much more accurate than using a pencil and string, which tends to stretch during use.

Although small-diameter circles can be drawn with a compass, a circle template is much easier and more efficient to use. When you must draw a curved design repeatedly, make a template of your own from plywood.

If you enjoy building furniture with curves, a set of *French curves* will enable you to smooth out the bumps in the layout. French curves are plastic templates that come in three or four sizes. Their flowing lines are helpful anytime you're drawing freeform curves.

Basic Shaping Tools

Often the most efficient way to cut a shape is to use power tools; however, don't discount the pleasure of using hand tools. They're quiet and create shavings rather than chips and dust. If you do use power tools, always keep safety at the top of your mind. Some of the most useful tools for cutting shapes are profiled below.

The *table saw* is one of the most versatile machines in any woodworking shop. Besides cutting stock to width and length, the table saw is also useful for cutting simple geometric shapes, such as rectangles and octagons. With the right jigs and accessories, you can also use your table saw to cut tapers, create coves, and even shape moldings.

The *jointer* works as an inverted plane to flatten and straighten stock before milling it to size. Although the 6-in. and 8-in. jointers are most common, a larger jointer will allow you to flatten wide, figured boards for tabletops and door panels. For a bargain on a 12-in. or 16-in. jointer, search the internet

A table saw, basic shop equipment, excels at dimensioning stock. It can be used for cutting bevels and tapers, raising panels, and cutting coves.

▶ TABLE SAW SAFETY

- Never saw freehand. Always use the fence, miter gauge, or a jig that rides the fence or the miter gauge slot.
- Use a splitter whenever possible.
- Use a guard.
- Use push sticks when ripping narrow stock.

A splitter helps prevent dangerous kickback. Always use a push stick when ripping narrow stock.

A jointer mills stock true and flat to create reference points for other dimensioning operations.

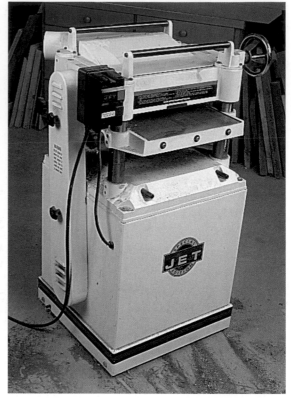

The planer serves two purposes: milling stock flat to the jointed face and thicknessing it to dimension.

▶ JOINTER SAFETY

- Stock should be at least 12 in. long.
- Always use the guard.
- Use push blocks and push sticks to keep your hands away from the cutterhead.

▶ PLANER SAFETY

- Keep your hands away from the infeed rolls.
- Stock should be at least 12-in. long.
- If a board gets stuck, turn off the machine before lowering the bed and removing the stock.

for used machines. Investigate any used machines closely to be sure of what you're buying.

After stock has been flattened on the jointer it can be run through a *planer* to achieve a smooth, parallel face. Be aware, though, that planers don't straighten stock; they only smooth it and mill it to thickness. So it's necessary to have a jointer as a companion for this machine.

A 15-in.-wide planer will handle most boards. Fortunately, as woodworking has grown in popularity a number of high-quality affordable planers have been introduced into the market.

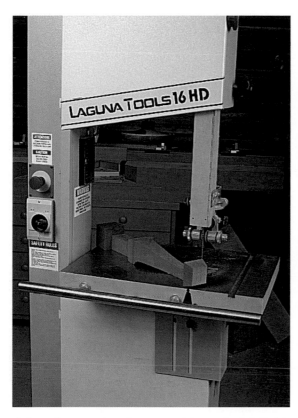

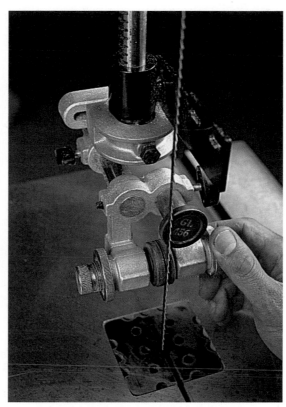

A bandsaw not only can cut broad and tight curves but can rip lumber and cut accurate joinery.

European bandsaws often have advanced blade guides that allow easy adjustments, without the need for additional tools.

The *bandsaw* is one of the most useful tools for cutting and shaping curves, but it does more than just cut curves. It's the tool of choice for ripping rough lumber. A bandsaw can also resaw thick boards into thin ones, slice veneer, and cut surprisingly accurate joints.

The common 14-in. bandsaw is a popular machine. And you can double its resaw capacity with a riser block that fits into the column. But an even better choice is one of the larger European bandsaws. For a little more money, you'll get more sawing capacity, a larger table to better support the stock, and a motor with greater horsepower. European bandsaws also come equipped

with unique guides that are quick and easy to adjust.

Once you've found a bandsaw, don't forget the blades. A small assortment of blades to choose from yields far better results than using one blade for everything. On the other hand, you can spend your evenings poring over a blade catalog, trying to determine the correct blade to use, and just end up more confused than ever. If so, just remember this simple rule: Use a narrow blade for cutting tight curves and a wide blade for broad, sweeping curves. When selecting the blade pitch (teeth per inch), use a blade with fewer teeth for thick stock and a fine pitch blade for thin stock. A good rule of thumb is to

▶ BANDSAW SAFETY

- Lower the upper guide to within ¼ in. of the work.
- Keep hands and fingers out of the path of the blade.
- If the blade breaks or runs off the wheels, do not open the covers until the machine has come to a complete stop.
- Close the covers before turning on the machine.
- Stop the saw before removing small chips that have become stuck in the throat.
- Decrease the feed pressure as you near the end of the cut.
- Keep the guard in place.
- Use push sticks when ripping or resawing.

▶ SCROLLSAW SAFETY

- As you follow the twists and turns of the outline, be aware of the position of your fingers and keep them from the path of the blade.
- Use the hold-down with the guard that comes with the machine.
- Turn the machine off immediately if the blade breaks.

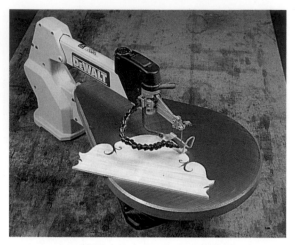

A scrollsaw makes quick and accurate work of cutting tight curves; and because the blade can be detached, it can be used for cutting interior curves.

Sometimes called a chop saw, the miter saw has replaced the radial-arm saw in many shops.

use a blade that places 6 to 12 teeth in contact with the stock.

The *scrollsaw* is the tool of choice for precise cutting of delicate stock and for sawing interior curves. Scrollsaws use short, narrow reciprocating blades, which reach into areas that a bandsaw can't. Because the blade is clamped at each end, it can be released and threaded through a hole in the stock to cut a trapped curve.

Scrollsaws have come a long way in recent years. The best saws are smooth running and virtually free of vibration. When shopping, look for a saw with electronic variable speed. This feature allows you to adjust the speed precisely for the thickness and density of the stock.

▶ MITER SAW SAFETY

- Keep your hands positioned at least 6 in. from the path of the blade.
- Use blades designed specifically for miter saws. The wrong type of blade can grab unexpectedly; read and follow the manufacturer's guidelines.

The miter saw has all but replaced the radial-arm saw for precision crosscutting. Miter saws are compact, accurate, and inexpensive. And although they are smaller than radial-arm saws, sliding-arm miter saws will typically cut stock up to a foot wide.

To get the most from your miter saw, build a stand for it with extensions that support long stock. Further, add a stop system for cutting multiples conveniently and accurately.

A *spindle sander* spins and reciprocates as it smooths the saw marks from curved surfaces. All spindle sanders come with at least five drums of different diameters, so you can easily match the drum size to the contour. A spindle sander is a perfect match for the bandsaw and the benchtop sanders are both compact and affordable.

Think of the *spokeshave* as a small plane with side handles. Its short sole makes it ideal for smoothing and shaping curves. The sole of the spokeshave works like the sole of a bench plane to span the ridges and cut them away.

A spindle sander is used to smooth away saw marks after machines like the bandsaw have cut curved shapes.

Spokeshaves excel at smoothing and shaping curves.

Like early planes, early spokeshaves were wooden. These shaves have an iron set at a low angle much like a miniature drawknife. With the introduction of metal planes in the nineteenth century, along came metal spokeshaves. During this time, spokeshaves became available in a wide variety of shapes. Some soles were concave; others convex. There were even shaves with specially designed fences for cutting chamfers. Although the variety isn't nearly as wide today, you can still find useful, yet inexpensive, spokeshaves at almost any flea market.

The *drawknife* also has a pair of side handles and is designed to be pulled or "drawn" toward you. By tilting the handle, you can

A drawknife is ideal for creating long, slender shapes—such as tapered octagons—and helps round stock.

A card or hand scraper is a quick way to smooth away saw marks and is often the best way to smooth highly figured stock.

The compass plane was designed to shape and refine rounded shapes. It can flex in either direction for shaping interior or exterior rounds.

achieve an amazing amount of control. Drawknives are most useful for shaping long, slender stock, such an octagonal taper.

▶ See *"Eight-Sided Taper"* on p. 53.

A *scraper* is a smoothing tool that actually cuts with a tiny burr that's on its edge. Scrapers are most useful for smoothing difficult figured stock that would tear out with

most edge tools. Unlike many hand tools, scrapers are still available in a wide variety of styles. The most common is the ordinary card scraper, which is flexed and pushed across the surface. Chair scrapers resemble spokeshaves. Their small blades are fit within a body with side handles to give greater control. Because of its short sole, the chair scraper works extremely well for smoothing tight contours.

Although there's a learning curve associated with sharpening scrapers, the time and effort are well worth it. When properly sharpened, a scraper cuts much faster than abrasives and leaves a scratch-free surface, too.

Sometimes called a circular plane, the *compass plane* has a thin, flexible steel sole. An adjustment knob turns to flex the sole in either a concave or a convex shape. Although it can be useful for smoothing any broad curve, the compass plane works best on segments of true circles.

For best results when using a compass plane, keep the iron sharp and set it for light cuts. Always begin cutting at the apex of the curve and cut "downhill."

Bench planes have flat soles and are useful for a variety of jobs, from smoothing away millmarks to planing drawers for a precise fit. The best bench planes have perfectly flat milled soles and precise adjustments. Unfortunately, many new planes won't do their job without undergoing lots of reworking and fitting of the parts. Some even have warped soles and cheap, stamped parts that don't fit together well. To avoid problems, purchase either an expensive new plane, such as one made by Lie-Nielsen Toolworks, or look for a good used plane. A good choice for a used plane is one of the old Stanley Bedrocks.

► See *"List of Suppliers"* on p. 285.

Block planes are small planes designed for one-handed use. They're extremely useful for smoothing and shaping chamfers, especially on small surfaces and in tight areas. Some block planes come equipped with a short fence and a removable side, which convert it to a rabbet plane. These features, along with the skewed blade, make this type of plane especially useful for beveling the edges of raised panels. Look for a block plane with a low blade angle and either a small throat or an adjustable throat (the opening around the iron).

► See *"Raised Panels by Hand"* on p. 91.

Rabbet planes have an open throat, which allows them to cut into corners. Although their obvious use is fine fitting of joints, they're also useful for minor shaping, such as smoothing the fillets that flank a bead and shaping the edge of a raised panel.

Rasps and *files* cut with rows of tiny teeth. They're available in a multitude of sizes and shapes, including flat, round, and half-round. Files are useful for smoothing contours after bandsawing and scrollsawing, especially in tight, awkward, or confined areas where other tools simply can't reach.

Rasps are really just files with large, aggressive teeth. For sculpting and shaping three-dimensional shapes and compound curves, such as a cabriole leg, the rasp is

Bench planes are shop workhorses for cutting away millmarks; but buy a quality plane, rather than struggle with a cheap one.

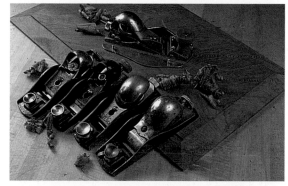

The block plane can get into tight spots. Used one-handed, it can create quick bevels.

Although primarily a joinery tool, rabbet planes have their use in shaping operations, especially when creating a raised panel.

Rasps and files are essential for creating sculptural shapes such as cabriole legs. A good selection includes different sizes, shapes, and tooth styles.

Although the possibilities for molding designs seem nearly infinite, all of the profiles are made up of basic shapes.

Shaper cutters can shape large profiles for moldings and can raise a panel in one pass.

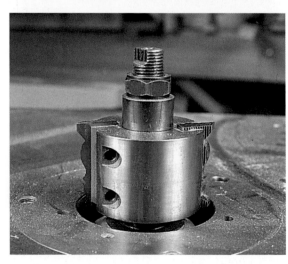

both an effective and an efficient choice. Of the various rasps available, the Nicholson no. 49 rasp works best. The staggered teeth cut aggressively, yet they leave the surface relatively smooth.

For serious shaping it's a good idea to have a dozen or so files and rasps in various sizes from 4 in. to 10 in. Unlike other hand tools, I would avoid buying used files and rasps. Their teeth are always dull from inevitable banging around, rust, and wear. Instead, buy new files and store them separately to protect the teeth.

It's always advisable to use a handle with a file or rasp. A handle makes the tool much safer to use and provides you with greater leverage and control.

Tools for Edge Treatments and Moldings

All *moldings* are made up from basic profiles—the ogee, bead, ovolo, thumbnail, cove, and chamfer. There are bits and cutters available for both the shaper and the router to create these profiles. So what's the difference? Shaper cutters are available in much larger profiles, allowing you to shape large moldings for furniture casework. Also, shaper cutters can be inverted, which gives them much greater versatility. So which is the best machine to own? The answer depends on the type of work you intend to do; in my own shop I have both a router and a shaper. Let's look at the machines and examine their pros and cons.

Without a doubt, the *router* has revolutionized woodworking; no other power tool has quite the versatility of the router. If you already own a router, the next step to

Mounted under a flat surface and fitted with a fence, a router can function like a light-duty shaper.

increasing its versatility is to mount it under a table. This, in effect, creates a mini-shaper. Although a table-mounted router doesn't have the power and capacity of a shaper, the operating principles are much the same. And in some ways, the router table is more versatile.

The short shank of router bits limit their reach, but used in a router table, they excel at shaping small stock. This is certainly another area where the router table excels. Because of the reduced power and small size of the router table, there's much less risk of it launching small pieces. Also, the reduced diameter of router bits allow you to use a small fence opening, which further lowers the risk.

▶ See *"Appendix: Shaping Small Parts"* on p. 282.

The shaper is a heavy-duty machine that can efficiently produce moldings, raise panels, and do template shaping.

► SHAPER SAFETY

- Always feed the workpiece against the cutterhead rotation.
- Do not exceed the manufacturer's recommended rpms for the cutterhead.
- Use the keyed lock washer to prevent the spindle nut from backing off.
- Don't use large cutterheads on small spindles.
- Cut from underneath when possible.
- Always use guards.
- Keep hands a minimum of 6 in. from the cutterhead.
- Always take light cuts by adjusting the fence and/or cutter height or by using larger rub bearings.
- Don't shape small stock; instead shape oversize stock and cut it to final size after shaping.

CUTTERHEAD FORCES

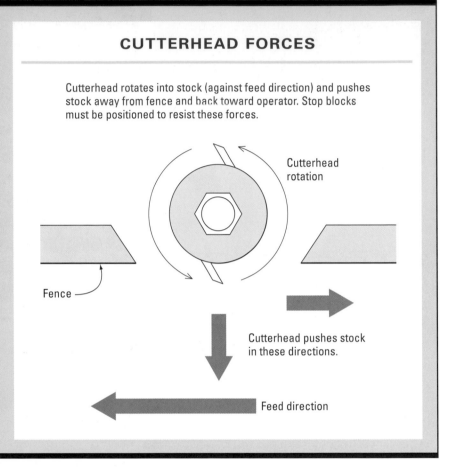

Cutterhead rotates into stock (against feed direction) and pushes stock away from fence and back toward operator. Stop blocks must be positioned to resist these forces.

Cutterhead rotation

Fence

Cutterhead pushes stock in these directions.

Feed direction

The *shaper,* on the other hand, is considerably more powerful than even the largest of routers. The motor and bearings of a router (the driving force for any machine) are no match for those of a shaper. The shaper excels at shaping wide stock; its long spindle can reach high toward the center of a wide panel.

A typical shaper cutter is, however, more expensive than the same profile in a router bit. So I use the router table for most smaller profiles, reserving the shaper for larger cuts.

Both the router and the shaper can flush trim and shape profiles on curves. But here's where a router has an advantage: Its small-diameter bits and bearing guides can shape into tight contours where a shaper spindle and cutter won't fit.

Although routers are capable of raising panels, the procedure typically requires three to five passes, depending on the density of the stock. This is because even the biggest routers lack the power for such a large cut. However, because of the larger spindle and

In tight spaces, a table-mounted router with its small-diameter bits can shape even the most detailed work.

Molding planes, once produced in a wide variety of profiles, can still be found at flea markets. Like any hand tool they leave tool marks behind that identify your work as made by hand.

► ROUTER TABLE OR SHAPER?

For most woodworkers, the router table is the smart choice. A router table and assortment of bits is far less expensive than most shapers. And a router table has a lot of versatility, too. In any case, a table-mounted router is good as a first purchase. Once you've learned to use it safely and understand its operating principles, you're more likely to understand the shaper. Later on, if you have a need to shape large profiles and gain greater efficiency for production work, you may want to consider a shaper.

motor, even a small shaper can bevel the edges of a panel in one pass.

Neither the router table nor the shaper can create a sharp inside corner. After shaping with these machines, you'll need to carve the corner by hand. But you'll do less carving if you use a router. The small diameter of the guide bearings allows it to reach far deeper into the corner than a shaper.

Wooden molding planes were the routers and shapers of their day. Both the sole and the iron of a molding plane are shaped with a reverse profile of the molding that is shaped. Each time the plane is pushed over the stock a shaving is produced and eventually the full molding profile is revealed.

Molding planes range in size from a small quirk-bead plane to a large crown-molding plane that requires two men to power it— one pushing and the other pulling. Many of these planes were produced in sets, such as hollows and rounds, tongue and groove, and rule joint planes for shaping the hinged joint of a drop-leaf table.

Although no longer produced in large quantity, wooden molding planes are still available through antique tool dealers and

While handplanes may take longer to achieve the same result, there's no comparison to the pleasure of using a well-tuned plane.

The Stanley 55 was one of a generation of planes meant to replace wooden molding planes. It was sold with inter-changeable cutters that make many different profiles.

flea markets. Remarkably, many old planes are still in excellent condition despite their age and need only cleaning and sharpening to be put to use.

Using wooden molding planes can be a quiet and romantic way to work wood. Although they may not be the tool of choice for shaping vast quantities of moldings, they can be an enjoyable way to produce a strip or two for a special project. And the unique textured surface that they create is unlike any produced by machine.

The Stanley Tool Company introduced the first *universal plane* in the second half of the nineteenth century, when wooden planes were rapidly being replaced by new planes made of metal. The Stanley 45 and, later, the Stanley 55 were designed to replace a multi-tude of wooden molding planes. As this type of plane evolved, its uses expanded, and it was advertised to be "a planing mill within itself."

The Stanley 55 came equipped with four boxes of cutters, each ground to create a dif-ferent molding profile. To accommodate the profiles of the various cutters, the plane had two skates, or runners, that adjusted both laterally and vertically. Other attachments included a third skate, two fences, and sever-al stops to limit the cutting depth.

Despite what some may say, the Stanley 55 is a working plane, albeit a heavy, awk-ward one. However, most Stanley 55s that I've seen have needed tuning. The most common problem is that the two-piece skates were sometimes misaligned during manufacturing. A few strokes with a mill file will bring the skates into one plane. Also, the cutters must be sharp—very sharp—if the plane is to work effectively. Using slip-stones, hone the bevel and back of the cutters as you would any plane iron or chisel.

A *scratch stock* is simply a scraper with a molding profile. It's pushed or pulled along the edge of the stock to shape simple moldings. The scratch stock is not practical for shaping large-scale profiles, but it is the tool of choice for shaping a small profile along a compound curve or for creating tiny details.

Although you can buy a scratch stock, making one is easy and takes only minutes. An old, inexpensive marking gauge is a ready-made scratch stock. Just bandsaw a kerf in the beam and insert the blade.

Making the blade is easy, too. Small pieces of bandsaw blade, scraper steel, or an old handsaw works well. You can easily shape the profile with small files.

There are certain times when the only effective way to create a profile is simply with a *chisel*. Chisels come in a variety of sizes. Although intended for chopping joinery, the short length of butt chisels makes them easy to maneuver in tight spots when shaping intersections that are difficult or impossible to shape by machine methods. Firmer chisels are much longer than butt chisels and so provide extra leverage when paring.

With their long pointed edge, skew chisels are the tool of choice for paring inside corners of raised panels, where routers and shapers can't reach. Although you can buy skewed bench chisels, the price is too high; it's easy and considerably less expensive to grind your own using ordinary bench chisels.

A scratch stock can make delicate profiles. You can buy one or can easily make one.

Although we usually think of chisels as a joinery tools, they have an important place in shaping operations.

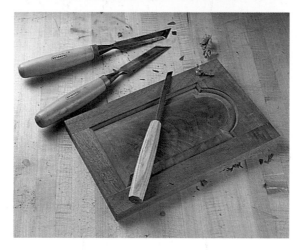

Skew chisels, which have one longer pointed edge, easily get into the inside corners of raised panels.

Tools for Carving

Carving tools are gouges and chisels that are available in a wide variety of sizes and shapes. To differentiate between the various tools, manufacturers use a numbering system. If you browse the pages of a tool catalog, you'll find that the size and shapes of carving tools seem almost endless. However, many are specialty tools; most furniture carving can be created with a little more than a dozen gouges of various sizes and sweeps.

When selecting carving tools, look for full-length tools with thin steel and polished edges. Crude, thick-bodied tools are difficult to use and usually cost as much as those of better quality. Although some manufacturers now offer shorter, lower-priced carving tools

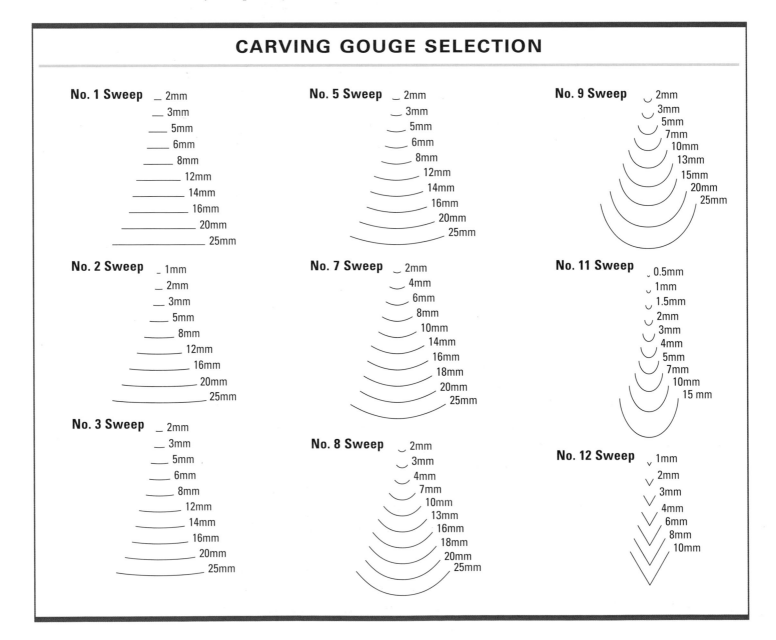

CARVING GOUGE SELECTION

No. 1 Sweep — 2mm, 3mm, 5mm, 6mm, 8mm, 12mm, 14mm, 16mm, 20mm, 25mm

No. 2 Sweep — 1mm, 2mm, 3mm, 5mm, 8mm, 12mm, 16mm, 20mm, 25mm

No. 3 Sweep — 2mm, 3mm, 5mm, 6mm, 8mm, 12mm, 14mm, 16mm, 20mm, 25mm

No. 5 Sweep — 2mm, 3mm, 5mm, 6mm, 8mm, 12mm, 14mm, 16mm, 20mm, 25mm

No. 7 Sweep — 2mm, 4mm, 6mm, 8mm, 10mm, 14mm, 16mm, 18mm, 20mm, 25mm

No. 8 Sweep — 2mm, 3mm, 4mm, 7mm, 10mm, 13mm, 16mm, 18mm, 20mm, 25mm

No. 9 Sweep — 2mm, 3mm, 5mm, 7mm, 10mm, 13mm, 15mm, 20mm, 25mm

No. 11 Sweep — 0.5mm, 1mm, 1.5mm, 2mm, 3mm, 4mm, 5mm, 7mm, 10mm, 15 mm

No. 12 Sweep — 1mm, 2mm, 3mm, 4mm, 6mm, 8mm, 10mm

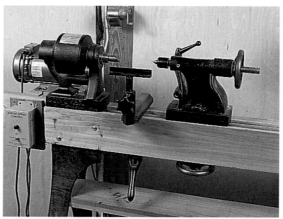

The lathe spins the stock around a center as a tool is pivoted into the stock to create beads, coves, tapers, urns and a wide variety of other shapes.

Carving tools come in a wide variety of sizes and shapes. Choose full-size tools, because the shorter ones are awkward to use.

often labeled for beginners, I would avoid these tools. The short length makes them awkward to use.

Tools for Turning

A *lathe* is totally unlike any other wood-working machine; the cutting tool is held by the craftsman as the motor spins the stock between a pair of centers. As the stock spins, the shapes are created by rotating, pivoting, and levering the tool along the rest. Learning to turn takes time and patience. And it helps to have a good lathe—one that is heavy and balanced to reduce vibration to a minimum. Although most lathes today are made of cast iron, a wooden bed lathe allows you to lengthen it to suit your needs.

A worthy, although expensive, option is a variable-speed motor. This feature allows you to adjust the speed quickly and easily to minimize vibration.

When spindle turning parts for furniture, you need only a handful of tools. The *roughing gouge* is a hefty tool with the end ground square. It's used for turning a square blank

Basic turning tools include (left to right) spindle gouges (first three), a parting tool, a roughing-out gouge, and two skew chisels.

into a round cylinder. *Spindle gouges* are ground with an elliptical pointed end. They're used for most shaping, including beads, coves, and vases or ogees. It's helpful to have about three sizes, such as ¼ in., ⅜ in., and ½ in.

The *skew*, as the name implies, is a chisel with a skewed edge. But unlike an ordinary chisel, the edge is ground with a double bevel so that the tool can be worked in two directions. The skew has a steep learning curve but it's an important tool that shapes into tight areas where gouges can't. For the greatest flexibility it's helpful to have at least a ½-in. and a 1-in. skew. I also have a heavy 1½-in. skew I use when turning bedposts.

The *parting tool* is used for quickly sizing the various diameters on a cylinder before shaping. Parting tools have a double bevel, and the best ones have a diamond-shaped shank to reduce friction.

Tools for Bending

The *vacuum press* has greatly simplified the processes of veneering and bent laminations. No longer do you have to fuss with mating forms, cauls, and multitudes of clamps.

A vacuum press uses atmospheric pressure to apply force to an assembly. The work is placed within a bag and the opening of the bag is sealed. Then a vacuum pump removes the air from the bag. The process is quick, simple, and hassle-free. Plus, the pressure inside a vacuum bag is uniform; so there's no worry that parts of the assembly lack sufficient pressure. I can't say enough about the advantages of a vacuum press. Once you've

tried one, you'll find that there's no going back to the old methods.

Building a *steam box* for bending wood is really quite easy. You'll need three items: a heat source, a container for the water, and a box to contain the parts as they are steamed. You can make the entire apparatus simply and inexpensively or you can spend some extra time and money to make it a bit more sophisticated.

For many years, craftsmen have used wood for the steam box. But wood is heavy, absorbs much of the steam during startup, and will eventually rot. Nowadays, schedule 40 polyvinyl chloride (PVC) pipe is a better choice. It's lightweight, yet strong, resistant to heat, and impervious to rot.

A portable camp stove works well for a heat source, especially if you already own one. But a better choice is the seafood cookers available from most home centers. They burn propane, which is safer to use, and they provide greater heat to boil the water faster.

An enclosed kettle or can may be used as a water container. Brian Boggs, a well-known chairmaker in Berea, Kentucky, uses a pressure cooker heated over a gas stove. A length of radiator hose works well to pipe the steam to the box. It's flexible and obviously designed to withstand high temperatures.

As a final note, as the steam condenses inside the box, a pool of lukewarm water will form and cool the contents. Avoid this scenario by drilling a couple of drain holes and sloping the box slightly when you set it up.

A vacuum press is normally used for veneering but is also an efficient way to make bent laminations.

A pressure cooker mounted over a gas stove provides steam for wood bending.

Materials

EVEN THOUGH LUMBER IS PLENTIFUL, finding local sources for quality lumber can often be difficult. For example, many lumberyards are stocked with boards that are stressed from being dried too quickly. In the rush to get lumber out of the kiln and into consumer's hands, kiln operators hurriedly push the lumber through the drying process. Often the result is boards that bear the scars of stress. Some of the scars are visible but others are not so easy to spot until you bring the lumber back to your shop and work it. Here are some examples:

■ **Case hardening** is evident during ripping, when the lumber twists and warps immediately upon passing the blade. As lumber is dried, it shrinks and develops different levels of stress from the core to the exterior. Although all lumber undergoes stress during drying, the stresses become severe when the lumber is dried too quickly.

■ **Surface checking** appears as cracks along the surface of a board where the cell structure has visibly separated.

■ **Honeycomb** occurs inside the board as the cell structure fractures from a speedy run through a kiln. Unlike surface checking, honeycomb is typically not evident until you begin milling the affected board.

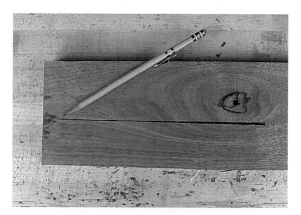

Case hardening is evident when ripping. The closed kerf is caused by warp and twist, caused by the wood being dried too fast.

The checks on the end of this board show one effect of drying lumber too quickly in a kiln.

One way to avoid problems like these is to buy green lumber and dry it yourself. Many woodworkers, including me, have found this to be a sure way of getting beautiful wide and figured lumber that is free of drying defects.

Of course, this method isn't practical for everyone. If it's not an option for you, ask around to find the most reputable lumber dealers—and when you find a good source, patronize it. As everyone knows, the lowest price isn't always a bargain. This principle applies to lumber as well.

Dry Lumber

As lumber dries, it shrinks; and because it shrinks unevenly, it often warps. Obviously it's important to work with lumber *after* it has shrunk and warped. This way you can

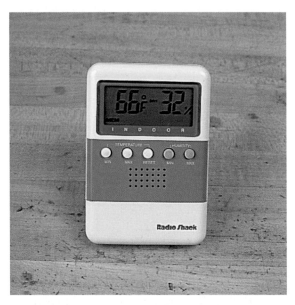

Storing lumber in stable humidity is important. An inexpensive hygrometer allows you to keep tabs on ambient humidity.

A moisture meter allows you to measure the moisture content of lumber.

straighten and flatten the stock with a jointer or handplane.

So, how dry should the lumber be when you begin working it? A rule of thumb is 6 percent to 8 percent moisture content. This places the lumber in balance with most environments that have a relative humidity of around 40 percent, including most indoor settings.

A common misconception is that only kiln-dried lumber is suitable for fine woodworking. But what's important is not how the lumber was dried but that it has the correct moisture content and that it is free of drying defects and stress. You can successfully air-dry lumber as long as the final stage of drying is done in an environment with a relative humidity of approximately 40 percent. This can be your shop, a garage, or even a spare bedroom. An inexpensive hygrometer will allow you to monitor the room's relative humidity accurately. When you suspect that the lumber may be dry, you can check it with a moisture meter. For the most accurate reading, cut a short segment from the end of a board and measure the core.

Stock for Sawn Curves

Unlike steam-bent curves or bent laminations, the grain in a sawn curve doesn't follow the curve. As a result, the short grain that occurs from sawing a curve weakens the stock. So when selecting stock for a sawn chair leg or other structural element, it's important to choose straight-grain stock for the greatest strength. Also, avoid stock with knots, because the grain is weakened around a knot. Save the wild and figured grain for

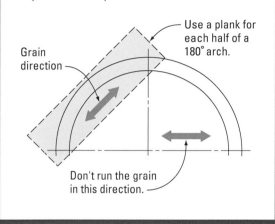

AVOID SHORT GRAIN IN CURVES

When bandsawing segments of a true circle, avoid short weak grain by using a separate plank for each quarter of the circle.

Use a plank for each half of a 180° arch.

Grain direction

Don't run the grain in this direction.

When choosing lumber for steam bending, make sure that the grain runs parallel to the edges of the board.

display in nonstructural areas such as table-tops and door panels.

After selecting the stock, orient the curved pattern to avoid short grain.

Whether curved or tapered, legs are created by sawing two adjacent faces of the stock. To avoid distraction and create visual harmony, it's a good idea to orient the grain to run diagonally across the end of the stock.

Stock for Bending

Stock for steam bending should have clear, straight grain than runs parallel to the edges of the board. Wood that is steam bent undergoes extreme stress as it is stretched at the convex area of the curve and compressed at the concave area. If the grain runs out along the edges, the stock will splinter and break during the bending process. So it's important to select grain that runs parallel to

the edges of the board. When lumber is sawn from the log, often the grain is not parallel. Knots also weaken the grain. Because of this, a break will usually occur near a knot.

There are two methods for creating stock with parallel grain. One way is to split the log into suitable sizes; a split naturally occurs along the grain. As you can imagine, this method is quite labor intensive.

A more practical method is to saw the stock with the grain. You can begin with straight-grain stock that is oversize. Mark layout lines that run parallel to the grain and rip the stock to size on your bandsaw.

Although it's important to select straight-grain stock for bent laminations, it isn't as critical as stock selection for steam bending. Before placing stock in a curved form for laminating, the stock is planed to a thickness that allows an easy, relatively stress-free bend.

Stock for Panels

To cooper a panel, strips of wood are beveled along the edges and glued together in a curved form. To avoid the distraction resulting from mismatched grain, it's a good idea to use quartersawn stock. The grain in quartersawn stock is straight and easily matched. As an added benefit, it creates a more dimensionally stable panel.

▶ See *"Coopered Panels"* on p. 102.

Wide, flat surfaces give you the perfect opportunity to show off a prized figured board. The challenge it to keep it flat. Old textbooks recommend gluing narrow boards together to create wide panels. But this method yields an unattractive panel with plenty of gluelines and mismatched grain.

I prefer instead to use wide figured stock for tabletops, door panels, and drawer fronts. In fact, I typically use only one board for tops of small tables, lids for slant front desks, and raised panels in doors. Often

the board may measure two feet in width. To keep the surface flat I follow these guidelines:

- Avoid boards that contain pith; they always warp.

- Use only dry, stress-free lumber. If a panel releases moisture after you mill it to size, it will warp. Once the panel is warped, it becomes difficult or impossible to shape. Although it may not be practical for some woodworkers, I prefer to dry my own wide lumber.

- Allow the stock to acclimate. Bring the lumber into your shop several weeks before you plan to use it to allow it to adjust to the humidity.

- Use the construction of the furniture piece to keep panels flat. Once assembled into the framework of furniture, wide stock is restrained. For example, raised panels are trapped within a stile and rail frame, tabletops are fastened to a base, and desk lids have breadboard ends. To

To avoid problems matching the grain in wide panels, try to find wide figured panels.

Avoid boards with pith when choosing lumber for wide panels, because they always warp.

➤ REMEMBER TO FINISH THE BOTTOM

I built the kitchen table we use in our home. The top was made from three wide, beautiful curly maple boards. It was a country design with breadboard ends, a painted base, and turned legs.

In my rush to complete the job, I forgot to finish the underside of the top. While it sat on sawhorses in my shop awaiting final rubout, the relative humidity changed as the result of an approaching storm front. I walked into the shop to find that the beautiful top had warped like an old phonograph record.

Fortunately, I had faced the same problem before so I knew what to do. When the sun came out, I placed the top outdoors with the convex, unfinished underside facing up. A few hours in the warmth of the sun, the tabletop dried and returned to its former flatness. I quickly took it into the shop and sealed it with a couple of coats of finish.

Years later, the top shows wear from daily use, including meals, birthdays, and home-school lessons—but it's still flat.

One way to keep lumber from absorbing moisture from the environment is to wrap it in plastic.

avoid warpage on wide stock, mill it, shape it, and assemble it on the same day.

- Wrap the board in plastic. Although this may sound odd, it works by preventing the exchange of moisture. Use rolls of industrial plastic available at home centers.

- Finish both faces of the board. All finishes slow down the exchange of moisture vapor. If you fail to finish the underside of a tabletop, for example, the moisture exchange will be uneven, usually resulting in a warped panel.

Straight-Edged Shapes, page 34

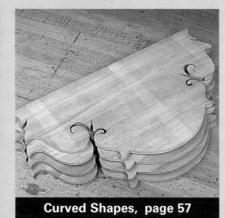

Curved Shapes, page 57

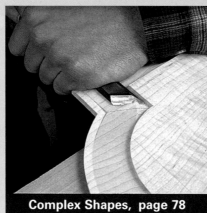

Complex Shapes, page 78

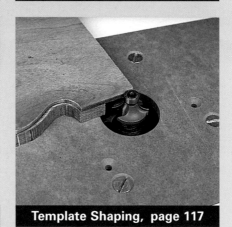

Template Shaping, page 117

PART TWO

Cutting Shapes

C UTTING SHAPES IS ESSENTIAL to making furniture because shape is the basis from which all other furniture design elements are drawn. In this part, you'll learned how to design and cut the basic geometric shapes of which furniture is composed:

■ **Rectangles and squares** are fundamental because all furniture elements, even curvilinear forms, will fit within a rectangle.

■ **Tapers and octagons** are often used in subtle ways, such as in table legs and bedposts.

■ **Circles, arcs, and ellipses** are used to relieve rectilinearity in bases, frames, and mirrors and to create the familiar round tabletop.

■ **Geometrical curves** are used to create flowing curves for moldings. Changing the radius alters the molding proportions.

■ **Freeform curves** are associated with cabriole legs, chair backs, and gooseneck pediment moldings on casework.

Straight-Edged Shapes

Milling

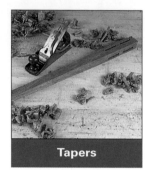

Tapers

Octagons

Chamfers

➤ Milling Stock to Size (p. 45)

➤ Milling Square Stock (p. 45)

➤ Two-Sided Taper Freehand on the Bandsaw (p. 46)

➤ Taper on the Jointer (p. 47)

➤ Taper on the Bandsaw with a Jig (p. 48)

➤ Two-Sided Taper on the Table Saw (p. 49)

➤ Four-Sided Taper on the Table Saw (p. 50)

➤ Eight-Sided Taper on the Router Table or Shaper (p. 51)

➤ Octagonal Post on the Router Table or Shaper (p. 52)

➤ Eight-Sided Taper with Hand Tools (p. 53)

➤ Stopped Chamfer on the Table Saw (p. 54)

➤ Chamfering with a Molding Head (p. 55)

➤ Shaping Stopped Chamfers on a Curved Workpiece (p. 56)

Learning to balance, proportion, and draw geometric shapes as well as freeform curves is essential to the design and construction of pleasing furniture. To cut a shape, you first need to define it, which usually means drawing it. Although shapes can be drawn freehand, achieving symmetry and accuracy is easier with measuring instruments and templates. A straightedge is a template for ensuring that a line is straight and true. A ruler is nothing more than a straightedge with graduated markings that enables us to measure and proportion rectilinear shapes.

Drawing Rectilinear Shapes

Knowing how to proportion rectangles (and series of rectangles) is essential to good furniture design (see the drawing on p. 36). Because all furniture, even curvilinear designs, will fit within a rectangle (remember, an ellipse fits within a rectangle; a circle, within a square), proportioning a rectangle is a good starting point from which to design a piece of furniture.

The *Golden Rectangle* has been used for centuries by designers and architects. In fact, the modern-day credit card fits within a Golden Rectangle. The proportions of the Golden Rectangle—1:1.618—are found throughout the natural world. The drawing at right shows how to draw a Golden Rectangle with a compass.

Using *ratios of whole numbers* is another easy and effective method of proportioning rectangles. For example, index cards, photographs, and stationary all use ratios such as 3 by 5, 4 by 6, 7 by 9, and so on.

This eighteenth-century secretary shows how simple and complex shapes can add interest and functionality to furniture.

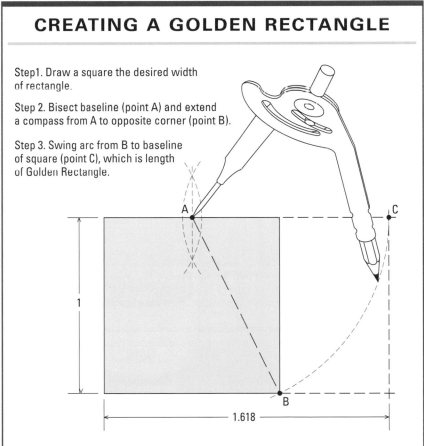

CREATING A GOLDEN RECTANGLE

Step 1. Draw a square the desired width of rectangle.

Step 2. Bisect baseline (point A) and extend a compass from A to opposite corner (point B).

Step 3. Swing arc from B to baseline of square (point C), which is length of Golden Rectangle.

A

C

1

B

1.618

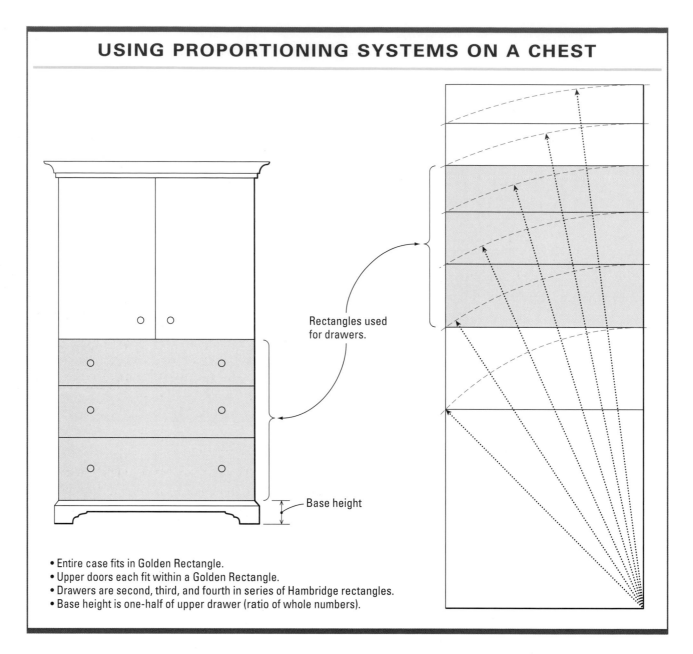

USING PROPORTIONING SYSTEMS ON A CHEST

Rectangles used for drawers.

Base height

- Entire case fits in Golden Rectangle.
- Upper doors each fit within a Golden Rectangle.
- Drawers are second, third, and fourth in series of Hambridge rectangles.
- Base height is one-half of upper drawer (ratio of whole numbers).

The illustration at top right demonstrates the method for constructing a series of *Hambidge rectangles*. Hambidge rectangles are a useful method for graduating drawers in a chest. Begin by drawing a square that equals the width of the chest. Next, position a compass so that each leg rests on a diagonal corner. Now strike an arc; extend the sides of the square to intersect the arc to cre-

ate the first rectangle. To repeat the process, keep one point of the compass in the lower corner of the square and extend the other point to the new corner.

Fibonacci numbers are a series of whole numbers in which each number is the sum of the two that preceded it. For example, a typical Fibonacci sequence is 1, 1, 2, 3, 5, 8, 13, and so on. The numbers in such a series

HAMBIDGE RECTANGLES

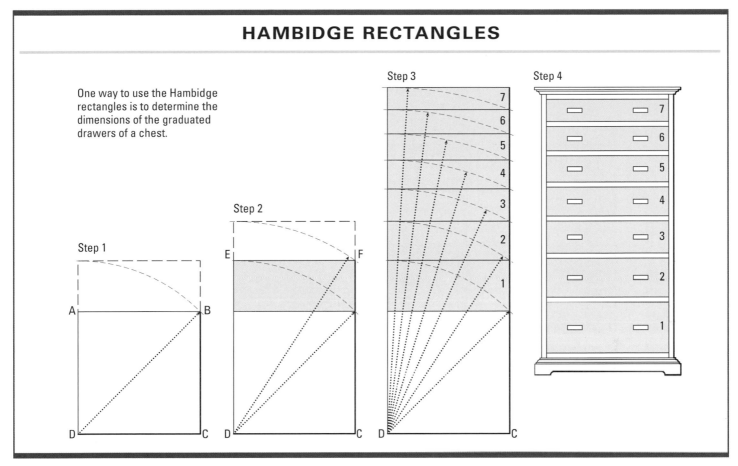

One way to use the Hambidge rectangles is to determine the dimensions of the graduated drawers of a chest.

Step 1

Step 2

Step 3

Step 4

can be employed as a quick and useful method for achieving pleasing proportions when designing furniture.

Squares are really special cases of rectangles. The only difference and the defining characteristics of squares is that all the sides are equal. Since a square is what it is, the main design concern is its size in relation to the rest of the elements in the piece.

Leaving the realm of 90-degree angles allows for shapes of more than four sides, of which the most useful is the *octagon*. This kind of shape is really just a matter of dividing 90 degrees into smaller segments. A protractor is useful for keeping track of the

FIBONACCI NUMBERS

1

1

2

3

5

8

Each number in the Fibonacci series is the sum of the previous two. As the numbers get higher, the ratio between consecutive numbers approaches that of the Golden Rectangle: 1:1.618.

angles. Octagons are familiar in table legs and bedposts. The illustration below shows a method of drawing this design.

A *taper*, which is a rectangle with one side cut at less than 90 degrees, does not have to be any particular angle; but a very slight angle will appear to be just not square. Too much angle will give a top- or bottom-heavy look. Although a protractor or a sliding bevel gauge helps keep track of the angles—mostly to make them consistent—sometimes the eye is the best measuring instrument of all. Experimenting with different angles and standing back to look at the result will help you get a pleasing result.

Designing Furniture with Rectilinear Shapes

Your best work, including curved work, begins with stock that is milled flat, true, and square. Flat milled surfaces create accurate reference points for cutting joints, sawing curves, and shaping profiles.

The simplest straight-edged shaped is a rectangle, which is essentially what we create by milling stock square and then cutting it to size. A square, as I've said, is just a special form of rectangle in which all the sides are the same length. But there are other straight-edged shapes that are useful in woodworking. Tapers help relieve the heavy

DRAWING AN OCTAGON

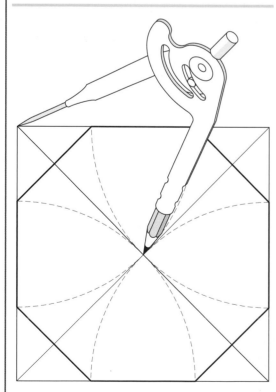

To draw an octagon from a square, first draw diagonal lines. Next, draw arcs with the compass. Connect the arcs to create the octagon.

FOUR TYPES OF WARPED BOARDS

Cup (warped across face)

Bow (warped on face for board's length)

Crook (warped on edge)

Twist

look of legs and posts. The octagon and its special form, the tapered octagon, are favorite stylistic elements for bedposts. Simple octagons and other multisided (more than four sides) straight-edged shapes represent a form of chamfering in which the chamfered sides are all equal in size; but a simple chamfer, which breaks the edge, can help relieve a heavy look as well.

Designing Tapered and Chamfered Shapes

Obviously, legs and posts are important structural elements, unlike purely aesthetic elements such as moldings and carvings. So from a design standpoint, a table leg or bedpost must have sufficient dimension for adequate joinery. So, to avoid creating a heavy, utilitarian look, the remainder of the leg can be reduced in size and shaped to enhance its

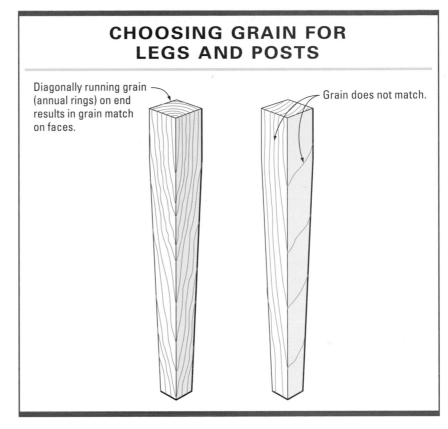

CHOOSING GRAIN FOR LEGS AND POSTS

Diagonally running grain (annual rings) on end results in grain match on faces.

Grain does not match.

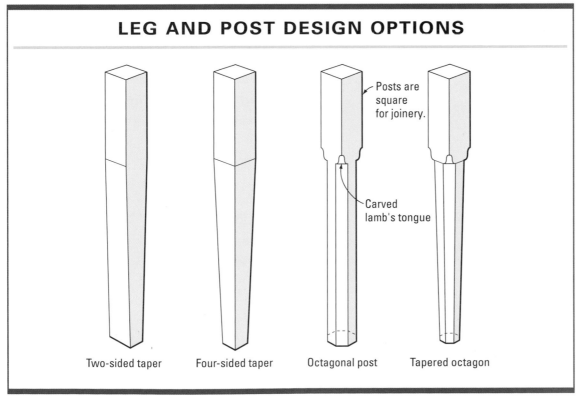

LEG AND POST DESIGN OPTIONS

Posts are square for joinery.

Carved lamb's tongue

Two-sided taper   Four-sided taper   Octagonal post   Tapered octagon

The popular pencil-post bed can look at home in both traditional and contemporary settings.

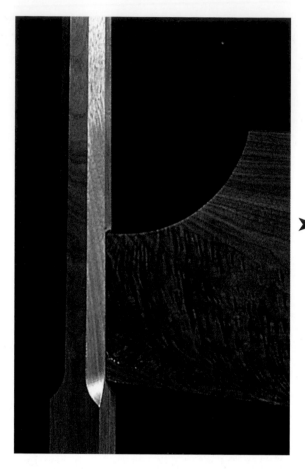

look at home in both traditional and contemporary settings

If you prefer a straight leg rather than a tapered one, you can reduce its mass by shaping the corners. A chamfer or other simple profile will add subtle embellishment while reducing the visual weight. Straight legs can also be fluted or otherwise molded to break up the flat, dull surface.

► See *"Flutes and Reeds"* on p. 212.

Jigs for Cutting Tapers

The table saw is undoubtedly one of the most efficient tools you can use for cutting a taper. You've probably seen adjustable tapering jigs offered in woodworking tool catalogs. I usually prefer to make my own jigs; doing so is inexpensive and I can make them dedicated to a specific application. This means that I don't have to waste time making adjustments the next time I want to use the jig. And the simple jig is quick and easy to make.

The tapering jig I use for the table saw is stone simple. It's a strip of plywood with a tapered notch for the workpiece. When the leg is positioned in the jig, the portion extending from the notch is ripped away, creating a straight, uniform taper.

Constructing the jig takes just a few minutes. Begin by cutting ¾-in. plywood approximately 7 in. wide by 4 in. longer than the stock to be tapered. After laying out the taper on the stock, position it on the plywood with the area to be cut off overhanging the edge. Next, trace the workpiece onto

appearance. Often, the shape is dictated by the style.

Perhaps the simplest and most familiar method of shaping a leg or post is the taper. By gradually reducing the mass, a leg appears lighter without sacrificing strength. Traditionally, legs are tapered on the two inside adjacent surfaces. Tapering all four surfaces yields a contemporary look. The inside legs on lengthy casework, such as a huntboard, have tapers on three faces.

Octagonal tapers, as the name implies, taper on eight surfaces. The most common examples are the posts on the pencil-post bed. This style of bed is popular and can the plywood and cut out the notched area with the bandsaw. It's that easy!

Usually when tapering, I turn to the table saw, but the bandsaw is sometimes a better choice for several reasons. The main reason is safety; the bandsaw can't kickback because the blade pushes the stock downward toward the table. Also, if you're tapering thick stock, such as bedposts, your table saw may not have enough cutting capacity. And even if it does, the thick blade on a table saw tends to bog down when ripping thick hardwood. In contrast, your bandsaw will taper thick posts much more efficiently because its blade creates a thin kerf (approximately half that of a

DEDICATED TABLE SAW TAPERING JIG

This edge is guided by the fence.

Friction-fit with leg or post.

Size to fit end of taper.

To make a simple table saw tapering jig, trace the taper from the marked stock to a piece of plywood.

To complete the jig, cut out the notch on the bandsaw.

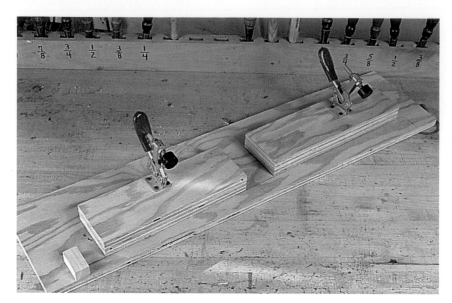

A simple jig for tapering on the bandsaw.

circular blade) so there's much less feed resistance.

If you've got a number of legs or posts to taper, it makes sense to build a jig to speed the process along. This jig is simply a tapered template that follows a guide stick next to the blade. Support blocks on the jig position the leg or post. A pair of toggle clamps secure the work while allowing you to swap workpieces easily.

➤ See *"Template Shaping"* on p. 117.

Shaping Octagonal Tapers

Undoubtedly, the most familiar use of the octagonal taper is the pencil-post bed. Still popular centuries after it first appeared, this design's simple, pleasing lines have broad appeal.

A typical bedpost has slender proportions; the post is commonly 2½ in. square by 80 in. tall. A short portion of the post is left square

TYPICAL PENCIL-POST DESIGN

1 in.

Tapered octagon

80 in.

Carved lamb's tongue

Square section for bed rail joinery

Octagonal

2½ in.

to accommodate the bed rail mortise-and-tenon joinery. The taper begins above the rails and gradually reduces in size until it reaches the top. The top of the post is typically 1 in. across.

You can make an octagonal taper several ways: by hand, with a router, or with a shaper. The first method involves using a drawknife and plane and is a quiet and enjoyable method. Laying out the taper in preparation for handwork is quick and precise with a spar-maker's jig. This special marking gauge uses two wooden dowels, which follow the edges of the post to guide the pins as they scratch the outline.

If you prefer using your router table or shaper, you'll need to build the jig shown at top right. The base supports the four-sided taper as the work passes a chamfer router bit or shaper cutterhead. To determine the degree of taper on the base, draw a pair of octagons. The first represents the start of the taper; the second represents the end. Cut the tapered base on the bandsaw and attach it under the plywood frame of the jig.

Smoothing Away the Saw Marks

No matter whether you use the bandsaw or table saw for tapering, you'll find that each machine leaves a distinctive pattern. To create a smooth surface suitable for finishing, I tap into any one of several methods.

For smoothing difficult grain such as curly maple, begin with a light pass over the jointer. If the knives are sharp, the cut is

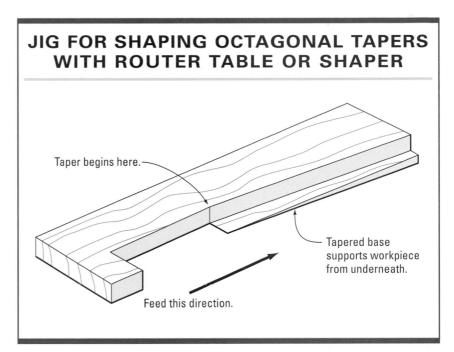

JIG FOR SHAPING OCTAGONAL TAPERS WITH ROUTER TABLE OR SHAPER

Taper begins here.

Tapered base supports workpiece from underneath.

Feed this direction.

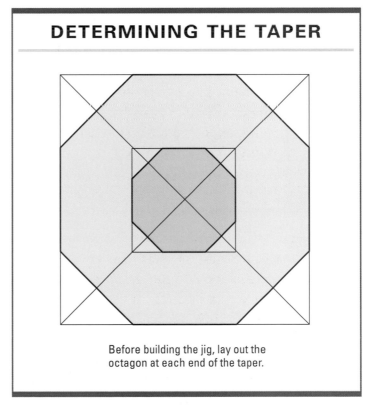

DETERMINING THE TAPER

Before building the jig, lay out the octagon at each end of the taper.

With sharp blades, a jointer can make quick work of saw marks.

A handplaned surface is so smooth it often doesn't need sanding.

A cabinet scraper is an efficient way to smooth tool marks.

light, and the feed rate is slow, the jointer will shear the curly grain with little or no tearout. Afterward, further smooth the surface with a sharp scraper. Finally, finish the surface with sandpaper.

If the grain is less troublesome (such as straight-grained walnut) you cut away the saw marks with a sharp bench plane. This method is very efficient and leaves a silky-smooth surface that often doesn't even need sanding.

Milling Stock to Size

Begin by cutting the stock to rough size, approximately 1 in. longer and ½ in. wider than finished size. The bandsaw is the tool of choice for ripping; crosscuts can be made on a radial-arm saw or sliding miter saw. This first step greatly helps remove warp from the stock. This is also the time to examine the lumber for defects, such as knots, sapwood, and checking, and to cut them away.

Next, flatten one face on the jointer (**A**). A long handplane—such as a no. 6, 7, or 8—will also work if your jointer is too small. Afterward, plane the stock to final thickness (**B**).

It's a good idea to check the jointer fence for squareness to the table before beginning the next step. Then, joint one edge of the stock 90 degrees to the face (**C**).

Now rip the stock to final width (**D**). If there are several pieces on your cut list of the same width, it's a good idea to rip them now, to ensure uniformity.

After jointing the sawn edge, crosscut the stock to final length. First, cut one end square; then, measure and cut the other end. If you're cutting multiple pieces, a stop on your miter gauge will help get them all the same length (**E**).

Milling Square Stock

When milling square stock for legs and posts, I take a slightly different approach. When ripping to rough size, I use the bandsaw. Cutting thick stock is safer on the bandsaw because there's no chance of kickback. Also, the bandsaw cuts thick stock with less feed resistance.

After cutting to size, true a face on the jointer (**A**). Then joint an adjacent face 90 degrees to the first. Finally, plane the stock to thickness (**B**).

A

Taper ends at foot.

Taper begins here.

No taper on this face

Line of taper

Apron stops here.

B

Mortise

Two-Sided Taper Freehand on the Bandsaw

Begin by laying out the taper on the stock (**A**). To simplify construction, tapers usually don't extend into the area of joinery (**B**). It's best to lay out and cut the leg mortise while the stock is still square (**C**).

Next, mount a wide blade, such as ¾ in., on the bandsaw. Using a wide blade greatly reduces the tendency for the blade to wander in the cut (**D**). Start at the foot and closely follow the layout line (**E**). Turn the leg 90 degrees and make the second cut (**F**). After all the cuts are made, remove the saw marks with a sharp bench plane (**G**).

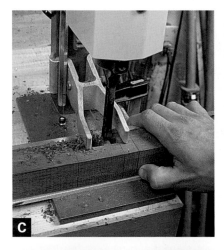

C

D

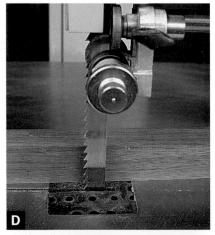

E

F

G

Taper on the Jointer

You can effectively cut a taper on the jointer by positioning the end of the workpiece beyond the cutterhead when starting the cut. You'll have to lower the stock onto the spinning head, so for the purpose of safety, it's important to clamp a stop block to the infeed side of the jointer, which also helps define the length of the taper.

Begin by laying out the taper on the stock (**A**). Next, divide the amount of stock to be removed by $\frac{1}{8}$ in.; this will determine the number of passes required. Set your jointer for a $\frac{1}{8}$-in. cutting depth. Clamp a stop block to the infeed table to position the start of the taper over the cutterhead (**B**). When you've completed these steps, you're ready to begin the process.

Rest the end of the workpiece against the stop block and carefully lower it onto the spinning cutterhead (**C**). Feed the stock past the cutterhead while applying pressure to the area to tapered (**D**). Use push blocks for safety. Finally, repeat the process several times to create the desired amount of taper.

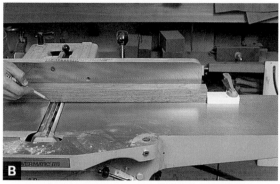

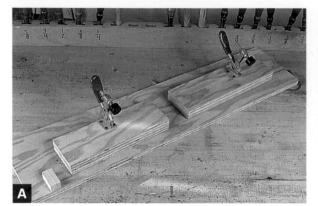

Taper on the Bandsaw with a Jig

If you've got a lot of stock to taper it makes sense to construct a jig to speed the process along. Although the table saw is a good choice for tapering, I prefer the bandsaw for tapering thick stock such as bedposts. This technique uses a template that follows a guide adjacent to the bandsaw blade. Best of all, you can create one-, two-, or even four-sided tapers with this technique.

First, make the jig to the desired degree of taper (**A**). The guide is simply a stick with a notch for the blade (**B**). Make certain that the guide is clamped firmly in position before you begin (**C**).

To use the jig, keep the base in contact with the guide throughout the cut (**D**). You'll need the off-cuts for support during the second cut. Afterward, rotate the stock to make the second taper (**E**).

You can use a guide and templates to rapidly bandsaw any number of identical parts.

Guide

This curve should match the tightest curve in the pattern.

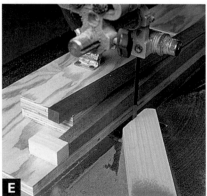

Two-Sided Taper on the Table Saw

Once you've made the jig and milled the stock, set the blade height so that the teeth are just above the workpiece (**A**). Next, set the fence at a distance from the blade that corresponds to the width of the jig (**B**). Position the stock for the first cut. As you feed the jig and workpiece into the blade, it's crucial to maintain contact with the fence (**C**). A splitter will dramatically increase safety during any ripping procedure such as this (**D**). Finally, rotate the leg and cut the second taper (**E**).

► See *"Taper on the Bandsaw with a Jig"* at left.

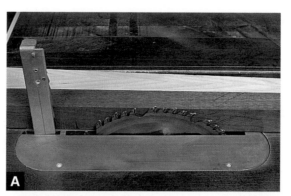

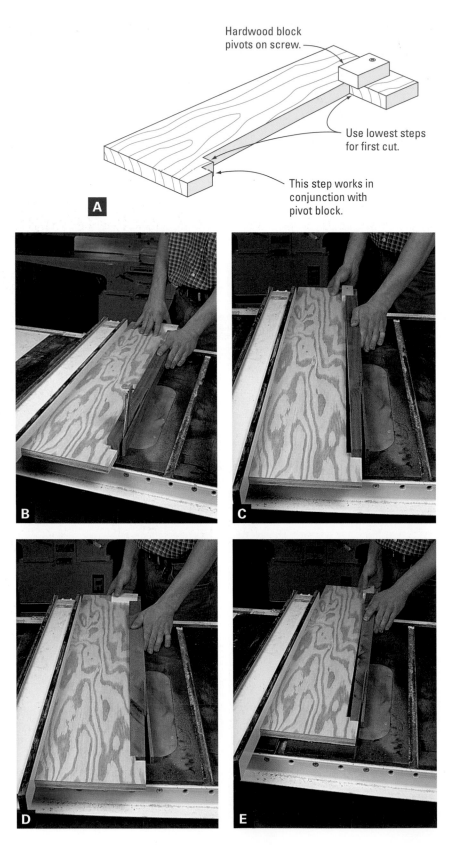

Hardwood block pivots on screw.

Use lowest steps for first cut.

This step works in conjunction with pivot block.

A

B

C

D

E

Four-Sided Taper on the Table Saw

The process for cutting a four-sided taper is much like the procedure for cutting a two-sided taper. The difference is the jig. There are two steps on the jig: one for the first two cuts and another for the final two cuts (**A**).

To use the jig, first pivot the stop block out of the way and cut two adjacent tapers (**B, C**). Then pivot the stop into position and use the second step of the jig for the last two tapers (**D, E**). Remember to use a splitter on your saw and keep the jig in contact with the fence.

Eight-Sided Taper on the Router Table or Shaper

Before shaping a tapered octagon, always begin by drawing two full-size octagons. The first represents the start of the taper; the second drawing represents the end.

Next, lay out a four-sided taper on the stock (**A**) and cut the four tapers using your favorite method (**B**). Now you're ready to chamfer the corners to create the eight-sided taper. But first smooth away the saw marks with a handplane or jointer (**C**).

To chamfer the corners, first build a jig to support the stock during the cut. Next, mount a chamfer cutterhead or bit on your shaper or router table (**D**). Adjust the bit height for the full depth of cut according to the drawing you made earlier (**E**). The jig will raise and support the small end of the stock to create the necessary amount of chamfer at each end (**F**).

Position the work in the jig with the trailing end of the stock resting firmly against the stop. Now feed the workpiece and jig past the cutterhead to cut the tapered chamfer (**G**). When you reach the end of the taper, stop and make a mark on the table or fence (**H**). This gives you a reference point when cutting the three remaining chamfers.

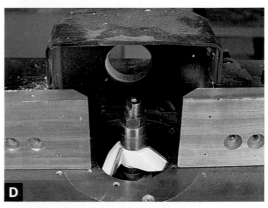

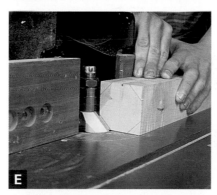

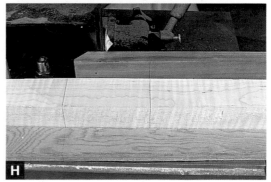

Octagonal Post on the Router Table or Shaper

Begin by milling the post square and drawing an octagon on one end. Next, mount a router bit or shaper cutter. If you're using a shaper, mount the cutterhead to cut from underneath the stock for safety (**A**).

The final step in the setup is to adjust the fence and cutter height. Your drawing on the end of the post makes it easy. Just position the post adjacent to the cutter and lock the fence and cutter height.

Now you're ready for the cut (**B**). If you're creating a stop chamfer, clamp a stop block to the outfeed fence or make a mark on the fence or table to align with a mark on the stock (**C**).

Eight-Sided Taper with Hand Tools

You don't need a router or shaper to create elegant octagonal tapers; as with any woodworking process, there's a way to achieve the same results with hand tools (**A**).

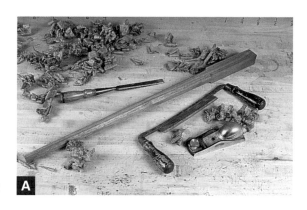

If you're unfamiliar with using hand tools, creating octagonal tapered bedposts by hand is a great way to get started.

Begin by shaping a four-sided taper using any of the previous methods. Next, lay out the chamfered corners. This step may seem complicated, but it's easy when you take a few minutes to build a spar-maker's gauge (**B**). If you keep the gauge's dowels against the stock, the pins will mark a perfect taper (**C**).

To remove the excess stock, use a drawknife, which will enable you to take large, controlled cuts (**D**). As for any hand tool, sharpness is a key to control. Once you've gotten close to the layout lines, finish the surface with a plane, taking the stock to the layout line (**E**).

Finally, carve a bevel at the termination of the cut to create a stop (**F**).

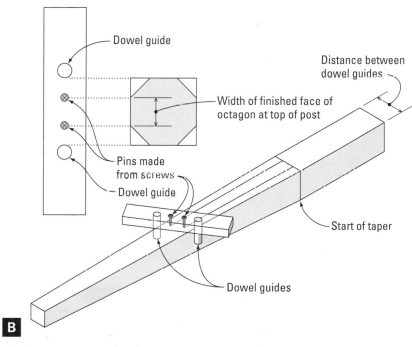

Dowel guide

Distance between dowel guides

Width of finished face of octagon at top of post

Pins made from screws

Dowel guide

Start of taper

Dowel guides

B

C

D

E

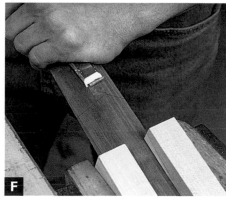

F

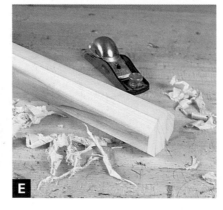

Stopped Chamfer on the Table Saw

Large chamfers that are beyond the capacity of your router table or shaper can be shaped on the table saw. The surface will have saw marks, but they're easy to remove with a plane. I like this technique for bedposts, which combine turning with octagonal sections. If the post is to be turned, chamfer it first and stop the chamfer before the square sections, which serve as areas of joinery for the bed rails.

Begin by drawing an octagon on the end of one post, which serves as a guide when positioning the saw's fence (**A**). Tilt the blade to 45 degrees and position the fence. Now rip the stock (**B**). If the chamfer stops before reaching the other end of the post, clamp a stop block to the fence or make a mark on the table to align with a mark on the post (**C**).

Remember to turn off the saw before backing out of the cut. Use a handsaw to remove the off-cuts (**D**). Afterward, the end of the chamfers can be turned or carved, and the chamfered surface can be smoothed with a plane (**E**).

Chamfering with a Molding Head

When chamfering with a molding head you can use a 45-degree cutter or, if you rotate the stock 45 degrees, you can use a straight cutter. I use a straight cutter, because it will create a symmetrical curve at the stop.

Don't shape a large cut on a slender piece of stock without a jig (**A**). A well-constructed jig positions your hands at a safe distance from the cutter and adds mass to the piece being shaped.

Begin by positioning the work in the jig (**B**). Tighten the wing nuts securely (**C**). Next, position the fence to center the work over the molding head and adjust the molding head height (**D**). Now you're ready to make the cut (**E**). If the chamfer is to be stopped, clamp a block to the fence or indicate the stopping point with a strip of tape (**F**).

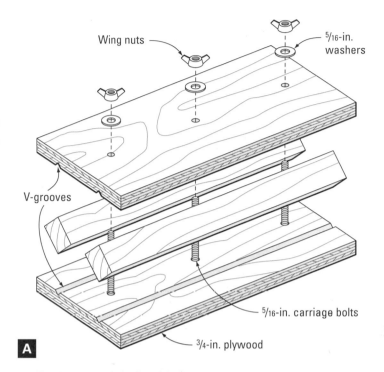

Wing nuts

5/16-in. washers

V-grooves

5/16-in. carriage bolts

3/4-in. plywood

A

B

C

D

E

F

Shaping Stopped Chamfers on a Curved Workpiece

When shaping a chamfer on a curved surface, the bearing on the router bit registers against the stock to limit the cutting depth. Any roughness or void in the surface will be re-created in the chamfer as the bearing rolls over the surface.

Begin by smoothing the curved surface. The bandsaw marks can be cut away with a spokeshave or compass plane. Another option is to flush trim the surface with a template and flush-trimming bit.

▶ See *"Flush Trimming"* on p. 125.

The next step is to mount a chamfer bit in the router table and adjust the height for a light cut, no more than ⅛ in. You'll also need a fulcrum to pivot the work into the spinning bit. Otherwise the stock could kick back violently. The fulcrum can be a pin or block; for the greatest mechanical advantage, it should be located as close as possible to the bit.

To make the cut, position the workpiece against the fulcrum and pivot it into the spinning bit (**A**). Once contact is made with the bearing, begin feeding the workpiece (**B**).

When making a stopped cut on a curved surface, it will be necessary to begin two of the cuts in the middle. Position the workpiece against the fulcrum and aim the start of the cut for the outer cutting circle of the bit (**C**). If you come up short of the line, don't back up! Instead, pull the work away and try again.

Curved Shapes

Arcs, Circles, & Ellipses

➤ Arcs, Circles, and Ellipses Freehand on the Bandsaw (p. 64)

➤ Circles on the Bandsaw with a Jig (p. 64)

➤ Arcs on the Bandsaw with a Jig (p. 65)

➤ Circles or Ellipses with a Template (p. 66)

Exterior Curves

➤ Bandsawing Tight Curves (p. 67)

➤ Bandsawing Broad, Sweeping Curves (p. 69)

➤ Sawing Multiples (p. 70)

➤ Scrollsawing on the Bandsaw (p. 71)

➤ Resawing a Curve (p. 71)

➤ Brick-Stacking Tight Curves (p. 73)

➤ Sawing Curves with a Coping Saw (p. 75)

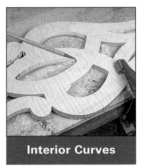

Interior Curves

➤ Interior Cuts with a Scrollsaw (p. 76)

➤ Beveling Curved Edges (p. 77)

STRAIGHT-EDGED SHAPES ALWAYS SEEM EASIER to cut because there are usually fences to guide the work. Curved shapes may seem challenging, but the effort is worth the options that sinuous forms can bring to your designs. Curves relieve the boxy look of rectilinear furniture, and they can provide a touch of imagination that sets your work apart.

Curves can be cut freehand on the scrollsaw or the bandsaw. Trapped curves are cut with a jigsaw or scrollsaw. If you like working with hand tools, a coping saw or fretsaw is handy. If you have many repetitive cuts to make, you can improve your accuracy by making templates. But all curved shapes need good design and a model. The shape must exist first in the mind and then on paper before it can be accurately cut from a piece of wood.

Use a compass or circle template for drawing accurate circles.

► See *"Making Patterns"* on p. 60.

Drawing Curved Shapes

Circles and arcs have a consistent radius and are easily drawn with a drafting template. For larger diameters, you can use a compass. The best tools have a thumbwheel for fine adjustments. To draw a circle that's beyond the capacity of your compass, clamp trammel points to a stick.

Simply stated, an *ellipse* is an oblique circle. An ellipse fits within a rectangle rather than a square. A beautiful form, the ellipse is easily drawn with templates that are available at drafting supply stores. To create a larger ellipse, I employ an old method that uses three trammel points clamped to a stick. Two of the points are guided by the edges of a framing square as the third point draws the ellipse. The size of the ellipse is determined by the position of trammel points along the stick. Because the ellipse is so pleasing to the eye, designers and architects have used it for centuries.

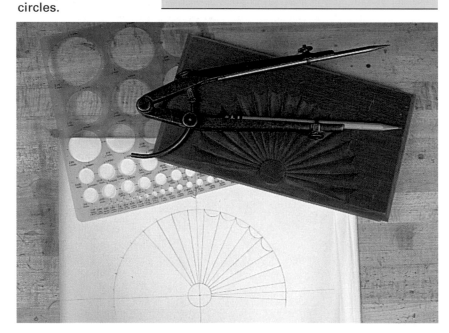

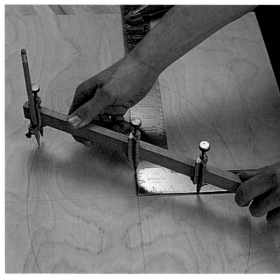

The three-trammel-point method for drawing an ellipse.

DRAWING AN ELLIPSE WITH TRAMMELS

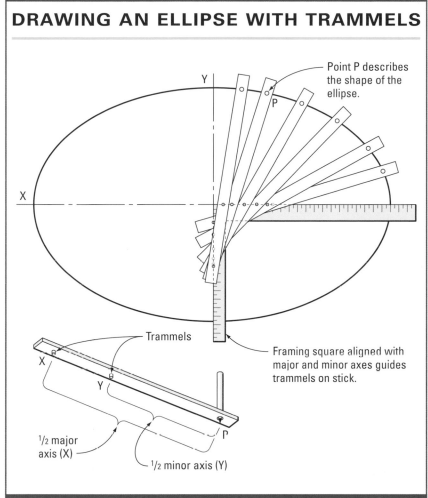

Point P describes the shape of the ellipse.

Trammels

Framing square aligned with major and minor axes guides trammels on stick.

1/2 major axis (X)

1/2 minor axis (Y)

DRAWING A SYMMETRICAL OGEE CURVE

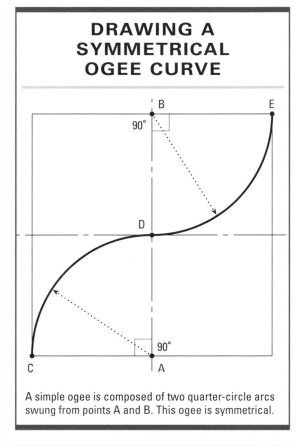

A simple ogee is composed of two quarter-circle arcs swung from points A and B. This ogee is symmetrical.

DRAWING AN ASYMMETRICAL OGEE CURVE

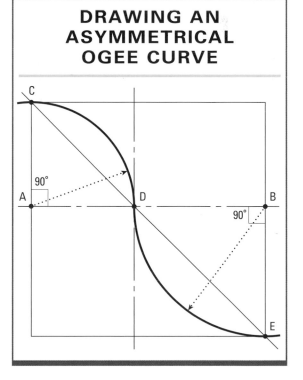

DRAWING SERPENTINE CURVES

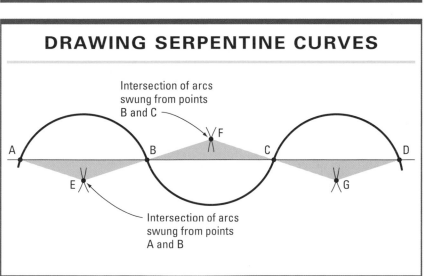

Intersection of arcs swung from points B and C

Intersection of arcs swung from points A and B

DRAWING A FREEFORM CURVE WITH A BATTEN

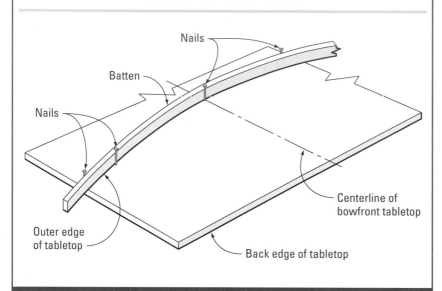

Nails

Batten

Nails

Outer edge of tabletop

Centerline of bowfront tabletop

Back edge of tabletop

Varying the radii of arcs enables you to design a variety of molding shapes.

▶ DRAWING FREEHAND CURVES

Although seemingly difficult, the drawing of freeform curves becomes almost second nature with practice. Begin by establishing a rectangle in which the curve fits. This proportions the relationship of the length to the width of the curve and provides guidelines you can use to sketch. When sketching the curve, try pivoting from the wrist, knuckle of the little finger, or elbow. By extending or shortening your grasp on the pencil, you can control the size of the curve.

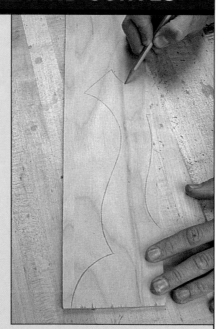

Adjusting where you grasp the pencil enables you to control the size of freeform curves.

Geometrical curves are drawn with the aid of a device such as a template or compass. By interconnecting the arcs, you can easily draw uniform, flowing curves for moldings. By experimenting with various radii, you can alter the molding proportions to achieve the desired effect. A *fair curve* is an arc with an inconsistent radius (such as ellipse). This element is often used to great advantage in contemporary furniture to create sinuous forms and relieve the boxiness of rectilinear shapes. A simple method for drawing a fair curve is to flex a thin stick, called a batten, to the desired curve and then trace it. The batten can be held in place by nails. Or thread a string through a hole on each end and pull it taut, like a bow string, to hold the batten's shape while the curve is drawn. Otherwise, a helper can keep the batten taut and in place.

Freeform curves are drawn by hand without the aid of a compass.

Making Patterns

Good patterns are one of the keys to good curves, because the lines and proportions are worked out before committing solid stock.

Afterward, the design can be stored for future use along with other information. For example, it's handy to note stock size, joint dimensions, and so on right on the pattern.

I like a stiff, strong material for patterns instead of heavy paper; ¼-in. birch plywood works well. The tight, diffuse porous grain provides a smooth surface for sketching and laying out.

When you've completed the sketch of the design on the plywood, carefully saw to the lines. After sawing, smooth and fair the curves with a spindle sander and/or a file. This is a real time saver: Removing irregularities in the pattern is far easier than working them out of solid stock later on!

Bandsaw Blade Selection for Curves

Your key to sawing accurate curves on the bandsaw is control. To get the most control, I use the widest possible blade for the job; it makes sawing to the line much easier, and I can avoid much of the tedious fairing of the curves afterward. You'll find that you can saw most curves with a ¼-in.-wide blade and avoid blade changes. However, narrow blades tend to wander in the cut; thus to saw a broad, gentle curve, you'll have to cut slowly. It makes sense to switch to a wider blade, because the blade is much easier to keep on path and you can saw faster with greater control. The drawing on p. 62 provides a guide for selecting blade width.

Blade pitch is the number of teeth per inch (tpi). If the pitch is too fine (too many teeth), the gullets fill with dust. When this

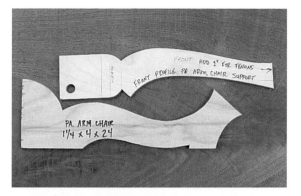

Noting dimensions right on the template enables you to keep the information handy for using now or making the same piece later.

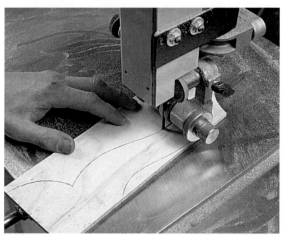

Cut the plywood pattern just to your line.

Remove any imperfections in a plywood pattern by sanding.

HOW BANDSAW BLADE WIDTH AFFECTS CUTTING RADIUS

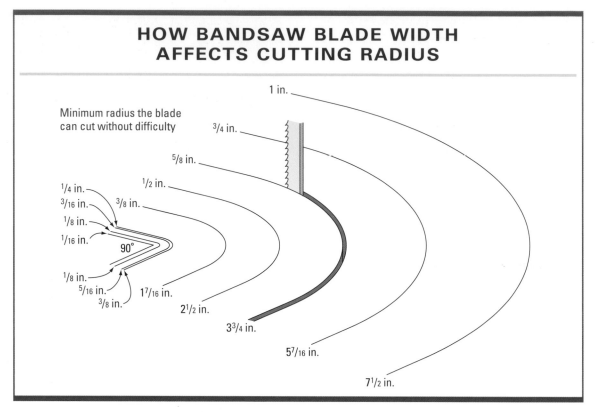

Minimum radius the blade can cut without difficulty

1 in.

3/4 in.

5/8 in.

1/2 in.

1/4 in.
3/16 in.
1/8 in.
1/16 in.
3/8 in.

90°

1/8 in.
5/16 in.
3/8 in.

1 7/16 in.
2 1/2 in.
3 3/4 in.
5 7/16 in.
7 1/2 in.

A CURVED FENCE FOR CUTTING SMALL ARCS

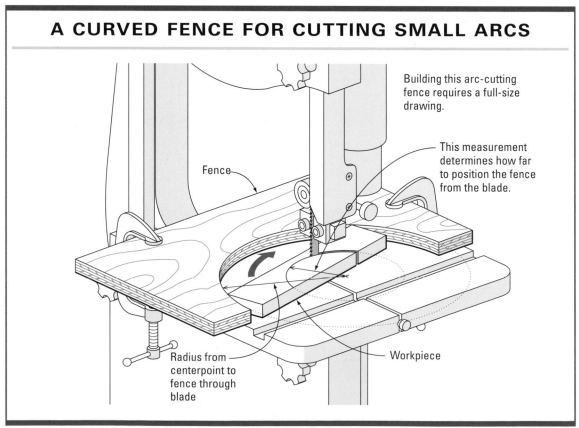

Building this arc-cutting fence requires a full-size drawing.

This measurement determines how far to position the fence from the blade.

Fence

Radius from centerpoint to fence through blade

Workpiece

▶ NEST PARTS TO SAVE LUMBER

Let's face it, sawing curves is wasteful. But one way to avoid needlessly wasting excessive stock is to nest parts together. When I select stock for chair legs, I look for pieces wide enough for at least two or three legs. This has the added advantage of getting a consistent grain and color match for the parts.

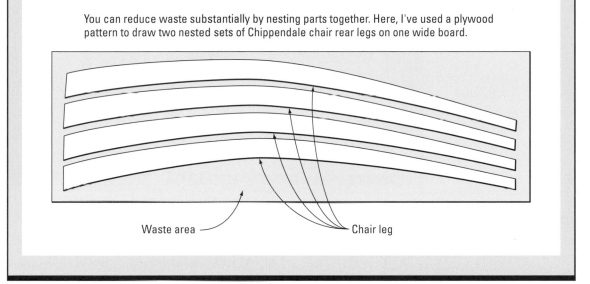

You can reduce waste substantially by nesting parts together. Here, I've used a plywood pattern to draw two nested sets of Chippendale chair rear legs on one wide board.

Waste area —   — Chair leg

happens, cutting slows down and the blade heats up. The rule of thumb to follow is to select a blade pitch that places 6 to 12 teeth in contact with the stock. For example, 4 tpi used with 2-in. stock places 8 teeth in contact with the stock. Thus the pitch is a good choice for the job.

Jigs for Cutting Circles and Arcs

Making many circles or arcs of the same radius can require tedious clean up if they are all cut freehand. There are several useful jigs for cutting arcs, circles, and ellipses with your bandsaw or router.

When cutting a number of true circles, you'll find it helpful to use a jig that allows you to rotate the stock. An arc jig clamps to the bandsaw table to pivot the stock past the blade. When cutting small arcs, a curved fence can be used to guide the work.

▶ See *"Circles on the Bandsaw with a Jig"* on p. 64 and *"Arcs on the Bandsaw with a Jig"* on p. 65.

Arcs, Circles, and Ellipses Freehand on the Bandsaw

Unless I've got a large number of pieces to cut, I prefer to do the cutting freehand on the bandsaw. Cutting freehand is surprisingly fast and, with a little practice, accurate. The key is to use the widest possible blade and follow the line closely (**A**). If your saw's table is small, space your hands farther apart to support the stock (**B**). After sawing, smooth the edges with a spokeshave (**C**). If you're careful to watch the grain direction, you'll avoid tearout.

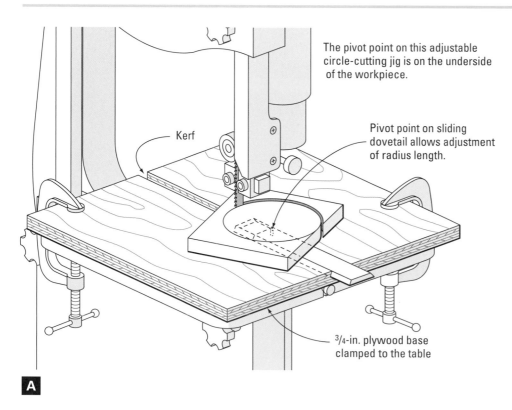

The pivot point on this adjustable circle-cutting jig is on the underside of the workpiece.

Kerf

Pivot point on sliding dovetail allows adjustment of radius length.

3/4-in. plywood base clamped to the table

Circles on the Bandsaw with a Jig

When cutting a number of true circles, you'll find it helpful to use a jig that allows you to rotate the stock. Build the jig shown here (**A**). The pin's location is adjustable by sliding the board that holds the pin to the desired distance from the blade. The pin-to-blade distance represents the radius of the circle. Make a small hole in the stock at the center of the circle you wish to cut. This will ride on the pin as you pivot the stock through the blade of the bandsaw (**B**).

Arcs on the Bandsaw with a Jig

Multiple arcs can easily be cut on the bandsaw. First build the jig shown here (**A**). Make sure the jig is sturdily supported, especially if it extends far past the edge of the bandsaw table; a post can be propped under the end. To use the jig, secure the workpiece with the toggle clamps. Swing the pivot arm and then pivot the workpiece into the bandsaw blade to make the cut (**B**). To make a small arc, you can make a circular fence in which the workpiece rides.

➤ See *"Jigs for Cutting Circles and Arcs"* on p. 63.

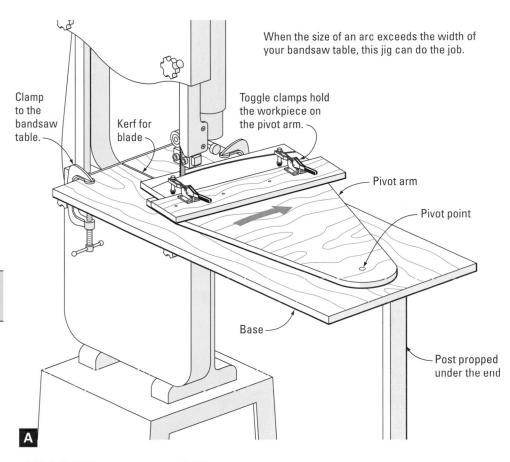

When the size of an arc exceeds the width of your bandsaw table, this jig can do the job.

Clamp to the bandsaw table.

Kerf for blade

Toggle clamps hold the workpiece on the pivot arm.

Pivot arm

Pivot point

Base

Post propped under the end

Circles or Ellipses with a Template

Whenever you're making a large number of circles or ellipses, a router and template will speed the process. Unlike the bandsaw, the router will leave a finished surface. The template can be made of plywood or medium-density fiberboard (MDF) and fastened to the workpiece with small nails, screws, or double-sided tape (**A**). A bearing-guided router bit will follow the plywood template and trim the work flush or create a molded edge, depending on the bit profile (**B**).

Bandsawing Tight Curves

Bandsawing should always begin with a pattern. This allows you to work out proportions and create smooth, flowing curves.

➤ See *"Making Patterns"* on p. 60.

Begin by carefully tracing the pattern onto the stock (**A**). If there are slight imperfections in the wood, you can often orient the pattern to locate them in areas of offcuts.

The example for this technique is two bracket feet joined by molding. Shape the molding before bandsawing, while the straight reference edges are still intact (**B**). The long, straight section that spans the feet is difficult to cut with a bandsaw. Instead, make a stop cut on the table saw. The stop block prevents kickback (**C**), and a second cut from the opposite face will reach into the corners (**D**).

[**VARIATION**] **You can get a straighter line between the bracket feet if you use the table saw instead of the bandsaw. It's called a stop cut, and the way to do it safely is with a stop block clamped to the fence or table.**

(Text continues on p. 68.)

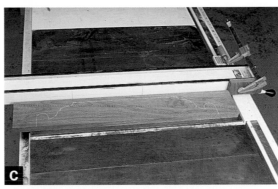

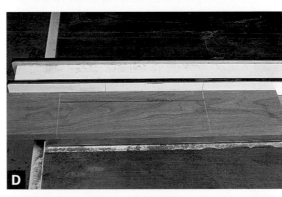

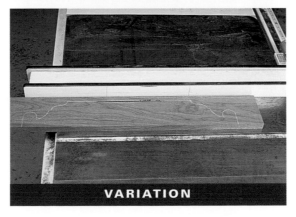

VARIATION

Before bandsawing, mount a blade that will turn the tightest contour without binding. Then plan the cutting sequence to avoid trapping the blade (**E**). Backing out of the turn is a sure way to pull the blade off the wheels (**F**).

You can avoid tedious cleanup of the surface by carefully sawing to the layout line (**G**). When the bandsawing is complete, smooth the curves with a spindle sander (**H**) and clean up the intersections with a chisel for a crisp, defined look (**I**).

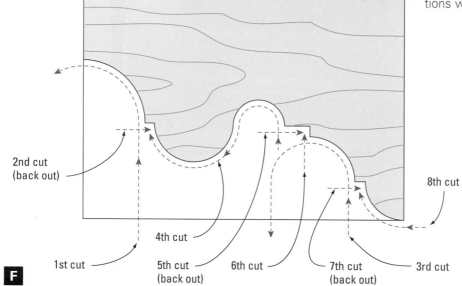

2nd cut
(back out)

8th cut

4th cut

F

1st cut   5th cut   6th cut   7th cut   3rd cut
                 (back out)   (back out)

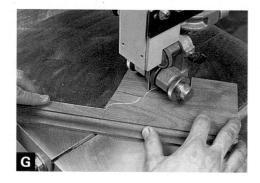

Bandsawing Broad, Sweeping Curves

Although you can bandsaw a broad curve with a narrow blade, it requires more concentration and effort because a narrow blade has a natural tendency to wander in the cut. I prefer to use a wide blade (**A**), because it naturally follows the broad curves of components such as chair rockers. After mounting the blade, trace the pattern onto the stock (**B**). Then carefully follow the layout line (**C**).

Use a compass plane to smooth the surface after sawing (**D**). The flexible sole will adapt to both convex and concave surfaces (**E**). Clamp the matching pairs of stock together to check for square (**F**). If you don't have a compass plane, a spokeshave can be used to clean up the surface.

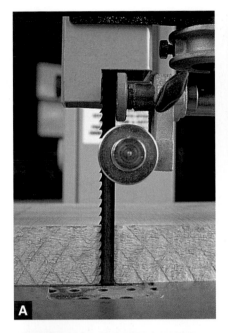

Sawing Multiples

If you've got several intricate pieces to saw, it makes sense to stack them together. Not only will the work be a perfect match (**A**) but you'll avoid the tedium of following detailed outlines on several pieces. Best of all, the time spent on the process is significantly reduced.

Begin by stacking the pieces and wrapping them with masking tape or use a good double-stick tape. Then draw the outline onto the top of the stack. Choose a blade with a pitch that is suited for the total thickness (**B**). As you saw, it may be necessary to stop occasionally and add a strip of tape to replace any pieces that are severed (**C**). When you've completed the pattern, smooth the surfaces before untaping them. A spindle sander is useful for concave areas (**D**), but convex contours are more easily smoothed with small files (**E**). A tiny needle file will reach into even the smallest spaces to smooth away any bumps in the contour (**F**).

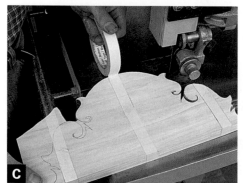

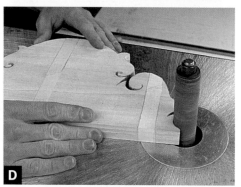

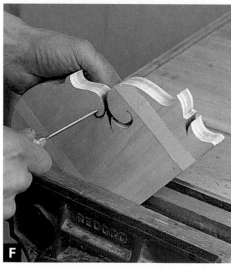

> ⚠ **WARNING** Stacking work in layers for scrollsawing or bandsawing is a great method for saving time. But I don't stack parts higher than their width. Otherwise the cut may not be safe or precise.

Scrollsawing on the Bandsaw

You can saw tiny, intricate curves with your bandsaw by mounting a 1/16-in. scrolling blade (**A**). However, although this technique is useful for occasional scrolling, you can't saw interior work as you can with a scrollsaw.

To give the tiny 1/16-in. scrolling blade the support it needs, you'll have to replace the steel guide blocks on your bandsaw with wooden blocks or Cool Blocks (**B**). Before mounting the blocks, cut a small V in one block for the blade. After mounting the blade, completely enclose it in the V with the blocks.

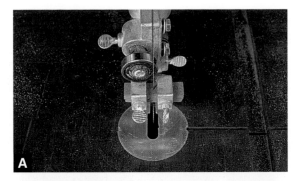

Resawing a Curve

Resawing is the process of ripping a board through its thickness. By resawing a shallow curve, you can create wide, curved panels such as chair backs.

Begin by selecting stock thick enough for the curve. To create a curve that is free of dead spots, it's best if the stock is thick enough to bury the blade throughout the entire cut.

I prefer a wide (1 in. or more) blade with a coarse, variable pitch (**A**). If your saw won't tension a wide blade, select a 3/8-in. variable pitch blade and tension it as much as possible. Also check the table for squareness to the blade before you begin.

Bandsaw the convex face first by carefully sawing freehand to the layout line (**B**). Then remove the saw marks with a spokeshave.

(Text continues on p. 72.)

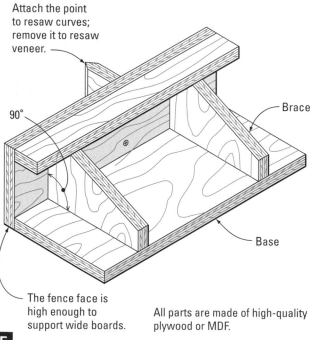

By skewing the spokeshave, you can avoid tearout in most instances (**C**). Otherwise, switch to a scraper (**D**).

To resaw the second face, use a point fence (**E**). This simple device is a great aid for keeping the two cuts parallel and the work of uniform thickness. Clamp the fence so that the point is positioned parallel to the teeth of the blade. Before making the cut, scribe a layout line parallel to the first fence. As you saw, follow the line precisely, making sure the work is in contact with the fence (**F**).

When smoothing the concave face, work with the grain, from the ends to the middle, to reduce tearout (**G**).

Attach the point to resaw curves; remove it to resaw veneer.

90°

Brace

Base

The fence face is high enough to support wide boards.

All parts are made of high-quality plywood or MDF.

Brick-Stacking Tight Curves

If you bandsaw tight, continuous curves of a quarter circle or more, you'll end up with *short grain* at the ends. Short grain creates structural problems because it is inherently weak.

One method for avoiding short grain is a traditional technique called "brick-stacking." This method involves mitering short blocks and stacking them up to create curved segments. As the "bricks" are stacked, the joints are staggered, which greatly increases the overall strength (**A**). Afterward, a curve is sawn into the stack and the curved assembly is covered with a sheet of veneer to hide the layers and variations in grain (**B**).

Although this is a time-honored technique, it has a drawback: The bricks creep somewhat with changes in seasonal humidity. Eventually, the brick layers telegraph through the veneer. However, if you saw your own thick veneer this will be less of a problem.

To create a brick-stacked curve, you'll first want to draw the curve full-scale and divide it into a number of individual segments (**C**). A small number of segments may introduce short grain, whereas a large number may complicate the process.

Once you've settled on the number of blocks needed, add the blocks to your drawing to determine the miter angle. Next, mill the blocks to length while mitering the ends. A stop on your saw will keep the blocks consistent (**D**).

When you've completed these steps, you're ready to begin construction. Glue the blocks end to end with yellow glue; it grabs fast and you'll avoid an awkward clamping assembly (**E**).

(Text continues on p. 74.)

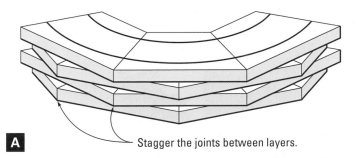

A Stagger the joints between layers.

B

C

D

E

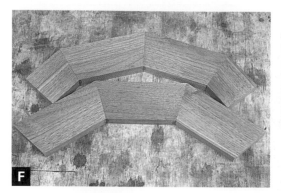
F

G

H

I

J

K

Next, stack the layers and glue them together. Make sure that you stagger the joints between layers (**F**). Clamp the assembly and allow the glue to set (**G**).

The next step is to bandsaw the curve. Lay out the curve on the top of the stack and follow the line closely (**H**). Now smooth away the saw marks with a scraper (**I**).

You can purchase veneer, but I prefer to saw my own (**J**); I can select the grain I want and I saw it thicker than commercial veneer to increase its strength and longevity. Finally, coat the veneer with glue and wrap it around the curved assembly. Place it in a vacuum press until the glue has set (**K**). Afterward, bandsaw the second face.

➤ See *"Bending"* on p. 272.

Sawing Curves with a Coping Saw

A coping saw has a frame to tension a narrow blade for sawing tight contours. If you need to saw scrollwork only occasionally, a coping saw is an inexpensive way to go.

The key when using a coping saw is to provide support for the stock. Make a simple device called a *bird's mouth* (**A**). It is a board with a deep V cut into one end. To use it, clamp it to the benchtop with the V overhanging the edge. Position the workpiece over the V and begin sawing (**B**). As you follow the outline, reposition the work as necessary to provide support close to the cut.

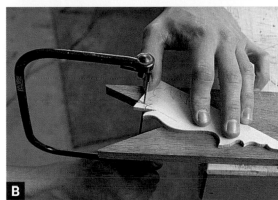

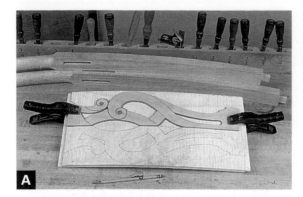

A

C

B

Interior Cuts with a Scrollsaw

The scrollsaw is the tool of choice for interior cuts. (A jigsaw can also be used, but it won't be as accurate and will require more cleanup with a file and sandpaper.) The blade of a scrollsaw can be unclamped at one end and threaded through a hole in the workpiece. Because the blade is clamped securely at each end, the cut is precise with minimal flex.

As an example of this process, I'm using a curved chair back. When tracing the pattern, it's necessary to flex it so it conforms to the curve of the work. You can hold it in position with clamps while tracing the outline (**A**).

Next, drill a small hole at each interior cutout for threading the blade (**B**). When sawing, take your time and follow the layout lines closely; this greatly reduces the amount of tedious cleanup later (**C**).

To create the illusion of thinness and delicacy, scrollwork is sometimes beveled on the edges. It's time-consuming work, but the refined appearance is worth the effort.

➤ See *"Beveling Curved Edges"* at right.

[**VARIATION**] You can also use a coping saw or fretsaw to cut interior curves by loosening the blade and freeing it so that you can enter the work through the drill hole.

Beveling Curved Edges

Beveling the edges of curves is a centuries-old technique for making the stock appear thinner than it actually is. This detail creates an illusion of lightness without sacrificing strength. The splat (the back center area) of the chair shown on p. 86 is a good example. The difficulty is that the work of beveling all those tight, interconnected curves is extremely tedious.

To help speed the process, first bevel the edges with a modified router bit. Beginning with an inexpensive high-speed steel router bit (**A**), grind away most of the steel to create a chamfer bit with a 15-degree angle (**B**).

Next, mount the bit in a laminate trimmer, which is really a small router (**C**). The small base will easily follow the curved surface of the splat, and the small-diameter pilot on the bit reaches into the corners (**D**). Before beginning the cut, adjust the depth so that the pilot of the bit just grazes the edges of the surface.

After routing, you will still need to carve the corners (**E**) and complete the bevel. But much of the tedious handwork has been eliminated.

A

C

B

D

E

Complex Shapes

Raised Panels

Door Frames

Coopered Panels

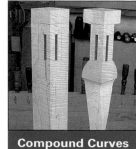

Compound Curves

MOVING FROM TWO DIMENSIONS to three looks pretty challenging. Just thinking about it is hard enough, and getting the all those cuts in the right direction on the right face of the stock is even more so. But really, it's not as hard as it looks. The key is marking out carefully and working methodically, step by step. After all, compound shapes are just simple shapes put together. The rewards for your effort are new design possibilities and, in some cases—such as frame-and-panel work—better construction.

The Beauty and Function of the Frame and Panel

The frame and panel is one of the most important elements of furniture design. Its construction allows for seasonal wood movement, yet it can usually be adapted to suit most any style or period of furniture. The most common use of frame-and-panel construction is in doors. But it's also used for lids and even for the sides of casework.

The broad appeal of the frame-and-panel design is its ability to overcome problems normally associated with seasonal changes in relative humidity. It works like this: A panel is trapped within a framework, yet the panel is free to expand and contract within that frame. This works because the thin edges of the panel fit within a groove in the frame. The frame gets its strength from the typically used mortise-and-tenon joinery. This prevents the panel from warping or distorting without limiting its natural movement. Frame-and-panel design allows you to cover a large expanse, yet keep the space around the door small, because expansion of the door is limited to its framework.

FRAME-AND-PANEL CONFIGURATION

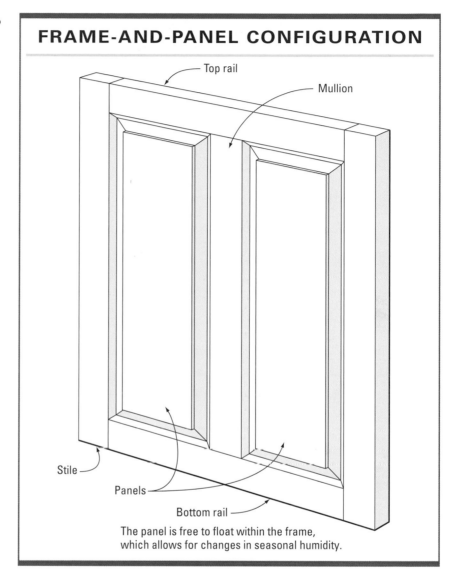

The panel is free to float within the frame, which allows for changes in seasonal humidity.

TYPICAL FRAME-AND-PANEL DESIGN

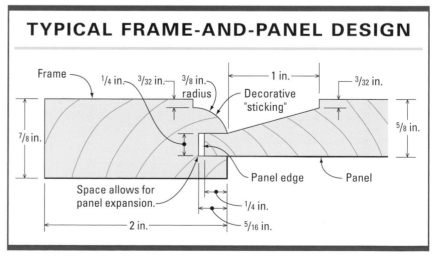

THE MORTISE-AND-TENON JOINT

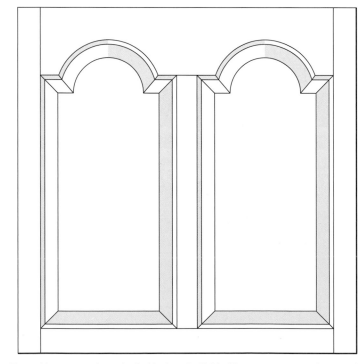

Mortise

Tenon shoulder   Tenon face

The time-honored mortise-and-tenon joint gets its unsurpassed strength from the mechanical interlock and long-grain surface area for glue.

RECTANGULAR PANELS

To avoid a square, boxy look this door is divided into two rectangular panels.

Because the grain in the panel normally runs vertically, the top and bottom rails are made wider than the stile to prevent panel distortion. For visual balance, the bottom rail is typically made slightly wider than the top rail. There are exceptions to this rule of thumb, however. For example, doors with an arched panel require a wide top rail to accommodate the arch. In this case, the remainder of the rail after cutting the arch is typically equal to the stile width.

Visually speaking, rectangular panels are more attractive than square ones. For this reason, square openings are usually divided into two doors (or one door with two rectangular panels). Otherwise, I like using a numerical proportioning system for calculating door size.

Once I've settled on the overall dimensions and proportions, I turn my attention to visual details. The most common panel edge is a flat bevel. But the edge can also be a

PANEL-EDGE DESIGN OPTIONS

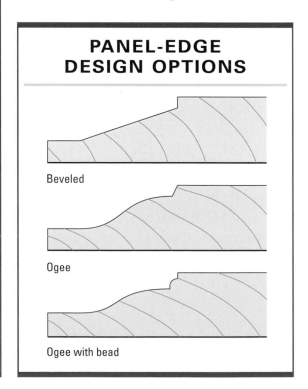

Beveled

Ogee

Ogee with bead

curve, ogee, or a simple bevel. The panel shape can be square, arched, tombstone, or cathedral. Once completed, the overall effect of the design is strong, so I'm careful to chose details and proportions that complement rather than compete with the overall design of the piece on which the panel is to be used.

Panel-Raising Jig for the Table Saw

Panels can be raised with any number of methods: with a shaper, on a router table, or by hand. Without a doubt, the shaper is the most efficient tool you can use to raise panels. But shapers are expensive and routers lack the power to cut the profile in one pass. Because of these limitations, for many woodworkers the table saw may be the best option. Most woodworkers own table saws and the machine can easily make the cut in one pass.

To set up your table saw for panel raising, it makes sense to build a jig. Of course you can instead tilt the blade and guide the stock with the fence. But the fence on most saws lacks sufficient height to provide good support for the panel. This jig overcomes the support problem and offers other advantages as well. The broad surface area of the jig provides plenty of support, and the bevel angle is built in. So there's no need to tilt the blade and check the angle. Each time you use the jig, you'll save time. In addition, it's safer than using the fence.

One final note: Construct the jig so that it fits in your saw's miter slot instead of just following the fence. This will prevent the jig (or work) from coming in contact with the back of the blade and causing kickback.

Tombstone Doors

Frame-and-panel doors can take on myriad designs. But certainly one of the most elegant examples is the tombstone door. A centuries-old design, the tombstone door is from a period when all woodworking was done by hand. Today, despite the beauty of the design, tombstone doors are not often seen. I'm sure that one reason is that the inside corners that flank the arch must be

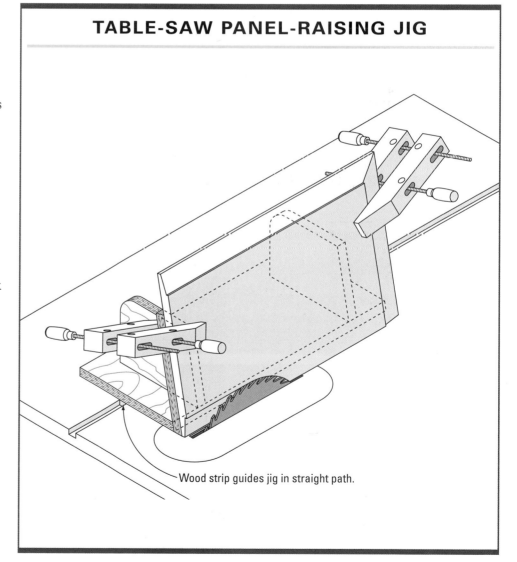

TABLE-SAW PANEL-RAISING JIG

Wood strip guides jig in straight path.

TOMBSTONE DOOR

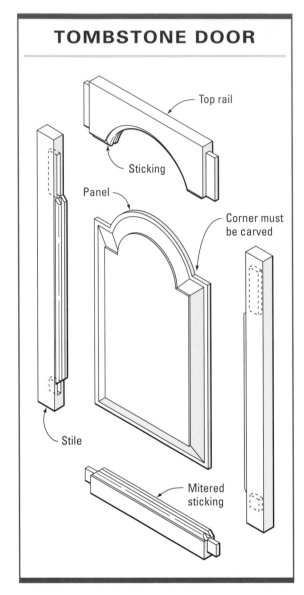

Top rail

Sticking

Panel

Corner must
be carved

Stile

Mitered
sticking

VARIATIONS ON THE TOMBSTONE PANEL

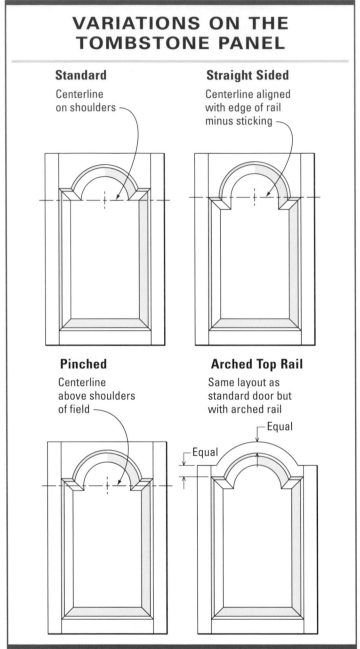

Standard
Centerline
on shoulders

Straight Sided
Centerline aligned
with edge of rail
minus sticking

Pinched
Centerline
above shoulders
of field

Arched Top Rail
Same layout as
standard door but
with arched rail

Equal

Equal

carved. That's because router bits and shaper cutters cut in an arc, and so they won't create inside corners. The solution is to carve the corners by hand. This process isn't really difficult—just a bit time-consuming.

If you would like to incorporate tombstone doors into your next project, there are several designs from which to choose.

Door Joinery and Structural Strength

Router bits and shaper cutters are available in several profiles, making it easy to achieve traditional door frame joinery. Cope-and-stick joinery is actually quite a simple concept. A profile is milled on the inside of the door stile (the vertical member), and its reverse profile or mirror image is milled on the rail (the horizontal member). In the process, a short tenon is formed that fits into the groove created for the panel. The drawing below shows a typical cope-and-stick router bit set. Single reversible bits are somewhat cheaper, but they can be fussier to set up.

Cope-and-stick joinery is fast and efficient and is best used when you have a large number of doors to make, say, for a kitchen. But this method of construction is not as strong as a traditional mortise-and-tenon

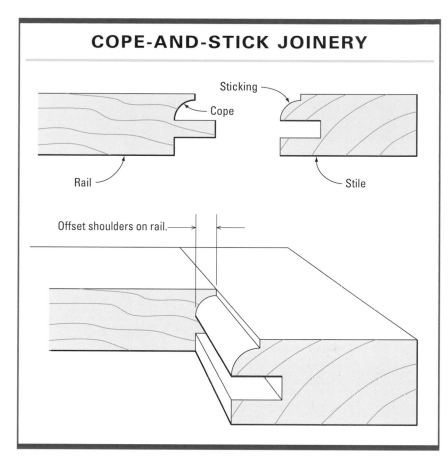

COPE-AND-STICK JOINERY

Sticking

Cope

Rail

Stile

Offset shoulders on rail.

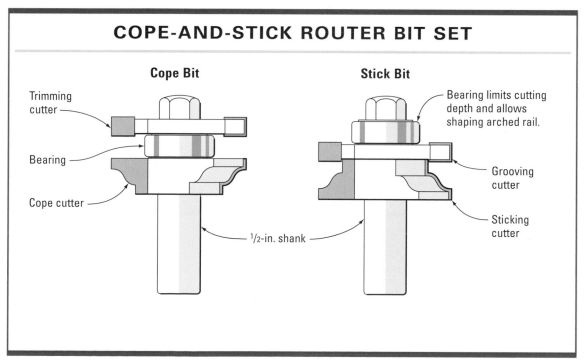

COPE-AND-STICK ROUTER BIT SET

Cope Bit

Trimming cutter

Bearing

Cope cutter

Stick Bit

Bearing limits cutting depth and allows shaping arched rail.

Grooving cutter

Sticking cutter

½-in. shank

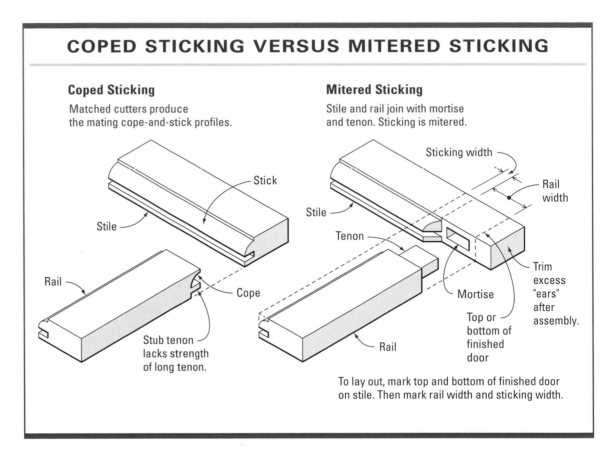

COPED STICKING VERSUS MITERED STICKING

Coped Sticking
Matched cutters produce the mating cope-and-stick profiles.

Stick

Stile

Rail

Cope

Stub tenon lacks strength of long tenon.

Mitered Sticking
Stile and rail join with mortise and tenon. Sticking is mitered.

Sticking width

Rail width

Stile

Tenon

Mortise

Top or bottom of finished door

Trim excess "ears" after assembly.

Rail

To lay out, mark top and bottom of finished door on stile. Then mark rail width and sticking width.

joinery. The short tongue or tenon created by the coping cut is typically only ⅜ in. and just doesn't have much long-grain gluing surface. So if you're building furniture for the ages, you'll want to consider the tried-and-true mitered sticking method, in which a regular tenon provides all the strength the frame will need to stand up to time.

Sash Door Construction

Constructing a sash-type door with interlocking bars is always a challenge. There are two keys to completing a successful project: accurate layout and precise machine setup. I've found that by checking each setup for fit to the previous one, success is virtually ensured.

First, design your door. The drawing at right shows the structure of a typical sash door. Once you've drawn a plan for your door, mill your stock to the correct width and length. Mark your layout on the stock using a sharp pencil with a hard lead (no. 4) to get an accurate reference mark. Your mark needs to be exact, so use a very sharp pencil. After the initial sharpening, sharpen the pencil to a chisel edge with very fine sandpaper. Carefully measure and mark the location of each joint. As you cut your profiles, check and double-check to make sure your setup is accurate.

SASH DOOR ANATOMY

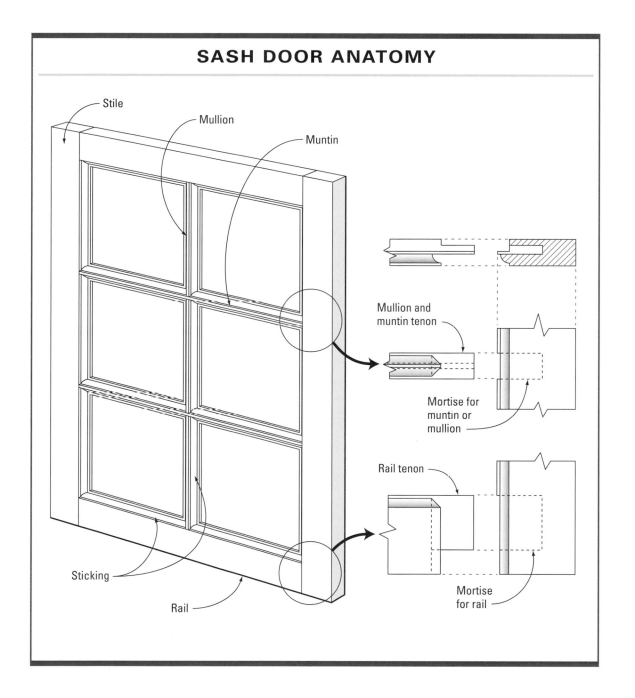

Stile

Mullion

Muntin

Mullion and
muntin tenon

Mortise for
muntin or
mullion

Rail tenon

Sticking

Rail

Mortise
for rail

SASH DOOR LAYOUT

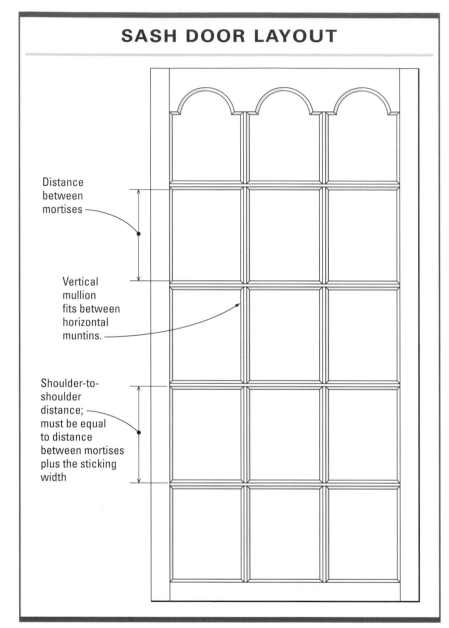

Distance between mortises

Vertical mullion fits between horizontal muntins.

Shoulder-to-shoulder distance; must be equal to distance between mortises plus the sticking width

Compound Curves Are Much Easier Than They Look

A compound curve flows in two directions simultaneously. Although the sculptural look appears difficult to execute, the technique is really quite easy. First bandsaw one face of the stock; then saw an adjacent face. When you've finished bandsawing, much of the effect has been achieved. The remaining handwork involves smoothing and blending the curves.

Probably the most familiar example of a compound curve is the cabriole leg. But you can see the influence of compound curves in many furniture styles, including contemporary pieces.

This eighteenth-century-style chair looks complicated; but when broken down into steps, these shapes are fairly straight-forward to create.

This coffee table shows how compound shapes can add interest to a contemporary design.

When designing furniture with compound curves, I find it necessary to build a prototype. It's very difficult to completely judge the curves and proportions by simply looking at a drawing (though it's a great place to begin). After sketching the design on plywood, bandsaw the curves to create a pattern. Then choose some inexpensive wood and model a prototype. Trace the pattern onto two adjacent surfaces. Next, bandsaw the outline on the first surface. Then tape the offcuts back in position and saw the second face.

After sawing, smooth and fair the curves with a spokeshave or rasp, depending on the tightness of the curve. As you work, examine the curve for irregularities. When you're satisfied with the lines, begin sculpting and blending with a rasp. As you sculpt, follow the outline you've already established.

Careful study of the prototype is one of the keys to success. When you're finished

Although drawings are a great place to start a design, a prototype brings the design to life.

Machines can do most of the rough work, but gouges and rasps refine the final shapes.

modeling the prototype, stand it on you bench for critiquing. This stage of the process is crucial; it gives you the opportunity to check out the design before committing it to a piece of furniture. I like to view the prototype from all angles, as I examine the curves and proportions. Usually, you'll find areas that need improvement. Perhaps the curve is too pronounced or maybe a dimension is disproportionate. If this happens, you'll be glad that you took the time to create a prototype.

Complex Designs Require Careful Planning

Asymmetrical compound curves (such as the chair arm and post in shown on p. 87) are a true test of a furniture maker's skill. Balance, curve, and proportion are critical for the piece to be visually successful. Added to the complexity is the joint where the arm and post meet. But a logical approach to the

problem combined with a systematic order of events help you avoid major setbacks.

For example, I usually prefer to cut joints before bandsawing curves. If the stock is straight and square, it easily registers against the milled surfaces of my machines. But this isn't always practical—or even possible with curved elements. Although I cut the tenons on the arm post before sawing the curves, I use an opposite approach on the arm itself. Otherwise, the stock is too wide to fit within my benchtop mortiser. Also, sometimes it's easier to cut the joint by hand than to consume time with an elaborate machine setup. Unlike most compound curves, asymmetrical curves require two patterns. In fact, the arm in this example uses three patterns: top, inside, and outside. After the patterns are traced onto the stock, extra care is needed when sawing the side. Following the pattern precisely on one side will result in a miscut on the opposite side. But if you take time to plan the cutting sequence, you can avoid spoiling the work.

You'll also find on this type of work that the bandsaw is really useful only for removing excess stock. Afterward, you'll need to shape the surfaces by hand with gouges and a rasp to remove stock in areas that the saw couldn't reach. This is the enjoyable part of the work—and the part that creates the details you can't match with machine work.

Finally, before I commit time and expensive stock to such a lengthy process, I model a prototype. Sculpted furniture parts are difficult to conceive without a three-dimensional model.

Raised Panels on the Shaper

If you're shaping a number of panels, the shaper is definitely the tool of choice. Most shapers have a hefty spindle and powerful motor, which enable you to shape a panel in one pass.

Use a box fence to shield your hands from the cutter. As an added benefit, the cutterhead opening in the fence is small. This prevents the work from tipping into the cutterhead, which can potentially cause a kickback.

Begin by mounting a rub bearing under the cutterhead. This provides additional support for the stock and aids in setting the fence. Mount the cutterhead over the bearing and lock it in place with the spindle nut. Next, adjust the height of the cutterhead (**A**). Then secure the fence (**B**). Use a straightedge to position the fence tangent to the bearing and clamp the fence firmly in place. Finally, adjust the front of the box fence for the panel thickness (**C**).

Make a trial cut and fit it within the frame groove. A snug (but not tight) fit allows for seasonal expansion but prevents the panel from rattling when the door is opened.

To avoid cross-grain tearout, first shape the ends (**D**) and finish with the sides (**E**).

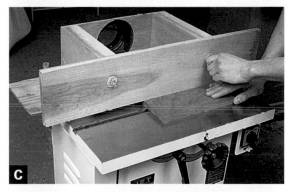

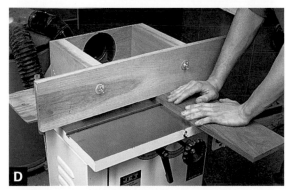

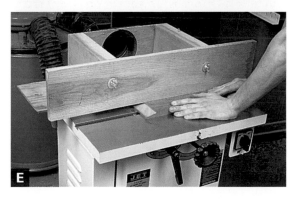

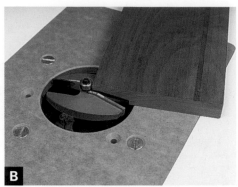

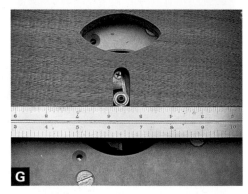

Raised Panels on the Router Table

Shapers are expensive and have a steep learning curve to master. So if you already own a router table, it makes sense to use it to shape panels—especially if you raise panels only occasionally.

Depending on the density of the wood you're shaping and the size of your router, you'll need to make the cut in two to five passes. This prevents the router from overheating and shutting down.

To set up the router table, first mount the bit securely (**A**). Make certain that the shank of the bit is clean and firmly locked into the collet. Next, adjust the bit height for the panel cutting depth (**B**). Then set the fence for a shallow cut (**C**). Note that the unique design of a box fence completely surrounds the cutterhead to keep hands safe. It also directs the shavings toward the dust collector.

Before connecting the router to a power source, make certain that the fence is clamped firmly and that the bit clears the fence. Finally, adjust the front of the box to the thickness of the panel (**D**).

Make the first cut starting with the end grain (**E**); then shape the edges. This way you'll avoid tearout on the ends (**F**). Shape all the panels before increasing the cutting depth (**G**) and check the final cut with the corresponding frame groove.

Raised Panels by Hand

Why raise panels by hand? It's quiet and safe—and there's a real pleasure that comes from shaping things by hand. Also, if you seldom shape panels, then shaping them by hand may be a viable alternative to purchasing a router table and accessories.

To try this technique, you'll first need to sharpen your tools; they must cut cleanly for you to have success raising panels by hand.

Begin by milling the stock for the panel flat and square and to thickness. Next, mark your layout by scribing lines on the panel face to indicate the perimeter of the field (**A**). Then scribe the edge of the panel (**B**).

➤ See *"Milling Stock to Size"* on p. 45.

Start the shaping process by planing a rabbet to establish the field perimeter (**C**). The rabbet plane's fence establishes the width of the cut, and a depth stop limits the cut to the scribe you made earlier. To prevent tearout at the ends of the field, stop occasionally and scribe the field edge with a knife (**D**). After planing the ends, reposition the panel and rabbet the edges (**E**).

Now you're ready to bevel the panel. Use a rabbeting block plane because the skewed blade cuts cleanly. Begin with the panel ends, so that any tearout can be cleaned up with the passes down the sides. As you push the plane, tilt it to create the bevel (**F**). When you approach the final pass, make any adjustment in the angle of tilt if necessary. After planing the ends, finish with the sides (**G**). The completed panel is shown at right (**H**).

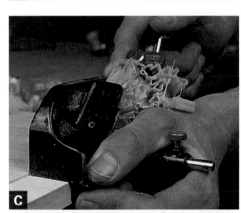

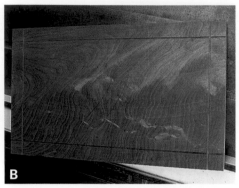

Raised Panels on the Table Saw

Shaping panels on the table saw is another good alternative to using a shaper. The table saw has plenty of power, and most woodworkers own this machine. But before you begin shaping on the table saw, take a few minutes to build a panel-raising jig. The jig holds the panel securely for a smoother cut. Plus the angle is built in, so you avoid having to tilt the sawblade each time you use this technique.

> See *"Panel-Raising Jig for the Table Saw"* on p. 81.

Once you've milled the stock for the panels, cut shallow grooves in the panel face (**A**) to score the perimeter of the field (**B**). Next, set the jig in position and adjust the blade height.

Now you're ready for the final cut. Clamp the panel in the jig and bevel the edges beginning with the end grain (**C**). Finish the process by beveling the long grain (**D**). Finally, use a scraper and sandpaper to remove the saw marks (**E**).

Arched Panel Door with Cope-and-Stick Router Bits

It may seem that making an arched door with a frame that matches the panel is complicated—but it's really not. The key is making an accurate, full-scale layout.

Begin by drawing a rectangle to represent the outside dimensions of the door.

➤ See *"Tombstone Doors"* on p. 81.

Next, use a compass to draw an arch to represent the top rail. Then, using the same center point, shorten the compass setting and draw an arch to represent the top edge of the panel. When you're satisfied with the drawing, mill the frame parts.

The next step is to set the bit height (**A**); then you're ready to shape the cope on the rail ends (**B**). Use a miter gauge for support.

Now bandsaw the arch in the top rail (**C**); use your drawing to determine the radius. Next, fasten a template to the rail and trim it flush with the router table (**D**); then switch router bits and mill the sticking and groove while the template is still attached (**E**). Remember to shape the stiles and bottom rail as well. Because the stock is straight rather than curved, it makes sense to use the fence (**F**).

(Text continues on p. 94.)

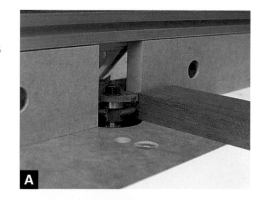

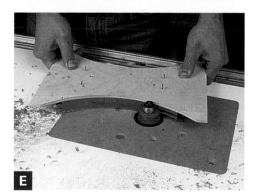

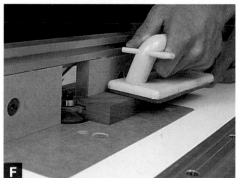

With the frame completed, turn your attention to the panel. First, mill the panel to size. Then band-saw the arch and trim it flush with the template (**G**). When fastening the template, drive the nails in the edges of the panel where they will be shaped away.

Now you're ready to shape the panel. Remove the template and begin with the arch. Use a box fence for safety. Position the arch against the fence (**H**) and pivot it into the spinning bit (**I**). Next, shape the opposite end and then the edges (**J**).

The last steps are to sand the panel and assemble the door (**K**).

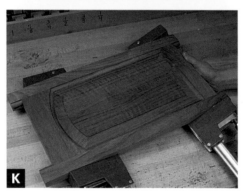

Door with Mitered Sticking

Mitered sticking adds structural strength to a door because it relies on longer tenons and deeper mortises than cope-and-stick joinery.

Begin by making an accurate, full-scale drawing of the door. This provides a layout reference to use throughout the process. Next, accurately mill the stock along with an extra piece or two for testing setups. Then lay out, cut, and fit the mortise-and-tenon joints (**A**). When laying out the tenons, add the sticking width to the shoulder at each end. This will compensate for the sticking around the mortise, which is removed before assembly.

The next step is to work the top rail. Begin by laying out the arch (**B**). After bandsawing (**C**), smooth the curve with a spindle sander (**D**).

Now you're ready to shape the frame. Begin by shaping the sticking profile; first on the top rail with a starting pin to begin the cut (**E**) and then on the stiles and bottom rail with a fence (**F**). Next, cut the panel groove using the same method as used for the sticking profile (**G**).

Once the sticking and panel grooves are shaped, you're ready to miter the sticking in the corners. First, tilt the table-saw blade to 45 degrees; then adjust the blade height to cut only the sticking.

(Text continues on p. 96.)

A

B

C

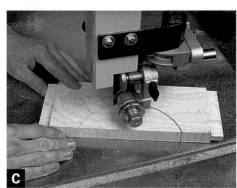

D

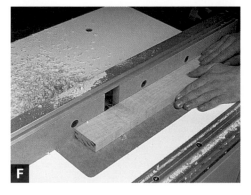

E

F

G

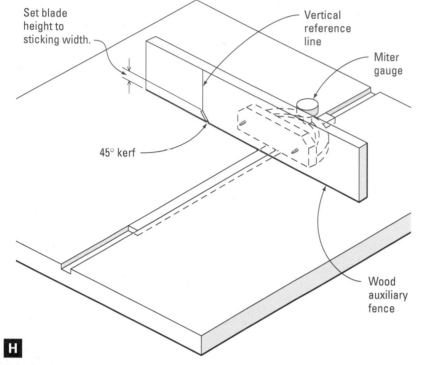

Set blade height to sticking width.

Vertical reference line

Miter gauge

45° kerf

Wood auxiliary fence

H

Next, mark a vertical line from the deepest point of the cut (**H**). Accuracy of the line is critical to the fit of the miters.

To use the setup, align the rail shoulders with the layout line and cut the miter (**I**). If you're mitering several pieces, clamp a thin piece of plywood to the miter gauge as a stop (**J**). To miter the stiles, align the mortise layout line with the layout line on the miter gauge (**K**). Before assembling the frame, you'll need to remove the excess sticking on the stiles with a chisel.

To make the panel, mill it to size and lay out the arch with a compass (**L**). The radius of the panel is typically ¼ in. greater than that of the top rail to allow for fitting into the panel groove.

Next, carefully bandsaw the panel arch (**M**) and smooth the curve with a file (**N**). Now the panel

I

J

K

L

M

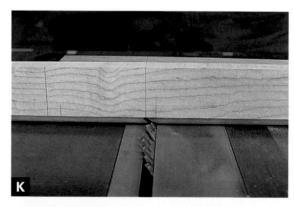

N

is ready for shaping. Shape the arch first, then the remainder of the panel (**O**).

To create an authentic panel, you'll need to carve the inside corners on each side of the arch. Although it's a bit time-consuming it's not at all difficult.

First, lay out the corner with a compass and square (**P**). Use the compass to complete the arch into the corner and the square to lay out the shoulder.

The next step is to cut away the excess stock in the corner (**Q**). Chisel across the grain to avoid splitting the panel (**R**). Next, incise the area indicated by the layout line. A chisel works well at the shoulder, but a carving gouge works best for the curve of the arch. Check the depth with a combination square to avoid cutting the area too deep (**S**).

With the initial carving done (**T**), you're ready to miter the intersection. First, incise the miter (**U**); then pare the beveled surfaces to the incision (**V**). You'll need left- and right-skewed chisels for this last stage of the carving.

Finally, sand the panel and assemble the door (**W**).

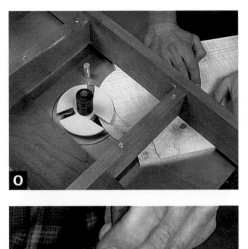

O

P

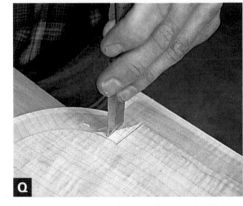

Q

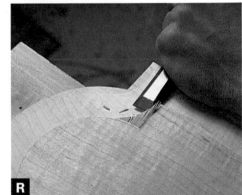

R

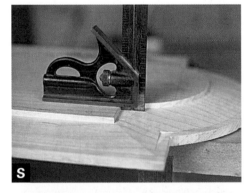

S

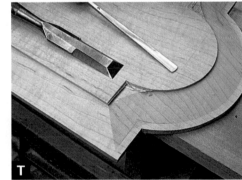

T

U

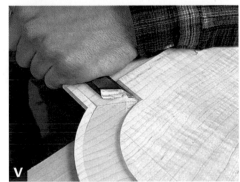

V

W

Small Tombstone Door

The process for making a small tombstone door is similar to the process for a large door. However, because the parts are very small, you'll need to use clamps and jigs to shape them safely.

Always begin with an accurate drawing, on which you've worked out details and proportions. After milling the parts of the door, lay out the arch in the rail (**A**). When bandsawing, follow the line carefully to avoid errors (**B**).

After smoothing the curve, shape the sticking (**C**) and then the panel groove. When shaping the curve of the top rail, use a large handscrew, which safely positions your hands and adds mass to the part being shaped.

When cutting the panel groove in the stile, remember to start the groove at one mortise and stop it at the other mortise (**D**). This will avoid having a gap in the top of the door frame after assembly. Use a stop block to prevent kickback. When milling the short bottom rail, always use a push block (**E**).

The next step is to miter the sticking.

▶ See *"Door with Mitered Sticking"* on p. 95.

With the frame complete. you're ready to shape the panel. The panel-raising bit has a bearing that follows the curve of the arch (**F**). To hold the panel safely while shaping, attach it to a push block with double-sided tape (**G**). This gives you

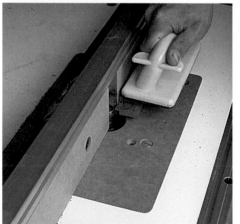

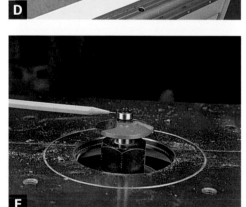

plenty of leverage while distancing your hand from the router bit.

[TIP] **When using double-sided tape, use woodturner's tape, which has tremendous holding power. Don't be fooled and use carpet tape. It doesn't work nearly as well.**

Apply the tape to the push block and peel the paper. Then position it on the panel and clamp it momentarily to strengthen the bond (**H**).

Shape the arch first (**I**), which is primarily end grain; then shape the rest of the panel using a fence to guide the stock (**J**). When shaping the arch, it's crucial to use a pin or block for a fulcrum when starting the cut. Once the work makes contact with the bearing on the bit, it's safe to pivot away from the starting pin or block. Positioning the fence for straight cuts is easy; simply align the fence tangent to the bearing (**K**).

Finally, carve the corners and assemble the door.

➤ See *"Door with Mitered Sticking"* on p. 95.

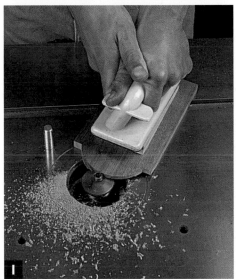

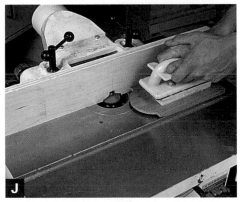

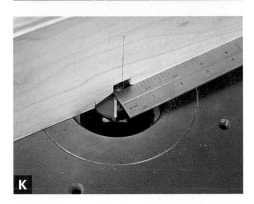

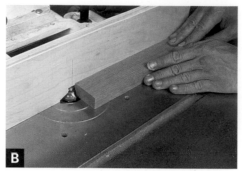

Arched Light Sash Door

Constructing a sash-type door with interlocking bars is another variation on the cope-and-stick construction shown on p. 83. The key is accurate layout and machine setup.

➤ See *"Sash Door Construction"* on p. 84.

Check the fit frequently and make any necessary adjustments.

Begin by accurately milling the stock. Make the stock for the bars wide enough for two; this makes feeding the work through machines safer and more accurate. For greatest accuracy, clamp matching pieces together and transfer the lines (**A**).

The location of the mortise in relationship to the sticking is critical. For this reason, shape the sticking on the stiles first (**B**). Then cut the mortises with a hollow chisel according to the layout (**C**). When correctly positioned, the mortise falls just on the edge of the sticking (**D**).

Next cut the tenons. Since the tenon shoulders are offset, cut the face of each tenon (**E**), and then adjust the setup for the second shoulder (**F**).

Before bandsawing the curves, cut the cope on the tenon shoulder (**G**). Then bandsaw the arches in the top rail (**H**) and smooth them with a spindle sander.

[**TIP**] **Remember to check the cope for fit to the sticking; it may be necessary to adjust the cutter height, fence position, or both.**

The last two steps are to shape the sticking and the rabbet. But first you'll need to rip the narrow sash bars to final width. To shape the bars safely, take a few extra minutes to shape the jig shown here (**I**). This jig will add much-needed mass to the otherwise narrow stock (**J**). When cutting the second rabbet, fill the first rabbet with a stick tacked into the jig (**K**). To shape the sticking and to rabbet the arches, it's necessary to use a starting pin or block as a fulcrum when entering the cut (**L**).

Once all the cuts are made, fit each joint individually and check the fit. To assemble the framework, fit the sash bars into the rails first (**M**) and then the stiles. Gently tap the joints together with a mallet (**N**). Finally, clamp the door and set it on a flat surface while the glue dries (**O**).

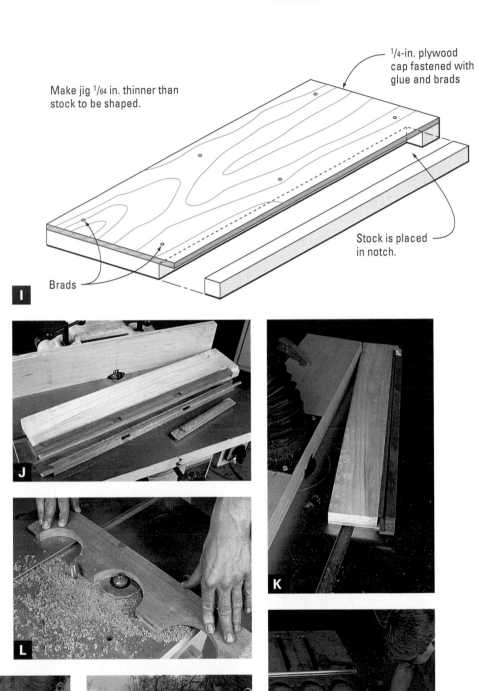

Make jig ¹/₆₄ in. thinner than stock to be shaped.

¹/₄-in. plywood cap fastened with glue and brads

Stock is placed in notch.

Brads

I

L

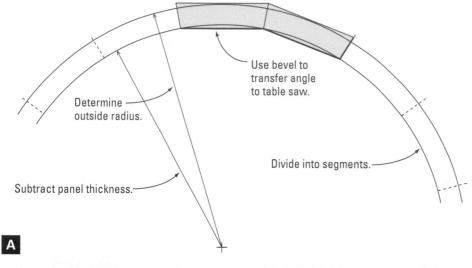

Use bevel to
transfer angle
to table saw.

Determine
outside radius.

Divide into segments.

Subtract panel thickness.

A

Coopered Panels

Coopering is a process of joining wood strips edge to edge to create a curve. The radius of the curve is determined by the degree of bevel on the edges of the stock (**A**).

Once the strips are milled and beveled, they are placed into a curved form (**B**) for gluing. Afterward, the facets are removed from the panel face with hand tools.

Begin by making a drawing of the curved panel. Next, divide the curve into a number of strips or staves. A smaller number of strips will result in large, flat surfaces that will require more time and patience to smooth with hand tools. Although using a greater number of strips requires that you match the grain carefully, it results in a smoother curve.

Next, mill the strips and bevel the edges on the table saw (**C**). To find the correct angle, set a bevel gauge from the drawing you created earlier. Then tilt the blade to match the angle on the gauge (**D**). Lay the strips in the form and arrange them for the best grain match before gluing and clamping.

[**TIP**] **Selecting quartersawn stock will make it much easier to match the grain.**

When clamping the panel, be careful to apply pressure evenly (**E**). After the glue dries, plane and scrape the corners away to create a smooth, fair curve (**F**).

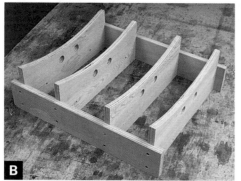

B

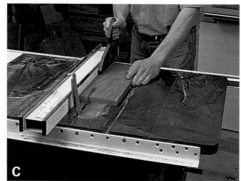

C

D

E

F

Raised Curved Panel

Raising a curved panel requires a vertical router bit and a curved fence to guide and support the workpiece (**A**).

First, bandsaw a curve into wide stock for use as a fence. After cutting a small opening for the panel bit, attach the fence to the router table fence.

To make the cut, feed the panel slowly and keep it firmly against the fence (**B**). After shaping the curved ends, shape the edges with the same bit and a straight fence. To maintain the correct angle while shaping, feel the panel between the fence and a stick clamped to the table (**C**). Pushing the panel face against the fence wedges it between the fence and the stick. This prevents it from rocking or tilting as it passes the router bit.

A

B

C

D

Simple Compound Curves

Compound curves flow in two directions simultaneously. They're most often used for the arms and legs of chairs. Although they can look complicated to build, they are actually quite easy to shape with a bandsaw. You simply saw the curves into one side, then rotate the stock to an adjacent side and saw the curves again. Afterward, the bandsaw marks are removed. For this example, I'm using a table leg.

Begin by sketching the curve onto thin plywood to make a pattern. After bandsawing and smoothing the pattern, trace it onto two adjacent surfaces of the stock (**A**).

Next, select an appropriate blade for the curve and stock thickness. A good choice for typical work is a ½-in. wide, 4-tpi blade. Begin by sawing the curves on one face (**B**); then tape the offcuts back in place and bandsaw the adjacent face (**C**). Smooth the curves with a spokeshave or compass plane. As you plane, examine the grain and work the tool "downhill" with the grain to avoid tearout (**D**).

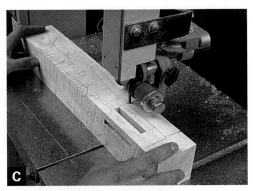

A Cabriole Leg

The cabriole leg is a beautiful example of compound curves. Although the shape appears complicated, it's relatively easy to create. In fact, most of the work is done on the bandsaw by sawing the contours of two adjacent faces of square stock. After sawing, the leg is further shaped and refined with hand tools.

Begin by sketching the leg onto ¼-in. plywood to make a pattern. When the sawing is completed, smooth the curves with a file. After selecting the stock, trace the contours of the pattern onto two adjacent faces of the leg blank (**A**). The pattern is oriented back to back rather than knee to knee. Next, cut the mortises while the leg is still square (**B**).

To avoid backing out of a long curve, begin sawing by making the short, straight cuts at the top of the knee and post block (**C**). Then saw the curves at the front (**D**) and back of the leg (**E**). After sawing the first face, use masking tape to reattach the offcut from the back of the leg and saw the second face (**F, G**).

(Text continues on p. 106.)

A

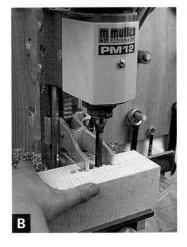

B

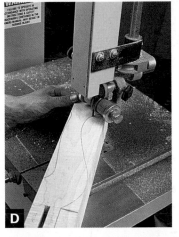

C

D

E

F

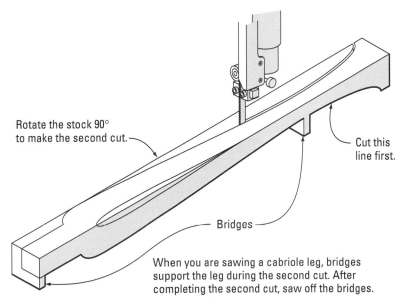

Rotate the stock 90°
to make the second cut.

Cut this
line first.

Bridges

When you are sawing a cabriole leg, bridges support the leg during the second cut. After completing the second cut, saw off the bridges.

G

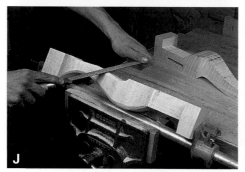

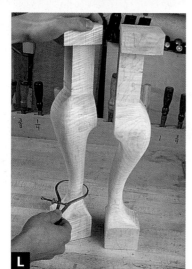

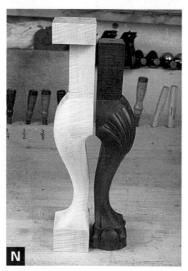

To further shape and refine the curves of the leg, use a no. 49 Nicholson rasp. It reaches into the sharp curves where a spokeshave can't.

[TIP] **To hold the leg secure while shaping, place it in a pipe clamp, which you can lock in the jaws of a bench vise.**

Begin by shaping the front corner, creating a chamfer with the rasp (**H**). Then rasp the back corner in the same way (**I**). Finally, rasp the corners on each side (**J**). As you shape the leg with the rasp, examine the curves for irregularities. Holding the rasp askew, cuts away high spots quickly. Next, round each of the four corners (**K**). Depending on the style of the leg, the ankle may be round (or nearly so) while the rest of the leg remains square with rounded corners. To keep uniformity between matching pairs of legs, check the final ankle size with spring calipers (**L**).

Once the shaping is complete, smooth the leg— first with a file and then with a scraper (**M**). Now you're ready to carve the foot (**N**).

► See *"Carving"* on p. 252.

Rounding a Simple Curved Leg

This method of rounding is useful when the leg is rectangular in section rather than square. When rounded, a rectangular leg becomes elliptical. By shaping it, you effectively lighten the look and add refinement without a loss of strength (**A**).

To make the process more efficient, first remove the excess stock with a chamfer router bit (**B**). Next, mark a centerline as a guide while shaping (**C**). Then clamp the leg in a vise and shape the leg with a rasp in the direction of the grain (**D**). When the grain direction changes, reverse the rasp and pull it toward you (**E**). Work gradually to the centerline to create an elliptical contour (**F**). When you're satisfied with the overall shape, smooth the leg with a file (**G**), followed by a card scraper (**H**).

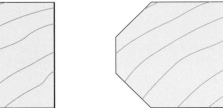

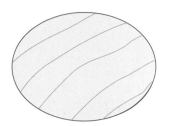
Chamfer the four corners with a router bit.

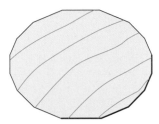

A Chamfer the eight corners with a rasp.

Round and blend surfaces with a file.

The first step in building an ogee bracket foot is making a pattern. The order in which you make the cuts is important.

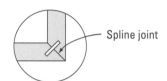

Spline joint

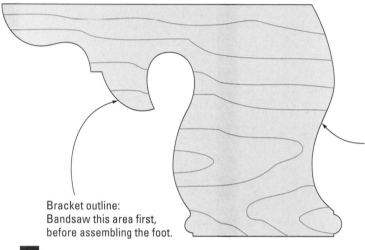

Ogee contour: Bandsaw this area after the two halves of the foot are glued together.

Bracket outline: Bandsaw this area first, before assembling the foot.

A

Shaping Ogee Feet on the Bandsaw

The curves of ogee bracket feet give a sculptural effect to chests, desks, and other forms of casework. Making them on the bandsaw is a four-step process of cutting the joints, sawing the bracket outline, assembling the feet, and band-sawing the ogee contour in the face (**A**). For the last step you'll need to construct a simple stand to support the foot during sawing.

> [**TIP**] **Because it's strong and doesn't require milling, ¼-in. plywood makes an excellent spline. Plywood is always less than the specified thickness, though, so cut the spline groove to fit the plywood.**

First mill the stock to size and cut the joinery. The front feet are joined with a miter and spline. However, the back feet are designed to fit flush with the back of the case so they are joined with a half-blind dovetail (**B**). Begin by cutting the miter on the table saw (**C**). Then cut the groove for the

B

C

D

E

F

spline (**D**). Once the joinery is cut and fit, trace the foot pattern onto the face of each foot (**E**).

[**TIP**] **Before sawing intricate scrollwork, save time by drilling segments that are circular.**

When sawing the tight curves of the bracket, drill areas that form part of a circle (**F**). Next, carefully bandsaw the remainder of the bracket outline (**G**).

Now you're ready to assemble the feet. I've found that four small clamps work well to hold the miter joint tight while the glue sets. The spline keeps the two halves from sliding out of alignment when clamp pressure is applied (**H**).

First, you'll need to build a support stand to hold the foot in position during sawing (**I**). Keep it simple: Use four boards joined with dadoes, glue,

(Text continues on p. 110.)

When bandsawing curves, you can save time and ensure accuracy by using a drill to form the parts of the curve that are true circles.

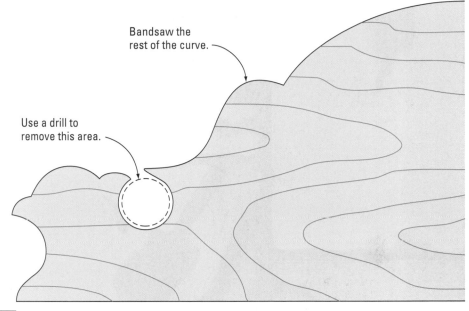

Bandsaw the rest of the curve.

Use a drill to remove this area.

TIP

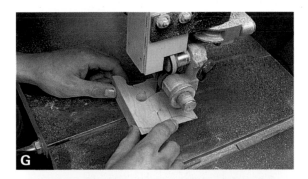

G

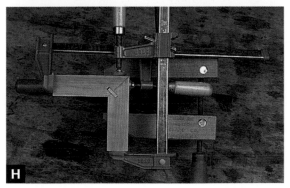

H

When bandsawing an ogee contour in a bracket foot, make sure the foot is securely supported slightly above the table so that it is parallel to the blade.

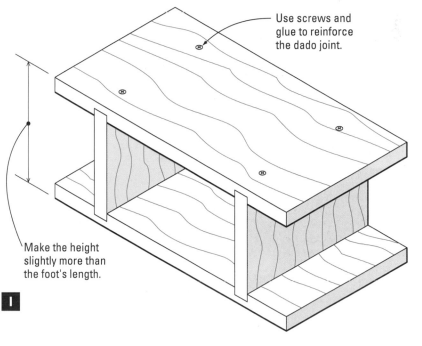

Use screws and glue to reinforce the dado joint.

Make the height slightly more than the foot's length.

I

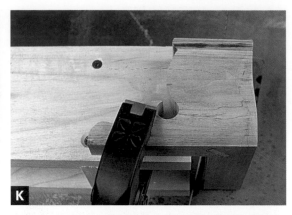

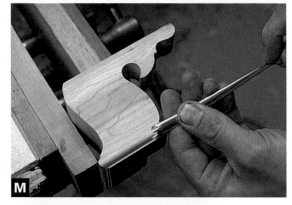

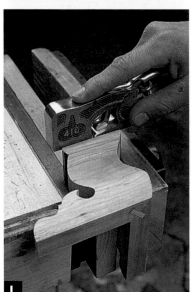

and screws. For the best results, you'll want to build the stand as short as possible—just high enough so that the bracket foot clears the band-saw table. This will enable you to keep the upper saw guide positioned low for the best blade support.

The next step is to bandsaw the ogee contour in the face. Secure the foot to the support stand with a small clamp while sawing (**J**). After sawing the first face, the outline for the second face is revealed in the miter (**K**). Afterward, work the surfaces with hand tools to remove the saw marks. A rabbet plane works well for shaping the fillets that flank the bead (**L**). To shape the bead, use a carving gouge (**M**); smooth the ogee contour with a file (**N**). Complete the smoothing process by using a scraper and sandpaper.

Ogee Bracket Feet on the Table Saw

Another method for shaping ogee feet uses the table saw to create the ogee contour. It involves cutting a cove on a long strip and mitering short lengths of the strip to create feet.

► See *"Coves"* on p. 204.

The first step is to mill a strip of lumber long enough for all four feet. Next, the concave portion is created by cutting a cove with the table saw (**A**). To shape the convex area, begin by beveling the strip (**B**). Then use a block plane to complete the contour (**C**).

When you're satisfied with the ogee profile, miter the two halves of the foot (**D**) and cut a groove for the spline (**E**). Next, bandsaw the bracket outline into the face of each foot (**F**). After gluing the two halves together (**G**), smooth and refine each foot with files before scraping and sanding (**H**).

A

B

C

D

E

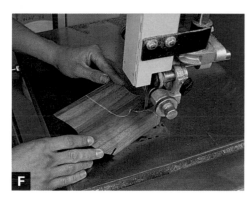

F

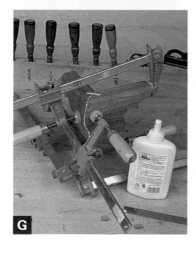

G

H

A

B

C

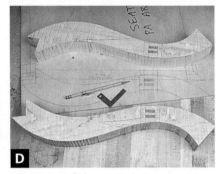

D

E

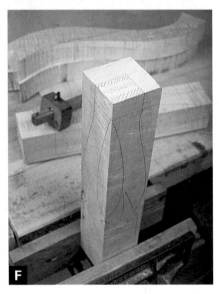

F

Bandsawing and Sculpting Compound Curves with Interconnected, Asymmetrical Components

The following techniques are useful for creating furniture (especially chairs) that is composed of flowing, sculptural curves. As an example, I'm going to use an arm and post from a chair.

As with any bandsawn component, it's important to begin by sketching the design and creating patterns (**A**). This provides an objective starting point for logical progression. After milling the stock to size, trace the arm pattern (**B**) and bandsaw the outline of the arm (**C**). It makes sense to saw the contour before cutting the mortise for the post; the convex curve of the arm works as a reference point for the joint.

After bandsawing the arm, lay out (**D**) and cut the mortise (**E**). Next, lay out the curves of the arms and the tenons (**F**). Then cut the tenons on the post while the stock is still square (**G**), because square surfaces are best when cutting joints on the table saw (**H**).

Next bandsaw the post—first the front (**I**) and then the side. Save the offcuts from the first series of cuts and tape them back into position with double-sided tape for sawing the adjacent surface (**J**).

Next bandsaw the curves on the top and bottom of the arm. Because the arm is asymmetrical, it's important to plan the cutting sequence carefully to avoid a miscut and spoiling the arm. More specifically, as the arm curves, the profile is simultaneously stretched and compressed.

After tracing the patterns (**K**), saw a relief cut at the base of the knuckle. When starting the cut, it's necessary to raise the back end of the arm so that the layout line is parallel to the blade (**L**). Next, cut from the post joint to the cut you

(Text continues on p. 114.)

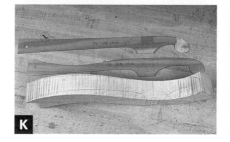

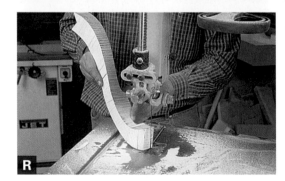

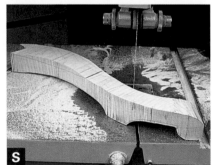

made at the knuckle (**M**). After making the turn, lift the arm again as the blade approaches the junction (**N**).

The next cut begins at the post joint (**O**) and continues to the back end of the arm. Afterward, make the simple, shallow relief cut on the top of the arm (**P**).

Finally, remove the square corners from the knuckle. Starting with the top, lift the arm so that the work is parallel to the blade (**Q**) and make a full turn to the bottom of the arm (**R**). Now the arm is ready for shaping (**S**).

Shaping the arm is a process of refining the curves with the appropriate tools to match the contour. Begin by smoothing the outside edges of the arm with a spokeshave (**T**). A carving gouge works well for the curve of the knuckle (**U**). Beginning underneath the arm, round the knuckle so that the curve flows continually to the top. A gouge is also used to remove excess wood behind the knuckle (**V**). For the subtle curves on the top (**W**) and bottom (**X**) of the arm, use a rasp to further shape and refine. The inside curve on top of the arm is dished out (**Y**) with the rasp, and the contour is blended with the rest of the arm.

(Text continues on p. 116.)

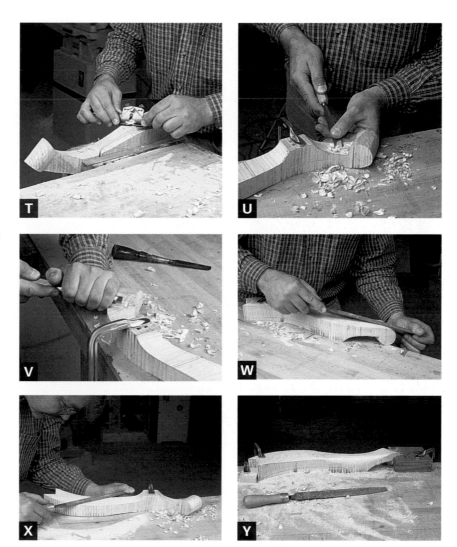

The front and back corners of the post are rounded, while the side corners remain relatively sharp. Secure the work in a clamp that is mounted in the vise. Beginning with a long, firm chisel, remove the excess stock (**Z**). Next, round the corner to blend the two surfaces into one flowing contour. As you're shaping, alternate between pushing (**AA**) and pulling (**BB**) the rasp to follow the grain and blend the curves effectively.

Once the major portion of the shaping is completed, dry-assemble the arm and post and blend the area around the joint (**CC**). At this stage, the knuckle is ready for carving.

➤ See *"Carving"* on p. 252.

Template Shaping

Cutting with Templates

Flush Trimming

Profile/Trim

Shaping Inside Corners

➤ Cutting with Templates on the Table Saw (p. 123)

➤ Cutting with Templates on the Bandsaw (p. 124)

➤ Flush Trimming a Broad Curve on the Router Table (p. 125)

➤ Flush Trimming Tight Curves in Small Stock (p. 126)

➤ Profile or Trim on the Router Table (p. 127)

➤ Profile or Trim from a Previous Template (p. 128)

➤ Shaping Inside Corners (p. 129)

Undoubtedly the most efficient method for shaping wood is with a template. The concept is simple: A shaped template is joined with the work; a guide or bearing mounted to the machine follows the template as the work is cut or shaped. Each piece—one or a hundred—is identical to the template. Although template shaping is the obvious choice for shaping multiples, it can also be extremely useful for shaping just one component. For example, intricate furniture parts, like the curved seat board of a desk interior, are time-consuming to shape entirely by hand. But with a template and profile router bit the job takes only minutes. Also, a template is the only machine

Piloted profile bits and a template make it easy to create complex shapes.

SHAPING THE ENTIRE EDGE

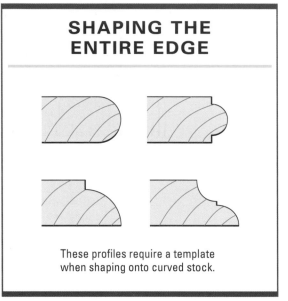

These profiles require a template when shaping onto curved stock.

THUMBNAIL PROFILE CREATED WITH ROUNDOVER BIT

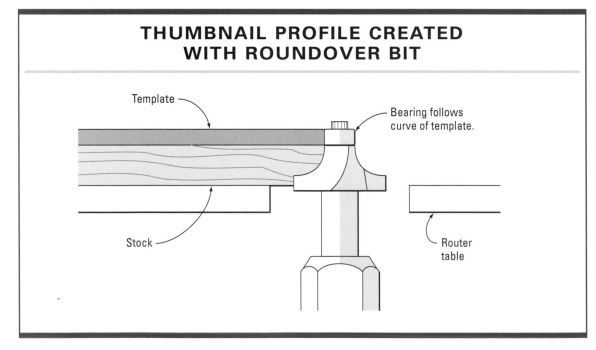

Template

Bearing follows curve of template.

Stock

Router table

method that can be used when the entire edge of a curved surface is to be shaped.

Flush trimming is another use for this technique. For example, bandsaws don't create finished surfaces, so the saw marks must be removed, often by hand. However, by using a flush-cutting router bit or shaper cutter with a bearing to follow a template, you can smooth the work much faster. The bearing can be located on top or underneath. As an added bonus, matching pairs, such as chair legs, are identical in shape and size. This allows you more time to devote to handworked details that add distinction to the piece.

The only disadvantage to template shaping is that you can't shape into an inside

corner. This is because router bits and shaper cutters rotate as they shape, which leaves inside corners rounded. Although one solution is to avoid designs with inside corners, I prefer to carve the corners by hand instead. This method creates visual

Flush-trimming and pattern bits leave smooth surfaces that don't need additional cleanup.

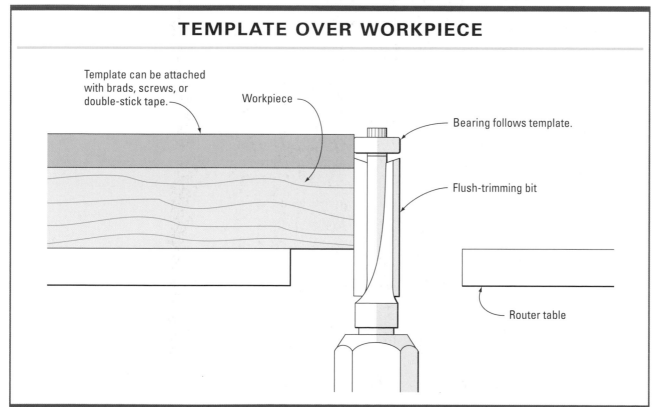

TEMPLATE OVER WORKPIECE

Template can be attached with brads, screws, or double-stick tape.

Workpiece

Bearing follows template.

Flush-trimming bit

Router table

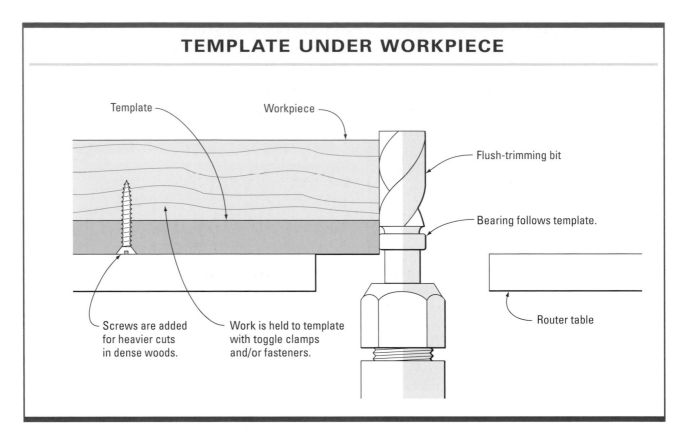

TEMPLATE UNDER WORKPIECE

Template

Workpiece

Flush-trimming bit

Bearing follows template.

Screws are added
for heavier cuts
in dense woods.

Work is held to template
with toggle clamps
and/or fasteners.

Router table

details that will set your work apart from
the rest.

Although the table saw and bandsaw can
be used to cut shapes with a template, the
shaper and table-mounted router are both
ideal for template work. The router has an
advantage over the shaper because its small
bearings reach into tight contours, whereas a
shaper simply can't. The shaper's advantage
is its size and power, which enable you to
shape large profiles beyond the capacity of a
router. That's why a well-equipped shop has
both tools.

Obviously, before shaping it's important
to spend time making the template. Any

irregularities, such as small bumps in the
curves, will be followed by the bearing and
shaped into the work. After bandsawing the
template, clean up the curves with a file
and/or spindle sander and closely inspect the
surface for flaws. Only when you're completely satisfied with the template's accuracy
and quality should you put it to use.

Securing Templates

There are three common methods for securing the template to the workpiece: toggle
clamps, fasteners, and double-sided tape.

Toggle clamps are fastened to the template
and make a jig into which the work is

► TEMPLATE SHAPING SAFETY

- Make sure the template is large enough to provide safe placement of your hands.
- Secure the work to the template with toggle clamps, fasteners, or double-sided tape.
- Make certain that clamps and/or fasteners are away from the cutter or bit.

- Extend the template beyond the workpiece when possible.
- Use a starting pin if the template does not extend beyond the stock.
- Feed the stock against the spindle rotation.
- Avoid making heavy cuts.

placed. Stop blocks are fastened to the jig in various locations to register the work and counteract the forces of the cutter. Although toggle clamps are quick to operate and work well, they can't be used when the work is to be shaped along with the entire perimeter. But they're a great choice when the work is to be shaped only along one or two edges.

Fasteners, such as small nails and screws, are also useful for securing work to a template. They hold well and are quick to install and remove. Of course, fasteners leave an unsightly hole in the work, so it's important to position them where the hole will be either hidden or later cut away. Also, it's crucial for safety to position any nail or screw well out of the path of the cutter.

Although *double-sided woodturner's tape* holds well, it's my last choice for securing a template. It's time-consuming to peel the paper from the tape and stick it in position.

But when the work is to be shaped around the entire perimeter and it's impossible to hide the hole from a nail or screw, then tape is a good option. Avoid carpet tape, however, because it lacks the strength of the cloth woodturner's tape. Also, never use tape for heavy cuts with the shaper; limit its use to small cuts on the router table.

Making a Template from a Template

Sometimes when making furniture it's necessary to match the curve (or a similar curve) on an adjacent element. The base, or seat board, is curved and above the seat board are drawers and dividers that must match, but they are stepped back. Matching the three elements—drawer, seat board, and divider—can be somewhat tedious.

To make a template from a template, first stack plywood to equal the thickness of the piece to be shaped.

Shape the new template from the old one using the same cutter you would use to make the finished part. The bottom-most piece of plywood is your new template.

Here's the method I use: Stack several layers of thin plywood together to equal the thickness of the seat board. The top layer of plywood is actually the template for the seat board; the bottom layer will become a template for the dividers and drawers. Next, shape the stack with the same router bit that was used for shaping the seat board. Afterward, separate the plywood layers; the bottom layer is now a perfectly shaped new template.

Carving the Corners

No discussion of template shaping would be complete without examining the technique's major shortcoming: You can't use it to shape inside corners. As router bits and shaper cutters spin, they cut in an arc, which is left indelibly on any inside corners. One solution is to design furniture that is void of shaped inside corners. But this often results in furniture that is void of detail and interest. I prefer instead to shape or carve the corners by hand once the machine shaping is completed. It usually takes just a few minutes, and the results are well worth it.

▶ See *"Shaping Inside Corners"* on p. 129.

Cutting with Templates on the Table Saw

The table saw can be used with a template to cut odd-shaped, straight-edged components. A good example is the shelf from a corner cabinet.

Begin by preparing the template and guide. A piece of ½-in. plywood is of sufficient thickness for the template; the guide must have a long, straight edge that is suspended over and parallel to the blade (**A**).

Once the setup is ready, attach the template to the workpiece. To make the cut, the template is pushed along the guide as the excess wood is cut from the stock to create the desired shape (**B**).

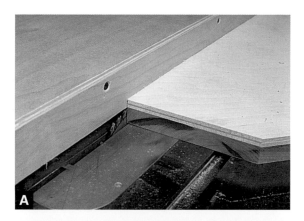

Cutting with Templates on the Bandsaw

Unlike the table saw, the bandsaw can cut curves. To cut curves with a template you must first equip your bandsaw with a guide. The guide is simply a stick with a notched end to fit around the blade. Of course, the end of the stick must be curved to follow the curved template. The other end of the stick is clamped firmly to the saw's table.

➤ See the drawing on p. 48.

Once the setup is complete, you're ready to begin sawing. Depending on the type of cut, use brads, double-stick tape, or toggle clamps to secure the work. To make the cut, simply maintain contact between the template and guide (**A**). As you feed the work, follow the curves of the template (**B**).

Flush Trimming a Broad Curve on the Router Table

Bandsaws don't create a finished surface; so after sawing curves, the saw marks must be removed. Without a doubt, the router is the most versatile tool for template shaping. It cuts curves, flush cuts, creates molded profiles, and shapes into tight corners. A template-guided straight bit will do the job quickly and efficiently. For this example, I'm using the rear leg of the chair shown on p. 86. A pair of toggle clamps secures the leg in the template, which is equipped with two edges: one for leg's face and the other for the leg's back (**A**).

To the shank of the bit, add a bearing that will follow the template (**B**). After bandsawing the leg heavy of the layout line, position the leg in the template for the first cut (**C**). The order that you complete the cuts is important, because the template is designed to remove equal amounts for each of the two cuts. Cutting out of order means that the first cut will be too heavy. In addition, if you cut out of sequence there will not be sufficient stock for removal during the second cut. Start the cut with the bearing in contact with the extended portion of the template base (**D**). This will give you a smooth entry into the cut. Feed the stock at a steady rate and listen to the machine to determine if you're feeding the stock too quickly (**E**). Afterward, reposition the leg and make the second cut (**F**).

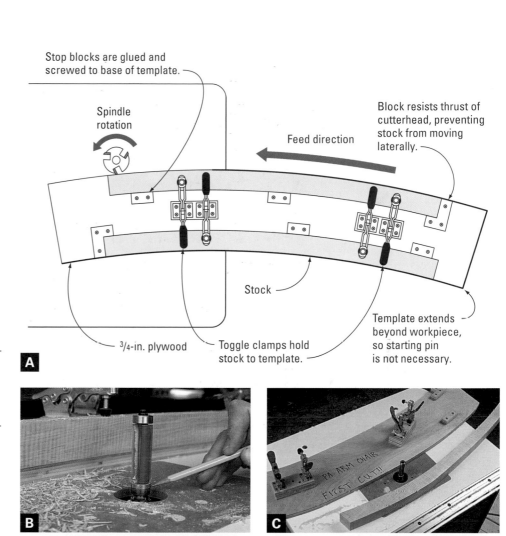

Stop blocks are glued and screwed to base of template.

Spindle rotation

Feed direction

Block resists thrust of cutterhead, preventing stock from moving laterally.

Stock

³/₄-in. plywood

Toggle clamps hold stock to template.

Template extends beyond workpiece, so starting pin is not necessary.

A

B

C

D

E

F

Template Shaping | 125

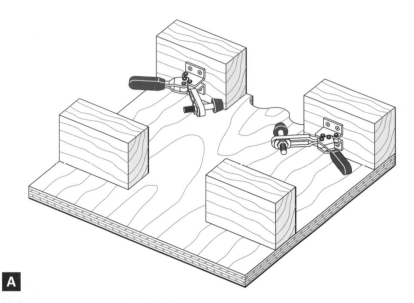

A

Flush Trimming Tight Curves in Small Stock

The small workpiece in this example, a drawer front from a desk, presents unique problems. The stock is small, and the cut is somewhat heavy because of the stock thickness. Also, the entry and exit portions of the cut are on end grain, which is tough and doesn't cut easily. As the bit exits the cut, tearout can occur on the drawer face.

To overcome the problem of the small stock size, use a jig (**A**) that positions the toggle clamps in the back, away from the cut. Blocks on the face of the jig counteract the clamp force and help prevent tearout as the bit exits the work.

[**TIP**] **Use a spiral bit; it cuts much cleaner than an ordinary straight bit and with minimal tearout.**

Begin by bandsawing the stock just outside the layout line (**B**). Secure the work in the jig (**C**). Make the first cut (**D**), and then raise the bit for the second cut (**E**). During the second cut, the bearing follows the surface created by the first cut instead of the template.

B

C

D

E

Profile or Trim on the Router Table

This example uses a seat board from a desk. The edge of the seat board has a thumbnail profile that must follow the curved contour at each drawer. The tight curves would be impossible to reach with a shaper and would be tedious to shape by hand.

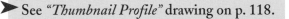

➤ See *"Thumbnail Profile"* drawing on p. 118.

Begin by tracing the template onto the workpiece (**A**). Be careful to match the centerlines, because the eventual curves must align with two more sets of curves in the desk. After bandsawing heavy of the layout line (**B**), adjust the bit height so that the bearing contacts the template.

To make the cut, start by contacting the bearing with the extended portion of the template (**C**). This makes entry into the wood smooth (**D**). Now reposition the template and make the next cut (**E**). Shaping the seat board with this method takes just a few minutes.

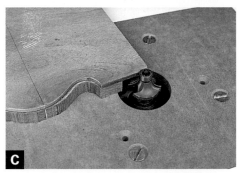

A

Profile or Trim from a Previous Template

Here's a unique method for making the template: Make the template from the previous template.

➤ See *"Making a Template from a Template"* on p. 121.

For accuracy, trace the contour onto the stock directly from the template (**A**). After bandsawing, fasten the template to the stock with brads (**B**). Although the brads will leave small holes, they won't be seen in the finished desk and the process is fast to set up.

B

The bearing on the bit follows the template, cutting away the saw marks and creating the profile—all in one light pass (**C**).

[**TIP**] **If you choose a bit that's slightly large, you'll avoid the ridges that occur with a smaller bit and the larger radius appears more refined.**

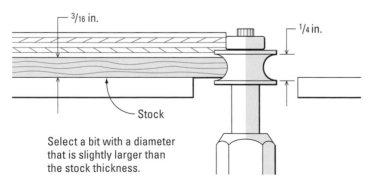

C

— 3/16 in.

1/4 in.

Stock

Select a bit with a diameter that is slightly larger than the stock thickness.

TIP

Shaping Inside Corners

Begin by shaping the work with a template. Next, select a tool for the job; in this case, I'm shaping a ³⁄₁₆-in.-thick divider from the gallery of a desk interior. The profile that I shaped was a ¼-in.-diameter bead, so I want a small gouge that approximates the bead's curve (**A**).

Before you begin carving, sketch the outline onto the work (**B**). Next, carve from both directions into the corner (**C**). To remove any facets, smooth the area with a small file (**D**). The finished divider is a result of combining power-tool techniques with hand-tool skills to create detailed work efficiently (**E**).

Edge Treatments, page 132

Beads, page 145

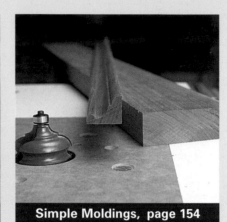
Simple Moldings, page 154

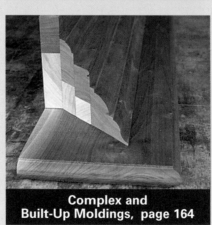
Complex and
Built-Up Moldings, page 164

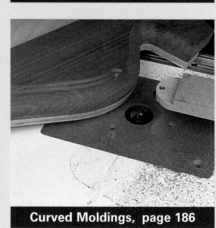
Curved Moldings, page 186

PART THREE

Edge Treatments and Moldings

EDGE TREATMENTS AND MOLDINGS have been used for centuries to add embellishment, detail, and visual interest to furniture. It's difficult to imagine furniture without moldings, because even the simplest styles, such as Shaker, use beads to soften edges and create interesting shadow lines. That's why an understanding of edge treatments and moldings is so important to furniture design. An edge treatment or the addition of even a simple molding can turn a boring box or a utilitarian table into a piece of beautiful furniture.

An edge treatment can be as simple as breaking the sharp 90-degree angle with a few passes of a block plane or cutting an ogee profile with a router or shaper. Simple moldings are easy to create with the wide variety of router bits now available. Even complex and built-up moldings are just a matter of combining basic shapes to create different effects.

Edge Treatments

Simple Shaped Edge

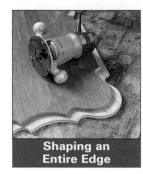

Shaping an Entire Edge

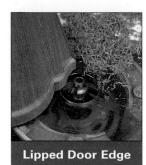

Lipped Door Edge

Shaping a Board's Face

Dished Tabletop

WHEN THE EDGE OF A TABLETOP OR DRAWER FRONT is shaped, it creates the same visual effects as a strip molding. But shaping an edge yields additional benefits; the square corners are removed, the resulting edges are softer to the touch, and the problems of wood movement associated with applied moldings are nonexistent, because the edge is part of the original stock.

Undoubtedly, the simplest edge treatment for tabletops is the roundover. By shaping a small radius on the edges, you remove the hard look and feel of the corner. The effect improves with age as the surfaces wear unevenly, creating a worn look. To create the worn look artificially, you can work the rounded surfaces with a file.

Another attractive table edge is the reverse ogee. The concave-convex profile creates an edge that appears thin and delicate. When designing an ogee edge, you can alter the effect by changing the center-point locations. The possibilities for edge treatments are broad, because router bits and shaper cutters are available in a wide variety of profiles.

► See *"Basic Molding Profiles"* on p. 155.

The edges of doors and drawers can also benefit from simple treatments. Adding a bead is a great way to frame the perimeter of flush-fitting doors and drawers. If a veneer is used on the faces, the bead will protect the fragile edges from chipping. You can add the bead after veneering; just cut a shallow rabbet around the drawer perimeter and miter a thin beaded strip.

You can also bead the edges of drawer fronts made from solid stock. The bead can be shaped into the front with a plane, router, or scratch stock. If you choose to shape a bead on the ends and edges, you'll need to miter the corners with a chisel.

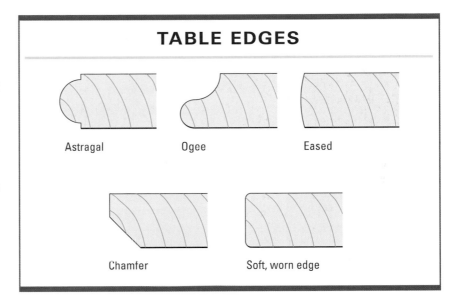

TABLE EDGES

Astragal   Ogee   Eased

Chamfer   Soft, worn edge

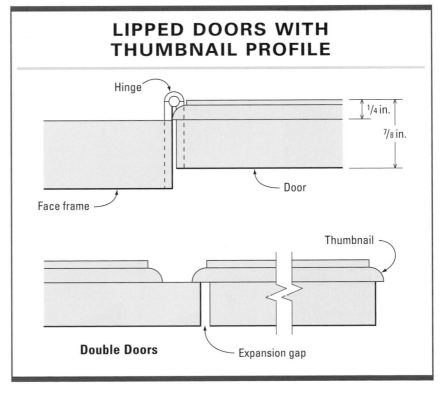

LIPPED DOORS WITH THUMBNAIL PROFILE

Hinge

1/4 in.

7/8 in.

Door

Face frame

Thumbnail

Double Doors   Expansion gap

The thumbnail profile is an attractive finish for the edges of doors, drawer fronts, and tabletops.

LIPPED THUMBNAIL EDGE FOR DOORS AND DRAWERS

3/16-in. radius

1/4 in.

7/8 in.

1/4 in.

When shaping an edge, a bearing or rub collar rides on the remaining portion of the edge to guide the cutter.

Almost any profile can be used on door and drawer edges. One popular and traditional profile is the thumbnail. It's most commonly used with lipped doors and drawers. A rabbet is cut around the inside perimeter, and the door or drawer front is fit within the opening. The lip that remains is shaped with a thumbnail profile. The result is a door or drawer that covers the opening, yet the edge is thin and refined.

Shaping the Entire Edge

The most efficient tools for shaping edges are the router table and shaper. Doors, drawers, and smaller tabletops are easy to handle when feeding through the machines. But large, awkward work is easier to shape with a handheld router.

When shaping the edges of round or curved tabletops you'll need to use a bit or cutter with a bearing to guide the cut. If the edge is partially shaped, the bearing can follow the remaining portion of the edge. However, if the entire edge is shaped, you'll need to make a template to guide the cut.

▶ See "Template Shaping" on p. 117.

Dished Tops

Still another form of molded edge treatments is the dished top. The surface of the top is recessed, and the raised rim is molded. If the top is rectilinear, it's simple to add a strip of molding to the edge and miter the corners. But if the top is round, the molding and top are easier to shape as one piece.

Dished tops were popular on eighteenth-century tea tables and candle stands. The traditional method used is to turn the top on

SHAPING EDGES

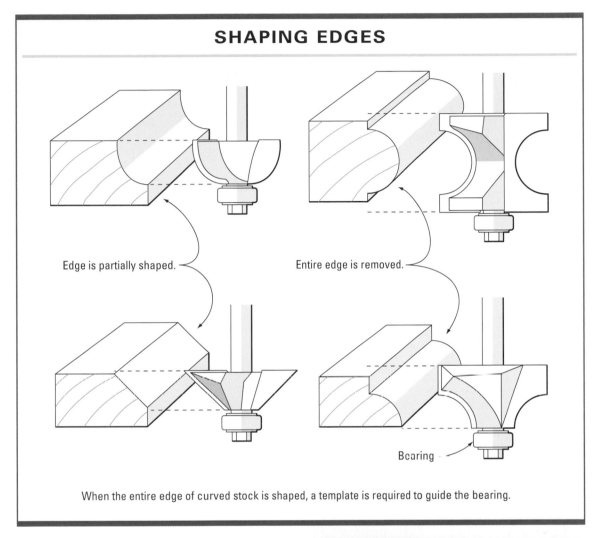

Edge is partially shaped.

Entire edge is removed.

Bearing

When the entire edge of curved stock is shaped, a template is required to guide the bearing.

a lathe. The molded perimeter and dished interior are both created by turning the top at a slow speed. A floor-stand tool rest is needed to support the tools during the turning process.

These days, a more efficient method for dishing circular tops is with a router. A jig is used to suspend the router over the top, and the router is held stationary while the top is rotated in the jig. A straight bit is used to dish the flat interior, and profile bits are used for the molded edge. Afterward, the interior is scraped and sanded smooth.

A jig allows the router to ride above the work while cutting to a specific depth. This setup creates the depression for a dished tabletop.

Shaped Edge with a Handheld Router

One of the advantages of a router over a shaper is that it is lightweight and portable. Profiling the edge of large, awkward stock such as a tabletop can be difficult without a helper—but with the router it's a snap. The chamfer shown here is just an example of the many edge treatments you can cut with a router.

First mill the stock to size and clamp it to your workbench. If you're creating a large chamfer, you may want to shape it in two passes. Otherwise, set the bit for the required cutting depth and guide it around the perimeter of the top in a counterclockwise direction. To avoid unsightly tearout on the edges, shape an end first (**A**) and slow the feed rate as you approach the corner. As you finish with the sides (**B**), any slight tearout will be shaped away.

Shaped Edge on the Router Table

The router table has replaced the shaper for most small tasks. Shaping a chamfer with the router table is a prime example.

Begin by adjusting the bit height (**A**) and set the fence tangent to the guide bearing on the bit (**B**). Then, starting with an end, feed the stock from right to left (**C**). When shaping the ends, slow down the feed as you approach the corner to avoid excessive tearout. When you shape the edges, any minor tearout will be shaped away (**D**).

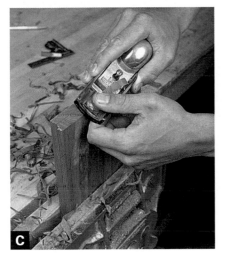

Chamfer with a Block Plane

Hand tools are a pleasure to use and are surprisingly efficient, especially when only a few pieces need to be shaped.

First, lay out the chamfer with a pencil to use as a guide while cutting (**A**). A combination square will guide the pencil and keep the layout consistent (**B**).

Next, begin chamfering the stock on the end of the board (**C**). Hold the plane at an angle that corresponds to the desired angle of the chamfer. As you approach the layout lines, you can adjust the angle if needed. Finish the surface with one continuous light pass. Any tearout that occurs will disappear when you chamfer the edges (**D**).

A "Worn" Table Edge

A worn, rounded surface is friendly to the touch and has a familiar look. Any surface can be worked to create an appearance of age; but the square, utilitarian edges of a tabletop work well for this technique.

First, use a ¼-in. roundover bit to remove the excess stock on the top and bottom of the edge (**A**). Next, use a coarse file to gently round and soften the corners (**B**). Be careful not to overdo it, or it can look artificial. A light pass with a scraper completes the job (**C**).

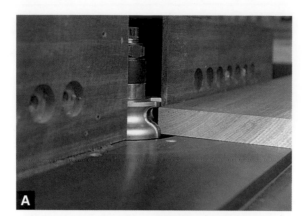

Entire Edge Shaped on the Shaper

Many attractive edge profiles, such as an ogee, involve shaping the entire edge. When shaping the entire edge, part of the stock width is removed. To compensate for the loss of width, a split fence is used; the outfeed half of the fence is adjusted forward the same amount as the stock being removed. In other words, the outfeed fence must be tangent to the smallest cutting diameter of the cutterhead.

Begin by adjusting the spindle height (**A**). To make the fence adjustment, first shape enough length of stock to reach the outfeed fence. Now turn the shaper off. Next, turn the micrometer screw on the fence back to advance the fence until it contacts the stock (**B**). Now lock the fence and make the cut beginning with the end (**C**). As you approach the corner, slow down the feed to avoid excessive tearout at the edge. Any minor tearout will be cut away as the edge is shaped.

Sometimes the back edge of a top does not need to be shaped. For example, the top of a dressing table that is placed against a wall. In this case, rip the top to final size after shaping to remove any tearout that may have occurred at the back edge (**D**).

Entire Edge of a Curved Shape on the Router

Anytime you shape a curved surface with a router, the rub bearing on the bit must follow a curve to guide the bit and limit the cutting depth. When only part of the edge is shaped, the portion that remains can serve to guide the bearing. However, when the entire edge is shaped, a template is needed to guide the cut (**A**).

▶ See *"Template Shaping"* on p. 117.

After making the template, trace it onto the workpiece. Now saw the outline slightly proud of the line, which will provide extra stock to be removed by the router bit. If the top is large and your bandsaw is limited in size, you may opt to use a portable jigsaw (**B**). If so, clamp the work to the bench to keep it stationary while sawing.

Next, attach the template to the underside of the top with screws (**C**). The screw holes will later be hidden, but make certain that the screw doesn't penetrate the full thickness of the top.

Before shaping, set the bit height with an offcut from the top (**D**). Now you're ready to make the cut. To have complete control of routers and shapers, it's important always to feed in the opposite direction of the cutter rotation (**E**). When hand feeding a router, move it counterclockwise around the top's perimeter.

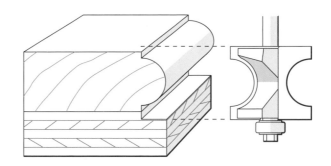

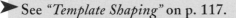

Because the entire edge is removed, a template is needed when shaping this profile on a curved surface.

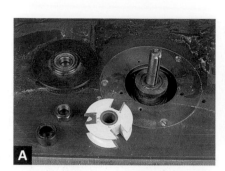

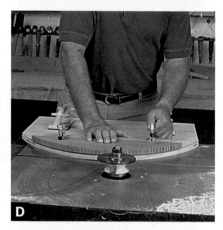

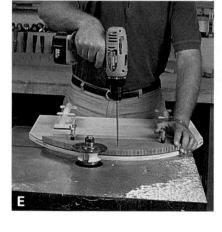

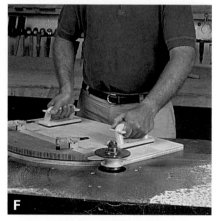

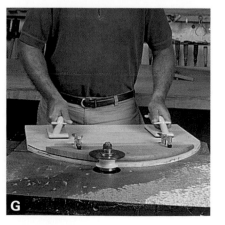

Entire Edge of a Curved Shape on the Shaper

If you own a shaper you'll find it to be a great tool for shaping edges. To shape curved edges, you'll need a rub bearing from the cutterhead manufacturer. You'll also need to construct a template to work in conjunction with the bearing.

Secure the work firmly to the template. Use a guard; keep your hands safely distanced from the cutterhead; and, if possible, extend the template beyond the workpiece. This will give you a smooth entry to the cut, because the template will contact the bearing before the cutterhead contacts the workpiece.

➤ See *"Template Shaping"* on p. 117.

The first step is to carefully set up the shaper. First mount the bearing (**A**), then the cutterhead (**B**), and finally the guard. Secure the assembly with a lockwasher and nut (**C**).

Next, secure the work to the template with a pair of toggle clamps (**D**) and a single screw (**E**). The screw holds the work to the template in an area that the clamps can't reach. Because the screw leaves an ugly hole, make sure it's located where it won't appear in the completed work; in this example, a handhold will be cut out in the area of the screw hole. Note, too, that the screw is placed well out of the cutterhead's path.

Start the cut by first positioning the template against the bearing (**F**). Then feed the stock against the cutterhead rotation (**G**).

> ⚠ **WARNING** Shapers can be dangerous, especially when used to shape curved stock. Take the necessary precautions.

Shaping a Lipped Door Edge

Unlike an overlay door that closes against the cabinet face, a lipped door looks refined. That's because most of the door's thickness fits inside the cabinet and the remaining lip is shaped with a delicate thumbnail profile.

The example I'm using here is the pendulum door from the waist of a tall clock. The top of the door has a decorative cutout. After bandsawing the top of the door, use a flush-trimming router bit and a template to remove the bandsaw marks (**A**). Then carve the inside corners where the router bit didn't reach (**B**). Next, use a roundover bit to shape the thumbnail profile around the perimeter of the door (**C**). Set the height of the bit to create a ⅟₁₆-in. fillet next to the thumbnail profile. This fillet is important; it creates another fine detail to capture light and create a shadow line.

After the thumbnail, shape the rabbet that allows most of the door to fit within the opening. The bearing on the rabbeting bit can ride along the thumbnail without damaging it; just don't press too hard (**D**).

[**TIP**] **A fence can be used to limit the rabbet's depth along the straight portions of the door.**

Afterward, carve the inside corners on the top of the door to complete the thumbnail profile (**E**).

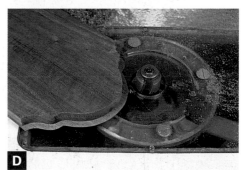

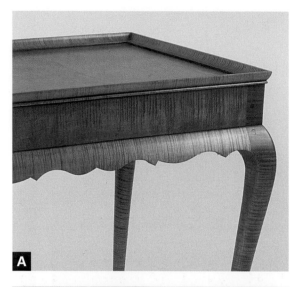

Face of a Board Shaped on the Shaper

Whenever you shape the face of a board on the shaper, it's necessary to mill the stock oversize in width. As the stock passes the cutterhead a portion of the original face remains intact to provide a reference surface on the outfeed fence.

The example shown here is a skirt from a tea table (**A**). The face of the skirt is a contoured molding strip that matches the knee of the leg to which it joins.

To provide stability, use a featherboard to keep the stock firmly in position against the fence. Note that the featherboard is mounted on a wood block to raise it off of the table (**B**). This provides pressure in the area that remains intact. After shaping, rip the molded skirt free from the stock (**C**).

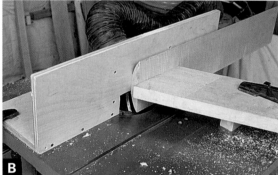

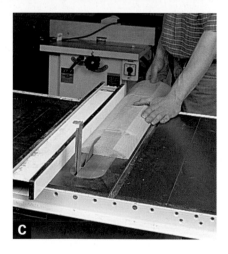

Dished Tabletop

A dished tabletop has a molded rim that sets slightly above the rest of the table surface (**A**). The molding is small and refined and the effect is dramatic as it reflects light and casts shadows. The design is a classic one but the router technique for producing it is relatively new. The router is suspended over the top, which rotates on a hub. To use the technique you'll first have to build a jig.

[**TIP**] **A one-board top looks best; but if you must use two boards, take care when matching the grain and color.**

Begin by milling the stock for the top. Now draw the radius of the top (**B**). Next bandsaw the top perimeter and glue the hub to the center (**C**). If you sandwich a layer of heavy paper between the top and the hub, it is much easier to remove the hub after the process is complete.

After the glue has dried, mount the top into the jig (**D**). Before shaping the molding, it's necessary to true the edge of the top. A spiral straight bit cuts cleaner and with less chatter than an ordinary straight bit (**E**).

Once the bit is mounted, you're ready to begin. Never attempt to start the router when the bit is in contact with the stock. Instead, start the router, slide it along the rails until it touches the top, clamp the router in position, and rotate the top. Always rotate the top clockwise against the bit rotation (**F**).

Next, switch to the roundover bit to create the bead. If you're not able to find a bit without a bearing it's easy to remove the bearing and grind away the bearing stud. To adjust the bit depth, use a block of plywood from the jig (**G**).

(Text continues on p. 144.)

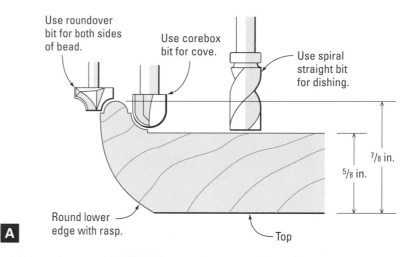

Use roundover bit for both sides of bead.

Use corebox bit for cove.

Use spiral straight bit for dishing.

$^{7}/_{8}$ in.

$^{5}/_{8}$ in.

Round lower edge with rasp.

Top

A

B

C

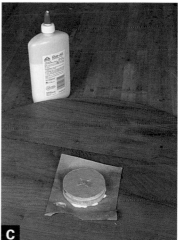

D

F

E

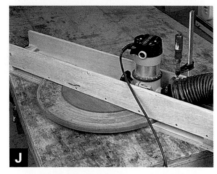

Shaping the molding is much the same as truing the perimeter: Start the router, clamp it in position, and rotate the top (**H**). To ensure that the molding isn't squeezed, begin from the outside edge and work inward (**I**). The molding is shaped in three steps: outside edge of bead; inside edge of bead; and cove, which is shaped with a bull-nose bit.

Once the molding is complete, switch back to the straight bit to dish the top (**J**). This process goes quickly, because there is no careful positioning of the router as there was with the molding. If you have a helper, one of you can hold the router while the other rotates the top, which sidesteps the process of clamping the router for each cut.

With the router work completed, you're ready for the handwork. Clamp the top to the bench and scrape the surface smooth (**K**). Use care to avoid scarring the molding. After smoothing the top, the edge will need shaping along the underside to remove the square corner. This step also gives the top a thin, refined appearance. A rasp works well for this process, but first draw a line with a compass for use as a guide. Now secure the top in the vise and rasp the edge (**L**). Work the surface from the fillet at the bead to the layout line. When you're satisfied, smooth the edge with a file, scraper, and then sandpaper.

> ⚠️ **WARNING   A dust collector is a must. Otherwise this process produces a choking cloud of fine dust and chips.**

Beads

Quirk Bead

➤ Quirk Bead with
a Wooden Plane
(p. 148)

➤ Quirk Bead on the
Router Table
(p. 149)

Beaded Backboard

➤ Beaded Backboard
with a No. 45 Plane
(p. 150)

➤ Beaded Backboard
on the Router Table
(p. 151)

Cock Bead

➤ Applied Cock Bead
for a Drawer Front
(p. 152)

➤ Integral Cock Bead
for a Drawer Front
with a Scratch Stock
(p. 153)

THERE'S PROBABLY NOT A MORE VERSATILE molding profile than the bead. A bead is a semicircular or semi-elliptical profile. It can be shaped flush along the edge of a table apron or proud around the perimeter of a drawer front. Used along the edge of backboards in casework, the bead will embellish the back while hiding the expansion joint between the boards. Beads are easily shaped with a router, plane, hand beader, or even scratch stock.

Undoubtedly, it's this versatility and ease of use that has made the bead so popular for centuries. Next time you need to soften a hard edge or add a bit of decoration, remember this simple, versatile profile.

When shaping beads, remember that you need to get to the full depth of the cutter's profile to achieve the right shape. Beads that aren't cut to full depth can appear flattened on one or more sides.

Making a Scratch Stock

A scratch stock is simply a scraper with a profile. By pushing the tool across the wood surface, you produce a molding profile. Why use a scratch stock instead of a router? There are several reasons. A scratch stock can shape tiny profiles that a router can't. Also, a scratch stock can easily shape a profile along a freeform curve. Plus you can customize the shape to suit your design requirements.

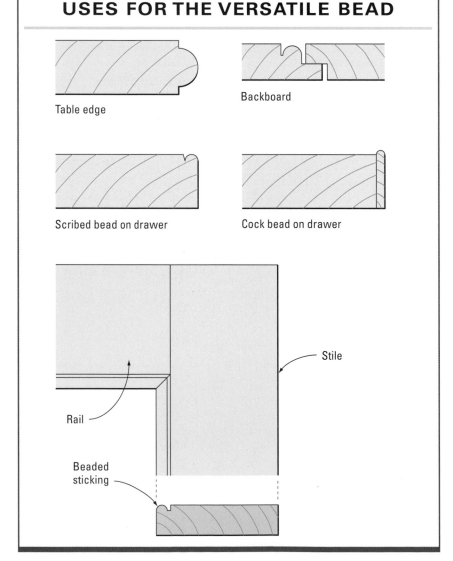

USES FOR THE VERSATILE BEAD

Table edge

Backboard

Scribed bead on drawer

Cock bead on drawer

Stile

Rail

Beaded sticking

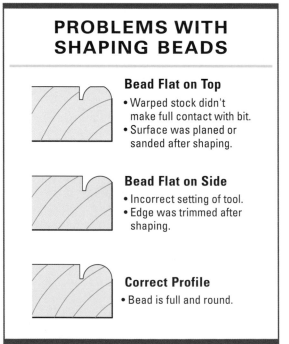

PROBLEMS WITH SHAPING BEADS

Bead Flat on Top
- Warped stock didn't make full contact with bit.
- Surface was planed or sanded after shaping.

Bead Flat on Side
- Incorrect setting of tool.
- Edge was trimmed after shaping.

Correct Profile
- Bead is full and round.

These days you can buy a scratch stock but it's just as easy to make your own. You can shape a scratch stock from a wood block or you can use an old wooden marking gauge. Pieces of an old handsaw work well for the blade. To shape the profile into the blade, I use small files of various shapes.

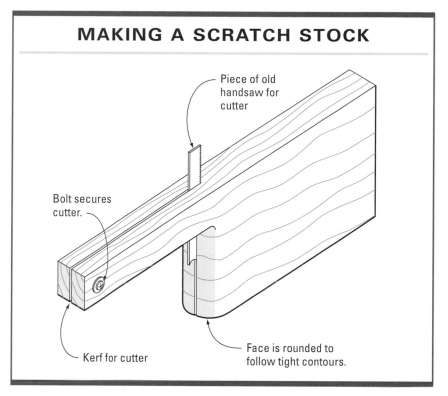

MAKING A SCRATCH STOCK

Piece of old handsaw for cutter

Bolt secures cutter.

Kerf for cutter

Face is rounded to follow tight contours.

A scratch stock is simply a device to hold a cutter and a fence to run against the work.

A simple scratch can be constructed by cutting a kerf in a block of wood. Shape the fence to a round to ensure good contact with the edge of the stock.

A scratch stock can cut elegant small beads and other profiles. You easily can make one from an old marking gauge.

Old bandsaw blades make good scratch stock blades. Small files are used to shape the profiles.

A

B

Quirk Bead with a Wooden Plane

Wooden quirk-bead planes are still widely available, and they're a pleasure to use. Best of all, the quirk bead has a wide variety of applications.

Begin by selecting clear, straight-grain stock for planing. Sight down the sole of the plane to set the plane iron for a light cut (**A**).

To make the cut, use one hand to keep the fence of the plane against the stock (notice I've added a strip a wood to my plane as a fence), while pushing the plane with the other hand (**B**). A quirk bead should have a full, round profile. If the plane comes away from the stock, the bead will be flat on the side. If you don't plane to the full depth, the bead will be flat on top. The plane's built-in stop will ride against the stock to prevent further cutting once the full profile is reached.

➤ See *"Problems with Shaping Beads"* on p. 146.

Quirk Bead on the Router Table

With your router table, you can shape a quirk bead quickly and easily and on curved stock. However, many beading router bits have too large of a quirk; it looks disproportionate to the bead. It pays to shop around and find a brand with pleasing proportions.

Begin by mounting the bit and setting the height (**A**). Next, position the fence tangent to the bearing (**B**). Set the router speed high and make the cut (**C**). If you experience burning, try increasing the feed rate or reducing the revolutions per minute (rpms).

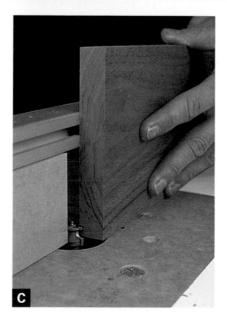

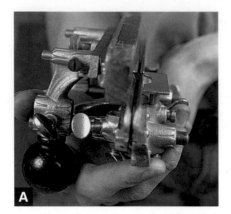

Beaded Backboard with a No. 45 Plane

You've probably seen no. 45 planes at your local flea market (**A**). Stanley Tools manufactured them for many years, and so they're quite common. They work well for shaping beaded backboards. The idea behind a beaded backboard is to hide the expansion joints in a solid-wood case back (**B**).

Begin by milling the stock for the backboards. I prefer to use random-width boards with minor defects. This allows me to use stock I have on hand that may not be suitable for more visible areas.

After milling the stock, cut a rabbet along both edges of each board. Keep in mind that the rabbets must be on opposite faces. First, mount a square cutter in the main body of the plane and position the second skate flush with the outside edge of the cutter. Lock the skate in position with the thumbscrews. Now adjust the cutter for a light cut and lock it in place. Finally, slide the fence in position on the arms and lock it in place next to the cutter (**C**). While cutting the rabbet, keep the fence firmly against the stock (**D**). As you reach the full depth of the rabbet on the first piece, adjust the depth stop to bear against the work.

After cutting the rabbets on all the stock, shape the bead (**E**). Follow the same set-up procedure as you did earlier: set the iron, then the second skate, and finally the fence. The no. 45 plane is equipped with a special fence for beading that rides the edge of the rabbet. To make use of it, you'll first need to remove the wood fence (**F**).

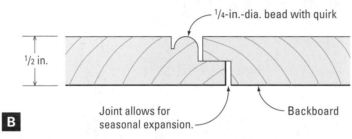

¼-in.-dia. bead with quirk

½ in.

Joint allows for seasonal expansion.

Backboard

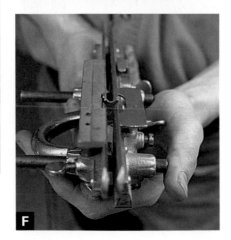

Beaded Backboard on the Router Table

Begin by mounting a rabbeting bit in the router. Set the height of the bit with a graduated square (**A**); then set the fence flush with the bearing (**B**). Finally, set a featherboard or other hold-down device in position to keep the stock against the table (**C**). Now you're ready to cut the rabbet (**D**).

Once you've cut the rabbet, change to the beading bit. Set the lower edge of the bead flush with the edge of the rabbet (**E**). To maintain pressure throughout the cut, clamp a featherboard to the table (**F**). As with any cut on the router, maintain a steady, uniform feed rate. Feeding the stock too fast will result in a coarse, washboard surface; feeding too slow may cause scorching.

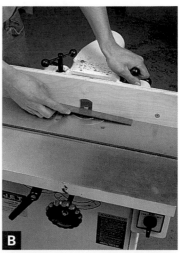

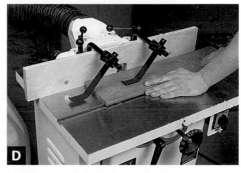

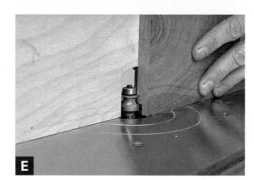

Veneer — | — 1/8 in.

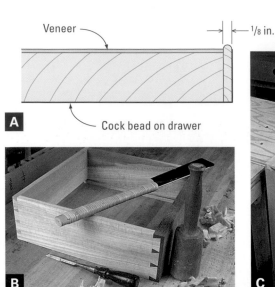

Cock bead on drawer

A

B

D

E

F

G

H

Applied Cock Bead for a Drawer Front

Cock bead is a small beaded strip applied to the perimeter of a drawer (**A**). The bead sits proud of the drawer front and protects the veneered edges from chipping. Obviously, the effect is attractive on solid fronts as well. This is another example of how to use the versatile bead.

Begin the process by building the drawers (**B**) and fitting them to the case (**C**). Don't fit the drawers after beading them, or you'll flatten the side of the bead.

Next, mill the strips for the cock bead. In this example, they measure ⅛ in. thick and are attached 1/16 in. proud of the drawer front. Make sure to mill the strips wide enough to safely shape them. After milling the stock, shape the bead with a ⅛-in.-diameter beading bit on the router table (**D**).

The next step is to rabbet the drawer (**E**). Mount a rabbeting bit in the router table and set it for the depth and height of the rabbet. If you've dovetailed the drawer, you may opt to cut the rabbet only to the base of the joint so that the joinery will be exposed for view. Cut the rabbet on the ends of the drawer first (**F**) and then on the edges. To provide support on the edges, tack a strip of thin plywood to the inside of the drawer (**G**).

Now rip the cock bead to final width and miter the ends. Next, drill small holes for the brads to avoid splitting the thin cock bead (**H**). Then attach the strip to the drawer with glue and small brads.

Integral Cock Bead for a Drawer Front with a Scratch Stock

Another method for cock beading is simply to shape the profile directly into the drawer front. Although the bead doesn't stand proud of the drawer front, it's a way to add a neat detail without all the fuss (**A**).

There are a couple of options for this technique. You can bead all four edges or simply bead the upper and lower edges. Both methods are attractive, but if you choose to bead all four edges you'll need to miter the corners with a chisel.

Although you can certainly shape the bead with a router bit, a scratch stock will yield the authentic irregularities that are associated with the provincial furniture on which this technique was first used.

[**TIP**] **Sharpen a scratch stock beading blade with a few strokes of a round file.**

To shape the bead, first secure the work on the bench. Then scrape the profile into the edge of the drawer with long, smooth strokes (**B**). As you work the tool, tilt it slightly in the direction in which you are pushing it (**C**).

A

B

C

Simple Moldings

Machine-Cut Molding

Hand-Cut Molding

➤ Simple Molding on the Router Table (p. 159)

➤ Simple Molding on the Shaper (p. 160)

➤ Simple Molding on the Table Saw with a Molding Head (p. 161)

➤ Simple Molding with a Molding Plane (p. 162)

➤ Simple Molding with a Universal Plane (p. 163)

Aᴸᴸ ᴍᴏʟᴅɪɴɢꜱ, even seemingly complex ones, are made up of shapes derived from about a half dozen basic profiles: bead, thumbnail, ovolo, ogee, chamfer, and cove. Simple moldings typically use just one of these profiles, whereas complex moldings use a number of them. By mixing sizes and variations of the basic profiles, the options become nearly endless.

Moldings are integrated into furniture in one of two ways: a strip of molding is mitered and attached to the work or the edge of a surface is shaped. Strip moldings perform several functions: They unify separate cases, frame the work, establish visual parameters, and provide visual unity. Most of all, strip moldings add visual interest by reflecting light and creating shadow lines.

▶ See *"Edge Treatments"* on p. 132.

BASIC MOLDING PROFILES

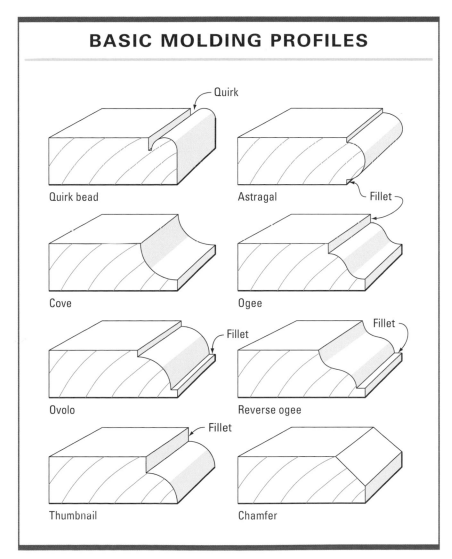

Quirk

Quirk bead

Astragal — Fillet

Cove

Ogee

Ovolo — Fillet

Reverse ogee — Fillet

Thumbnail — Fillet

Chamfer

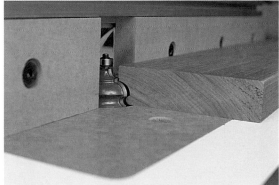

A molding can be either cut directly into the stock or ripped from the board and applied.

Use a wide piece of stock when making applied moldings to allow a safe margin for hand placement when ripping it from the original board.

MOLDINGS ON A CORNER CABINET

Crown molding

Neck molding adds detail.

Ovolo edge frames glass light.

Fluted pilaster emphasizes vertical lines.

Waist molding visually separates upper and lower cases.

Thumbnail edge frames panels.

Base cap provides transition between cabinet and foot.

Stock Selection for Moldings

Strip moldings are shaped on lengths of straight-grain stock and then attached to the work with glue and/or fasteners. Strip moldings can consist of one or more profiles shaped onto a single wood strip or several strips joined together to make a wide and/or deep complex molding.

It's best to select straight-grain stock when making strip moldings. When using hand tools, such as planes and scratch stock, straight-grain stock will produce less tearout.

Moldings add refinement to this eighteenth-century corner cabinet.

When using machines, it's often necessary to shape a wide board and rip the molding free afterward. This method will keep your hands a safe distance from the cutter or bit. If you select straight-grain stock, the strips will be less likely to distort when you rip them free.

Also, when milling stock for strip molding, it's a good idea to make extra for a miscut or other any other problem that may occur. Otherwise, if you need another piece it can often be difficult to mill it for an exact match to the original—especially if the molding is a complicated design made from several profiles.

Attaching Moldings

When attaching moldings, it's helpful to follow a few guidelines to ease the process. Parallel strips—such as those that wrap around a table edge—must be of the exact same length for the miter to fit. This is easily accomplished by using a stop on the miter saw.

When fitting molding to casework, it works well to miter the front strip first and then the returns or side strips. If adjustments need to be made for a precise fit, they can be made to the returns. Afterward, the ends of the returns are cut 90 degrees to be flush with the case back.

One of the most important points to remember when attaching strip molding is to allow for cross-grain seasonal wood movement. Small moldings can be effectively fastened with brads, which are set below the wood surface. As the wood moves, the soft brads will flex. Large moldings, such as a crown molding on casework, can be fastened with screws from the inside of the case.

For an applied molding, rip the molded profile from the main board on the table saw. For safety, always use a push stick to feed the stock.

> ## ▶ MAKE A LITTLE EXTRA MOLDING

Don't shortchange yourself when making moldings; a little extra is always useful. If you run short of your original estimate, the extra will match the grain and profile of the other molding exactly. If you need to cut more later, you'll have to set up your machinery again, and it has to be spot-on to match.

Furthermore, always save a short section of molding when the job is complete. It provides a reference sample for designing or shaping molding at a later date.

Remember to slot the holes in the case so the screws will be able to slide as the case expands and contracts. Always use glue in the miter joints of moldings; it keeps the joint closed tight through the years.

Using Hand Tools to Create Moldings

There's something addictive about making moldings with hand tools, watching the shavings pile up like confetti. It's quiet work; and for period projects, you get the tool marks and slight imperfections that lend an authentic look. For small moldings, you can use a scratch stock. Molding planes were once made in an amazing variety of profiles;

When using hand-planes or a scratch stock to cut mold-ings, always select straight-grain stock to avoid tearout.

they can still be found at flea markets and in antiques shops.

► See *"Making a Scratch Stock"* on p. 146.

The so-called universal plane—the Stanley 55—was developed around the turn of the twentieth century to replace a multitude of wooden planes. Although it's sometimes a useful tool, it's too impractical to be the "planing mill within itself," as it was originally claimed to be. However, it is an enjoyable tool to use and can create many profiles.

Whenever you use hand tools to cut molding, be sure to choose straight, even-grain stock to reduce the possibility of tearout. Keep the blades sharp by using rounded files and polishing with slipstones.

THE STANLEY 55 PLANE

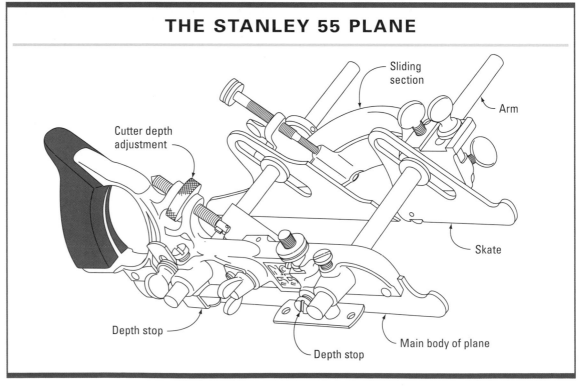

Sliding section

Arm

Cutter depth adjustment

Skate

Depth stop

Depth stop

Main body of plane

Simple Molding on the Router Table

Anytime you're shaping strip molding on the router table you'll want to select wide stock to distance your hands safely from the spinning bit. After securing the bit in the collet, set the height to create the cutting depth you desire. A small, graduated square works well for gauging the bit height (**A**).

Next, set the fence in position by aligning it tangent with the bearing on the bit (**B**). Now set the stock in place and lock the guard in position (**C**).

When you've finished these steps, make the cut by feeding the stock from right to left (**D**). Listen to the router for an indication of the proper feed rate and rotations per minute (rpms). After shaping, rip the molding free on the table saw (**E**). The finished molding is now ready to apply (**F**).

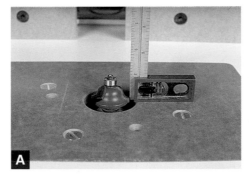

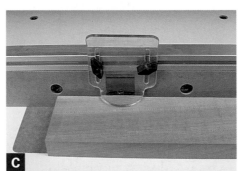

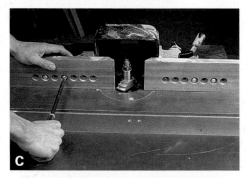

Simple Molding on the Shaper

When using the shaper, safety is always the most important issue, even when shaping a basic profile. Resist any temptation to shape narrow stock without a power feed or appropriate jig. Instead, select wide stock, which positions your hands a safe distance from the cutterhead.

After mounting the cutterhead, check the height with a combination square (**A**). Next, adjust the fence tangent to the smallest cutting circle (**B**); then adjust the fence for the smallest possible opening (**C**). Next, check the spindle rotation. To position the cutterhead underneath the stock for safety requires reversing the spindle to a clockwise rotation (**D**). Now add a featherboard for additional safety and make the cut (**E**). Afterward, rip the molding free on the table saw (**F**).

Simple Molding on the Table Saw with a Molding Head

A molding head has insert cutters that lock securely in the head. The entire assembly mounts on the saw arbor. Why use a molding head when the router table is just a few feet away? When shaping the face of a board, you are not limited by the board's width when you use a molding head in the table saw. This is a distinct advantage when shaping window trim and other wide stock that is beyond the reach of a router bit.

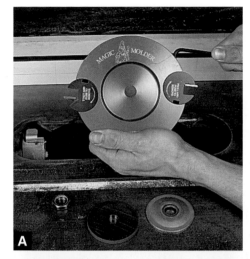

The first step when using the head is to lock the cutters securely in position (**A**). Head styles vary so read and follow the manufacturer's instructions carefully. Next, mount the head on your table saw (**B**). Make certain that the head spins freely and fits within the throat plate opening. It may be necessary to add a spacer to center the head (**C**). Lower the head for a light cut. The next step is to position the fence and clamp a featherboard in place to hold the stock firmly to the table (**D**). Now you're ready for a trial cut; a quick check of the profile depth and you're ready to begin.

[**TIP**] **Make test cuts on inexpensive stock, such as pine or poplar. This saves your best stock for the project.**

Keep your hands clear of the molding head and use push sticks or blocks (**E**). After shaping, rip the molding free (**F**).

Simple Molding with a Molding Plane

Wooden molding planes have been around for centuries. Despite the array of power tools available, the wooden plane is still an effective and enjoyable tool for shaping moldings. Molding planes are readily available from tool dealers and flea markets; if you've never experienced the pleasure using them, I encourage you to find one and give it a try.

Stock selection is important; wooden molding planes are lightweight and work best on straight-grain stock.

Check the iron for sharpness and set it for a light cut (**A**). Most asymmetrical profiles (like the ogee in this example) require that you hold the plane at an angle in relationship to the work. As an aid in gauging and maintaining the correct angle, planes usually have spring lines scribed into the front end of the plane (**B**). As you begin each cut, keep the spring lines parallel to the stock and the fence in contact with the edge of the stock (**C**). When you reach the full depth of the profile, the stop will contact the surface of the work and prevent the plane from cutting farther (**D**).

Simple Molding with a Universal Plane

Begin by selecting the stock. Anything but the straightest grain makes planing difficult. Although soft woods plane easily, you can also achieve good results with a moderately hard wood, such as walnut or cherry. The next step is to set the iron in place and adjust the cutting depth (**A**).

[**TIP**] **Check the iron for sharpness first; like any chisel or place iron, the edge should be smooth and polished.**

Adjust the iron with the thumbwheel for a light shaving. Next, set the second skate in position flush with the cutter or slightly inset (**B**). Then slide the fence onto the arms and lock it in place with the thumbscrews (**C**). When shaping asymmetrical profiles such as this ogee, it works best to position the cut inward slightly from the edge of the stock. This way, the cutter will be trapped by the stock as you plane, which prevents it from sliding off of the profile.

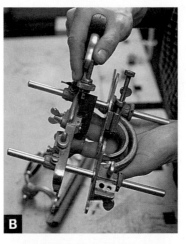

Now you're ready to make the cut. Keep the fence against the stock with one hand and push the plane firmly with the other (**D**). As the shavings peel away and the profile is revealed (**E**), set the plane's stop to bear against the stock (**F**). The stop will ensure that all subsequent moldings are identical in profile depth.

Complex and Built-Up Moldings

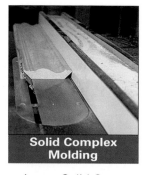

Solid Complex Molding

Built-Up Molding

Dentil Molding

COMPLEX MOLDINGS ARE COMBINATIONS of two or more simple profiles. They are used when a more dramatic or formal look is desired. A typical example of a complex molding is the crown molding on most casework. Generally, a crown consists of a large cove flanked by smaller profiles, such as a thumbnail, bead, or ogee. As the molding steps upward, it also steps outward to "look down" toward the observer.

Waist moldings on casework are another example of complex moldings. Chests, clocks, desks, and other tall pieces are usually constructed of several cases or "boxes." To unify the cases, a waist molding is used at their junction.

There are three options for making complex molding: shaping thin, flat stock and attaching it to the case at an angle,

A SAMPLE OF COMPLEX MOLDINGS

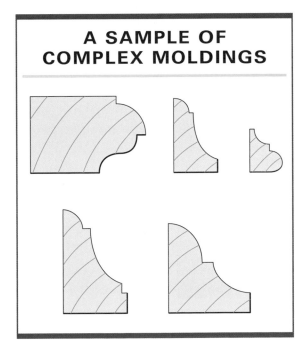

MOLDINGS ON A CHEST

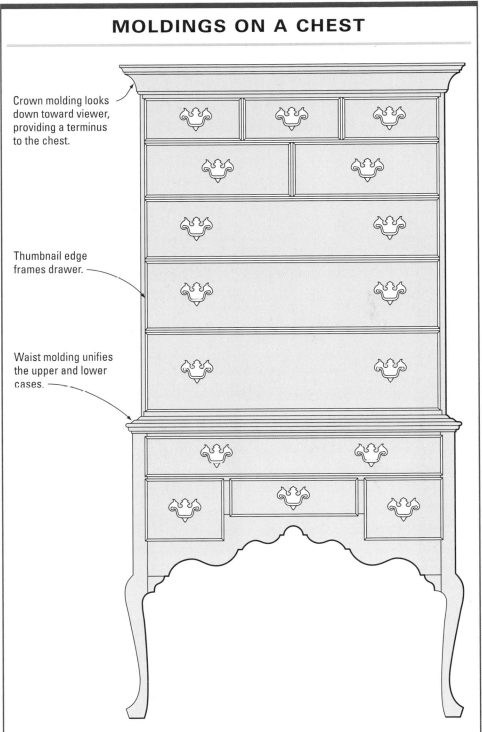

Crown molding looks down toward viewer, providing a terminus to the chest.

Thumbnail edge frames drawer.

Waist molding unifies the upper and lower cases.

COMBINING A FLAT CROWN MOLDING WITH STACKED STRIPS

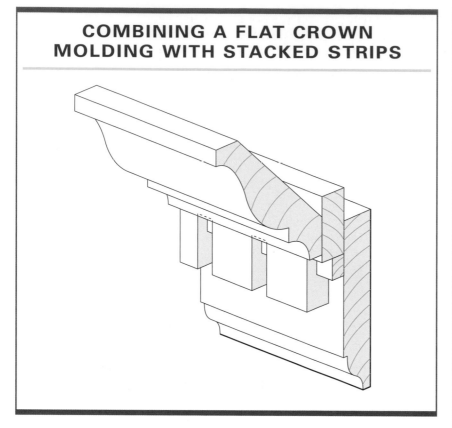

THREE METHODS FOR SHAPING CROWN MOLDING

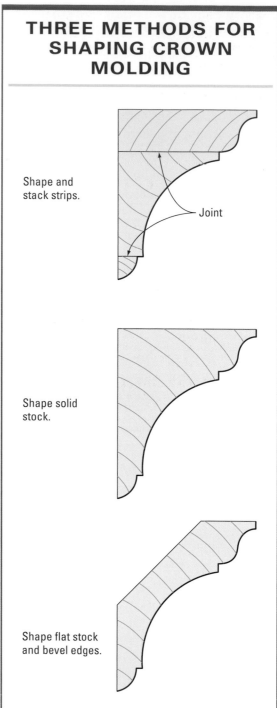

Shape and stack strips.

Joint

Shape solid stock.

Shape flat stock and bevel edges.

shaping thick stock, and shaping and stacking strips of simple profiles. You can also use a combination of these methods to create a cornice. But first let's discuss each method individually.

Flat Stock Moldings

Architectural crown moldings are commonly shaped out of flat stock and mounted. This also works well for furniture. A flat crown molding is beveled on the bottom edges and applied at an angle. This method uses thinner stock, yet gives the appearance of depth. The downside is that flat moldings are diffi-

➤ SAFETY FOR CUTTING COMPLEX MOLDINGS

Cutting complex moldings from a single piece of stock presents some safety challenges. Here are some guidelines to help you make the process as safe as possible. Remember, as with any woodworking technique, if you feel uncomfortable, try to find another method with which you feel more confident.

- Make the largest cut first, while the stock has the greatest mass and resistance to chatter and kickback.

- Make certain that there is sufficient surface area in contact with the table and fence to prevent the possibility of the stock tipping into the cutter and spoiling the work.

- Position the workpiece to expose the least amount of cutter, thereby exposing less cutting surface to your hands. When possible, position the cut underneath the stock so that the stock shields your hands.

USING A FLAT CROWN MOLDING TO CREATE A CORNICE

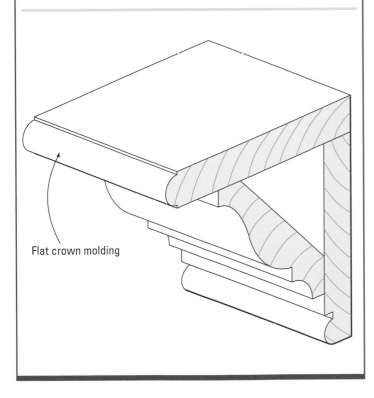

Flat crown molding

A SAMPLE OF FLAT CROWN MOLDINGS

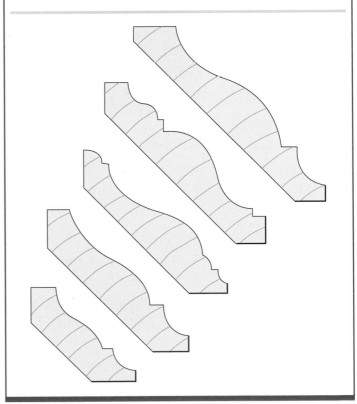

Making moldings from wide, flat stock requires a shaper with a long spindle. Another option is a table saw fitted with a molding head.

This corner cupboard cornice was shaped as two separate strips to avoid waste; then it was fastened to the case.

- Bead
- Cove
- Ovolo
- Cove and bead
- Joint
- Fillet
- Bead
- Thumbnail

cult to apply; it's awkward to align the molding and attach it. In addition, if the molding isn't capped off, it will need to be supported by triangular glue blocks.

The main advantage to this method is that it avoids using thick stock. To shape wide, flat stock you'll need a shaper with a long spindle, some molding planes, or a table saw molding head. Unfortunately, a router can't reach to shape wide stock.

Thick Stock Moldings

The second method of shaping a complex molding uses thick stock. This method works well when a large, elliptical cove is the centerpiece of the molding. First, the cove is cut on the table saw; then smaller profiles are shaped on each side of the cove. Because it's shaped from thick stock, the molding is self-supporting and easier than flat stock to apply to a case. It appears more finished, too. This can be especially important when the case is short enough to view from the

SHAPING A COMPLEX MOLDING ON THICK STOCK

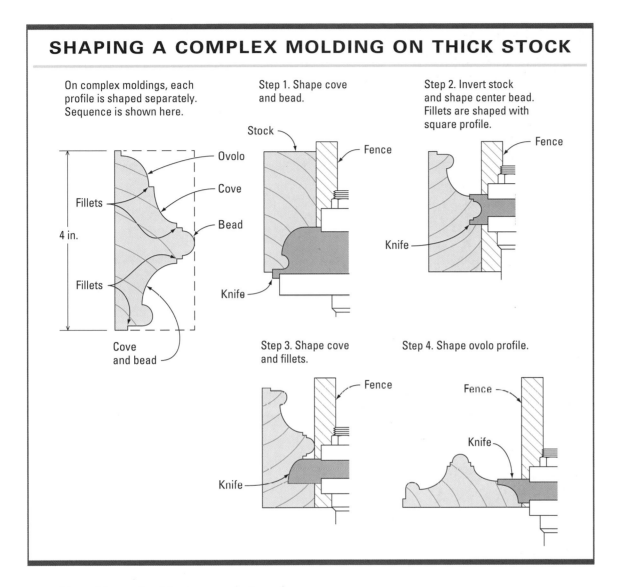

On complex moldings, each profile is shaped separately. Sequence is shown here.

Ovolo

Cove

Bead

Fillets

4 in.

Fillets

Cove and bead

Step 1. Shape cove and bead.

Stock

Fence

Knife

Step 2. Invert stock and shape center bead. Fillets are shaped with square profile.

Fence

Knife

Step 3. Shape cove and fillets.

Fence

Knife

Step 4. Shape ovolo profile.

Fence

Knife

top. Also, this method is a great choice when the molding curves, such as a semicircular or gooseneck pediment molding.

Stacked Moldings

The third method involves stacking strips of simple molding profiles to create a wide, dramatic effect. To avoid using a lot of valuable stock, the strips can be glued to

a secondary wood, such as poplar. Once the strips are stacked, the secondary wood will be hidden.

Still another option is to combine the methods described above. The decision of which method to use is often based on the tools and materials at hand.

▶ ORDERING A CUSTOM CUTTERHEAD

If you need to create moldings efficiently, it's tough to beat the power and speed of a shaper. Unfortunately, you may not always be able to find the exact profile that you require. The solution may be to order a custom cutterhead. To do this, you'll need to supply the manufacturer with the following information.

- **Number of wings.** Two wing cutterheads are less expensive and are better suited to the slower pace associated with hand feeding the work. If you're using a power feeder, opt for three wings; you'll be able to choose a faster feed rate.

- **Bore size.** Shaper spindles are sized from ½ in. to 1¼ in. so specify your machine's spindle size.

- **Sketch of the cutter pattern.** A full-scale drawing is best. Make certain that it is accurate.

- **Cutter diameter.** Do you need a specific diameter? It's important that the diameter doesn't exceed the spindle and throat capacity of your shaper.

- **Cutterhead rotation.** The most common is a counterclockwise rotation with a right-to-left feed.

Talk with the manufacturer to see if you must provide additional information. And be prepared for sticker shock. Like creating custom furniture, making custom shaper cutterheads is labor intensive, and the price will most likely reflect that. But for a special job, the extra cost may be well worth it.

▶ See *"List of Suppliers"* on p. 285.

Using Dentil Molding for a Formal Look

One of the most versatile complex moldings is dentil molding, essentially a strip of wood with a series of cuts that leave blocks. These blocks resemble teeth, giving the molding its name. Because the cuts are shallow, the teeth remain intact; it's much easier to work with a strip of evenly spaced block than with dozens of individual blocks. But the blocks, or teeth, appear individual because the upper portion of the dentil molding is hidden by another applied molding.

The whole process of laying out, cutting, and applying dentil molding is a bit time consuming. But the result is certainly worth the extra effort. Using dentil molding is an easy way to add formality and distinction to almost any cornice.

There are several options to choose from when designing a cornice with dentil molding. For example, you can leave the bottom of each cut flat or you can carve a convex

ARCHITECTURAL CORNICE

This cornice can be made on the shaper from six separate molding strips using simple knife profiles. Dentils can be made on the table saw with a dado head.

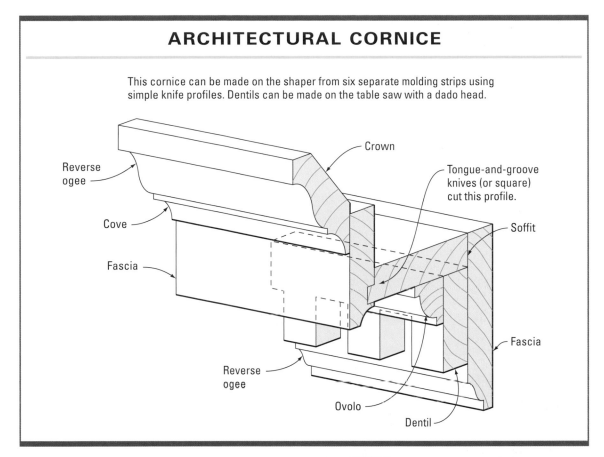

Crown

Reverse ogee

Tongue-and-groove knives (or square) cut this profile.

Cove

Soffit

Fascia

Fascia

Reverse ogee

Ovolo

Dentil

arch into each one. Another option is to drill a series of shallow holes above the spaces. This adds additional detail, which gives the molding more distinction.

Spacing and proportion are also important. The blocks look best if each is a vertical rectangle rather than a square. The proportion of the blocks should fit with the rest of the cornice, whether it's an arrangement of small profiles for, say, a clock case or a large group of moldings in an architectural cornice.

Finally, dentil molding looks best if the miters meet at blocks rather than at a space between the blocks. To space the blocks accurately you'll need to lay out the dentil strip with dividers before you begin cutting.

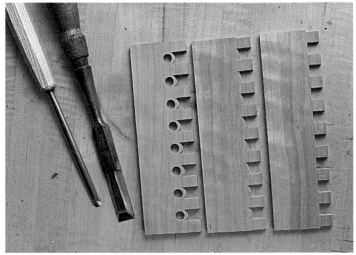

The design options for dentil moldings are nearly limitless and can make a piece of furniture quite distinctive.

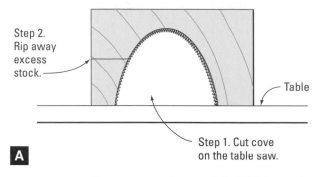

Step 2. Rip away excess stock.

Table

Step 1. Cut cove on the table saw.

A

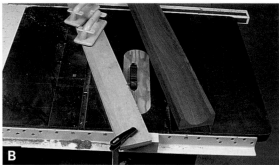

B

C

Large, Solid Crown Molding on the Table Saw and Router Table

The molding shown here is used as a crown for a large case, such as a Connecticut-style tall chest. But the technique, like most in this book, has broad applications.

Many furniture crown moldings use a deep, elliptical cove as the large focal point, with smaller, basic profiles flanking it. Making the molding from one piece of solid stock ensures continuity of grain and color and greatly simplifies application to the casework

Begin by drawing the profile full-scale. This ensures good proportions and allows you to plan each cut more easily. Next, shape the cove on the table saw while the stock is still square (**A, B**).

▶ See *"Machine-Cut Coves"* on p. 209.

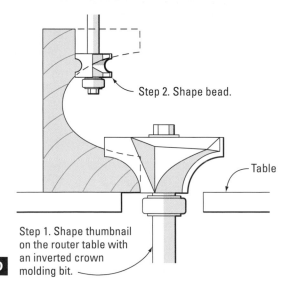

Step 2. Shape bead.

Table

Step 1. Shape thumbnail on the router table with an inverted crown molding bit.

D

Before you begin shaping with the router, rip away the excess stock at the base of the molding. Now turn your attention to the thumbnail profile at the top of the molding. If you have a shaper, you can invert a roundover cutter (**C**); or you can use a special inverted router bit, available from CMT USA, Inc. (**D**).

➤ See *"List of Suppliers"* on p. 285.

Shape the bead next. The tall fence that came with your router table will obstruct the cut. Instead, use a flat, wide piece of stock. Cut it the same length as your router table and clamp it to the top after cutting a small opening for the bit. Now stand the molding on edge and shape the bead (**E**).

There is only one profile remaining: the small cove at the base. To cut the cove, you can use the shaper (**F, G**) or a corebox bit on the router table.

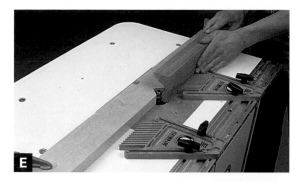

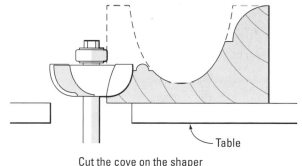

Cut the cove on the shaper
with an inverted cutterhead.

Another Large, Solid Crown Molding on the Table Saw and Router Table

Here's another example of a solid crown molding. Many design variations can be accomplished with the use of different profiles. This example uses a large cove flanked by an ogee at the top and a thumbnail profile at the base (**A**).

Begin by shaping the large cove on the table saw (**B**) and then rip off the excess stock (**C**).

▶ See *"Machine-Cut Coves"* on p. 209.

Next, invert the molding to shape the ogee at the top (**D**). Finally, lay the molding on its back to shape the thumbnail (**E**).

This and the profile shown on p. 172 are from the CMT USA, Inc., crown-molding set.

▶ See *"List of Suppliers"* on p. 285.

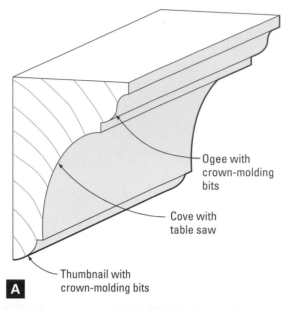

Ogee with crown-molding bits

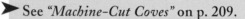

Cove with table saw

Thumbnail with crown-molding bits

A

B

C

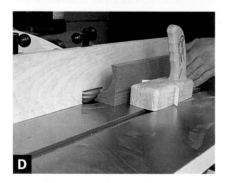

D

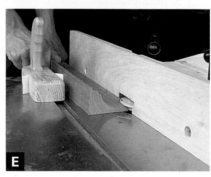

E

Flat Crown Molding on the Shaper

For shaping this molding. you'll need a tall cutter-head designed for crown molding (**A**). A power feed works best for feeding the stock but you can also use featherboards (**B**) and push sticks.

Begin by milling the stock oversize in width; this provides a flat surface on either side of the profile to contact the outfeed fence (**C**). Next, adjust the cutterhead height so that it is centered in the stock. Then set the fence for a light cut. I prefer to shape a profile this size in two passes for a smoother surface that is free of milling defects. As you feed the stock, keep the ends butted together to reduce sniping (**D**).

After shaping the first pass on all of the stock (**E**), reposition the fence and make the second pass.

The last step is to bevel the edges of the molding. Tilt the table-saw blade to 45 degrees and position the stock between the blade and fence for uniformity (**F**). Then rip the second edge (**G**).

> ⚠ **WARNING** Dust collection is a must with a cutterhead of this size.

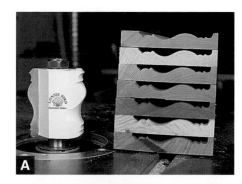
A

C

E

G

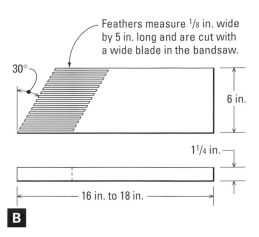
Feathers measure 1/8 in. wide by 5 in. long and are cut with a wide blade in the bandsaw.

30°

6 in.

1 1/4 in.

16 in. to 18 in.

B

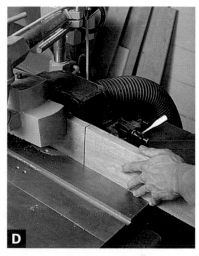
D

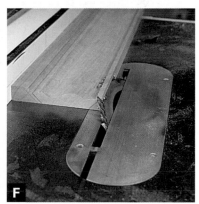
F

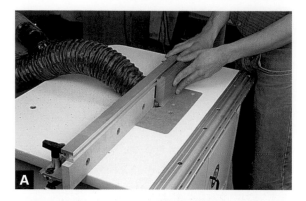

Complex Molding on the Router Table

This two-step profile is commonly used as a transition molding between stacking casework. As with all narrow strip moldings, it's important to mill wide strips for safe handling and then rip the molding free.

Begin by shaping the cove (**A**). Set the fence tangent to the bearing and shape the stock on edge. Afterward, raise the bit and cut the stock a second time (**B**). Now switch to the roundover bit for shaping the thumbnail. Turn the stock 90 degrees and shape it on the face (**C**). Now rip the molding free (**D**). Use a push stick and splitter for safety.

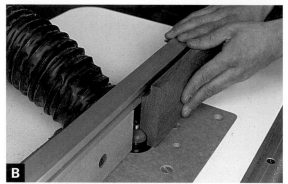

Another Complex Molding on the Router Table

Here's another example that shows the wide variety of applications associated with making moldings on the router table. This small molding forms the base and capital on the fluted pilasters for a desk interior. After the strips are shaped, they are cut into small blocks and shaped on the ends to complete the detail.

➤ See *"Template Shaping Small Parts"* on p. 282.

[**TIP**] **Whenever I design a new molding, I first make a drawing. It's a great aid for the setup; I can take measurements directly from the drawing to set the bit height. At each setup, I compare the test cut to the drawing to check accuracy.**

The first step is to shape the bead. To set the bit height, I used a molding sample that I saved from a previous run (**A**). Shape the bead with the molding inverted (**B**). The next step is to lay the molding face down and shape the large cove at the top edge (**C**). Now turn the molding end for end, which will position the remaining flat surface against the fence, and shape the small cove (**D**). Finally, use a straight bit to cut the fillets next to the small cove (**E**).

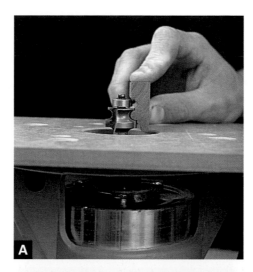

A

B

C

D

E

TIP

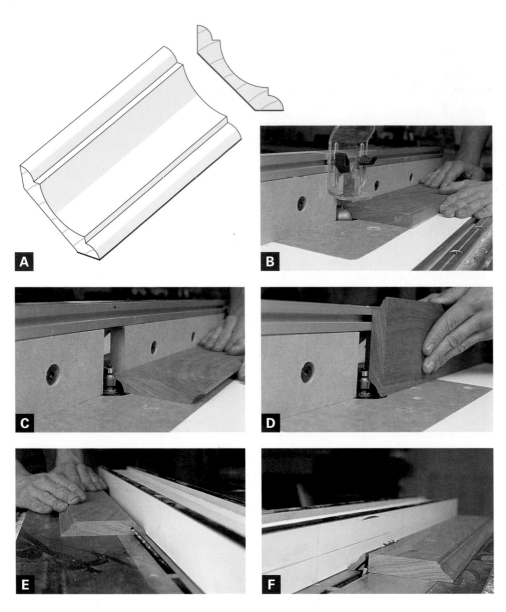

Flat Molding on the Router Table

Like an architectural cornice, this molding is attached to a case at a 45-degree angle (**A**).

After milling wide stock for safety, start by shaping the cove. I've removed the bearing on the cove bit to allow it to cut deeper. Shape this profile with the stock face down (**B**). Next, shape the thumbnail profile at the base of the molding (**C**). Now turn the stock on edge and shape the second thumbnail (**D**).

Because the back of this molding can be seen inside the lid, it's necessary to bevel the back corner for refinement. Begin by tilting the table-saw blade to 45 degrees and lowering the blade so that it doesn't penetrate the stock thickness. Now rip a kerf along the back of the molding (**E**). Return the blade to 90 degrees and set the height just above the stock thickness. Position the fence for the width of the molding and rip it free (**F**).

Flat Crown Molding with Wooden Handplanes

Wooden handplanes still have a place in the small shop. Here's a good example: To shape a wide, flat crown by a machine method, you would need a large shaper or a molder. Yet you can easily shape crown moldings with a few hollow and round planes.

Begin by drawing the crown molding full-size. Next select clear straight-grain stock for the molding (**A**).

The first step in shaping is to saw the fillet that separates the two profiles. Tilt the sawblade to 45 degrees and position the fence to align with the drawing you made earlier. Next, saw V-grooves to guide the planes (**B**). Now, shape the cove that is part of the ogee. Then shape the cove that is adjacent to the fillet (**C**).

The final step of the process is to bevel the edges of the molding to 45 degrees. Simply tilt the blade and position the fence for this ripping cut. This completes the crown molding (**D**).

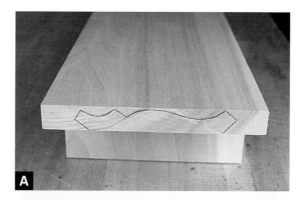

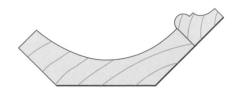

Shape cove separately; then glue on bead strip.

A

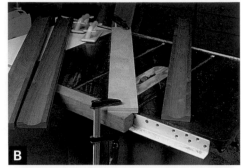

B

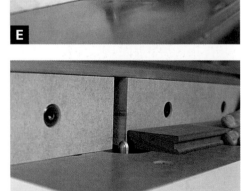

C

D

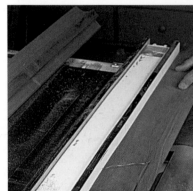

E

F

G

Complex Flat Molding

Many crown moldings, including the one in this example, incorporate a large cove flanked by a small bead at the base (**A**). With this style of molding, it becomes necessary to shape the cove and bead separately and join them after shaping. Otherwise, the bead will be cut away during the cove-shaping process.

Begin by shaping the cove (**B**). Next, bevel the edges of the cove strip. First bevel the front edges (**C**); then the back edges (**D**).

▶ See *"Machine-Cut Coves"* on p. 209.

Now shape the small secondary molding strip. Start by shaping the bead (**E**) and then complete the strip with the cove (**F**). Finally, glue the strip onto the base of the cove (**G**).

Stacked-Strip Complex Molding

The ability to make broad, dramatic moldings is typically limited to large shops with heavy, expensive industrial molders. But you can make broad moldings by shaping and stacking small strips (**A**). The shelf in shown here is a good example. Originally, the design was used as a shelf that was attached to a large architectural mantelpiece over a fireplace, which is typically the focal point in a room. You can create the same effect in your own shop. Let's get started.

First mill the stock for the shelf. The shelf and backboard are attached at a 90-degree angle and all the other moldings are stacked between them. To create the large astragal on the shelf edge, use an insert cutterhead (**B**) on the shaper; note that you can create this same profile with a router bit. When creating the top, shape the ends first using a miter gauge for support; then shape the profile onto the front edge (**C**). Afterward, rip the shelf to final width to eliminate any tearout at the back edge.

The next step is to shape the quirk bead on the backboard. Shape the returns on the ends first; then shape the face (**D**).

[**TIP**] **To save valuable lumber, glue strips of primary and secondary woods together. For this example, I used walnut and poplar.**

Now glue the shelf and backboard together and allow the glue to dry while you shape the other strips of molding. Notice in the drawing (**A**) how the moldings stack to create the wide cornice. After shaping, miter and stack the strips to complete the cornice (**E**).

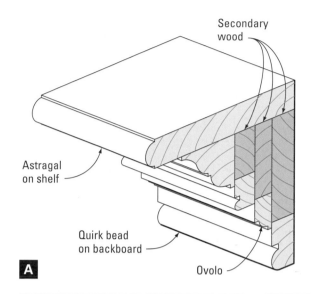

Secondary wood

Astragal on shelf

Quirk bead on backboard

Ovolo

A

B

C

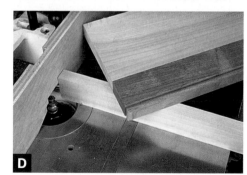

D

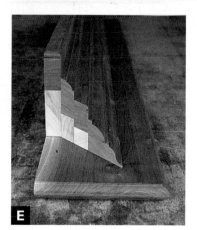

E

Cornice with a Flat Crown and Stacked Strips

This method for making a wide cornice combines the two previous methods. By attaching a wide, flat crown molding to a stack of strip molding, a very dramatic effect can be created. This technique has many applications—from crowning fine casework to use as an architectural cornice within a room.

Begin by shaping the crown molding. I produced the molding on my shaper with a tall cutterhead (**A**). But you can create it in other ways, too. For example, you can use a large cove on the table saw flanked by smaller moldings, you can shape the crown with wooden planes, or you can even purchase the crown from your local millwork shop or home center.

After shaping the crown molding, bevel the edges on the table saw. Next, shape a simple profile onto a wide strip to serve as a backboard. Then cut a dentil mold that fits within a wide groove cut into the face of the backboard. The dentil is quite simple to cut on the table saw with a dado head (**B**). After the dentil has been cut, the stock is very fragile until it's glued into the groove. The last step is to apply the crown molding to the top of the stack (**C**). To ease the process of fitting the cornice, the crown is added after the strips are applied to the casework or wall.

Basic Dentil Moldings on the Table Saw

As with all moldings, it's important to draw the dentil design before cutting it, allowing you to work out the proportions (**A**). This is especially true for dentil molding because, unlike many other moldings, it is never used alone.

Next, fasten a backboard to the miter gauge. Stack the dado to equal the kerf in the dentil and make a cut into the backboard (**B**). Using dividers, transfer the dentil spacing from your drawing to the backboard. Now tack a small brad into the board at the point indicated by the dividers and allow the head to protrude slightly. With the setup complete, you're ready to begin.

Place the end of the stock against the bead and make the first cut (**C**). To space each subsequent cut, slip the previous cut over the brad (**D**). It's that simple.

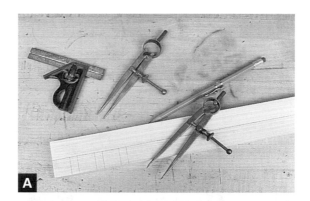

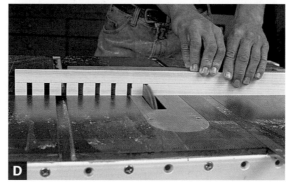

A

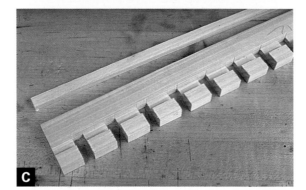

B

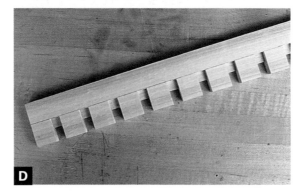

C

D

Dentil with a Stepped Block Detail

Now that you've seen how easy it is to make dentil you can add a strip of thin wood to the back to create a step between the blocks.

Lay out the dentil spacing and set up the table saw as in the previous example. Position the end of the stock against the brad for the first cut and slip the kerf over the brad for each successive cut (**A**).

➤ See *"Basic Dentil Moldings on the Table Saw"* on p. 183.

Now rip a narrow groove in the back of the dentil molding (**B**). The groove is positioned at the top edge of the blocks, and the depth of the groove equals one-half the dentil thickness. After cutting the groove, mill a strip of wood to fit snugly within the groove (**C**) and glue it in place (**D**).

Dentil with a Carved Detail

Furniture dentil is often more elaborate than architectural dentil. The dentil shown here is a good example (**A**). The bottom of the space between each dentil block is carved with an arch. Above each arch is a small hole, which accentuates the arch, adding even greater detail. The time involved in producing many linear feet of this dentil for a room is more than most people are willing to spend. But 7 ft. or so for a chest isn't enormously time consuming.

Before beginning, it's essential to understand the importance of accurate spacing on furniture dentil molding. The miters at each end should fall precisely on the edge of a dentil block instead of at a space or in the middle of a block. Therefore, the brad-spacing technique used in the previous examples isn't effective here. Even the smallest spacing error is multiplied many times over, which may affect the location of the blocks at each end.

➤ See *"Basic Dentil Moldings on the Table Saw"* on p. 183.

Thus it's best to lay out the entire length of dentil strip with dividers (**B**) and a square (**C**). After making the layout, saw each space to the line (**D**). It's not nearly as tedious as it sounds, because you need only a few feet of molding.

The next step is to carve the arch at the top of each kerf. Finally, drill a small hole above each kerf to complete the job (**E**).

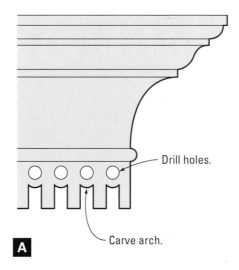

Drill holes.

Carve arch.

A

B

C

E

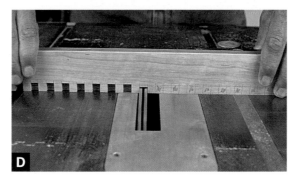

D

Curved Moldings

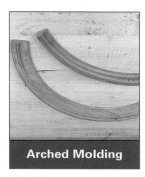

Arched Molding

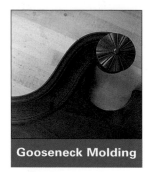

Gooseneck Molding

BUILDING CURVILINEAR FURNITURE presents many challenges, one of which is shaping curved moldings to match the contours. To shape curved moldings successfully it's important to understand the type of curve so that you can approach the problem logically. For all practical purposes, curved moldings fall into four broad categories: arcs, S curves, elliptical curves, and compound curves.

Arcs are segments of true circles. Arched moldings are used over semicircular doors and openings on casework, such as clocks, desks, and chests.

There are two methods for shaping arcs: First you can shape from the edge with a bearing to guide the work and limit the cutting depth. The second option is to shape the molding from the face with a curved cradle to support the stock. The decision of which method to use is determined by the width of the molding and the shape of the profile. It's much easier and less time consuming to shape the work from the edge; however, if the molding is wide, it's safer to shape from the face and limit the amount of exposed cutter. Also, some profiles, such as a quirk bead, can't be shaped from the edge.

Moldings that follow an *S curve* are usually referred to as "goosenecks" and are used as pediment moldings on casework. Gooseneck moldings can be shaped from the edge with a shaper or the face with a router. Again the determination is made by the molding profile and its size. If shaped from the edge, a template jig is necessary to guide the cut and position your hands a safe distance from the cutterhead.

If you use the router, you'll also need to first construct a jig to guide the work. The

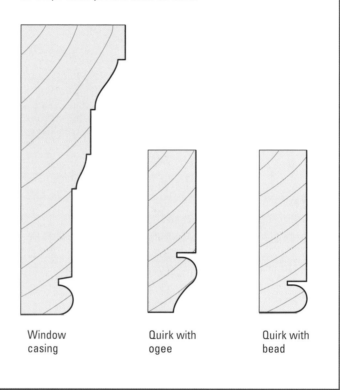

PROFILES THAT MUST BE SHAPED FROM THE FACE

Some profiles are impossible to shape from the edge without using dangerously long knives. So shape these profiles from the face.

Window casing

Quirk with ogee

Quirk with bead

When using the router table to cut curved molding on the face of the stock, use a cradle to support and guide the work.

CREATING A GOOSENECK MOLDING ON THE SHAPER

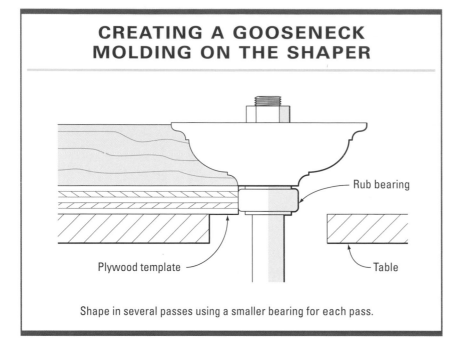

Rub bearing

Plywood template

Table

Shape in several passes using a smaller bearing for each pass.

TEMPLATE JIG FOR THE SHAPER

Stock is also fastened to jig with screws from underneath.

jig shown at top right clamps to the edge of the router table to convert it to a pin router. The work is secured to a template, which is guided by the pin.

With either a router or a shaper setup, plan on making multiple passes. This prevents bogging down the machine and reduces the chance of kickback. Also be aware that the router setup requires skill and patience to keep the work moving tangent to the guide pin at the point at which the cut occurs. It's a good idea to develop

Cutting a gooseneck molding on the shaper requires a dedicated jig to secure the work.

Gooseneck moldings can be cut on the face on the router table. The jig creates a setup that works like a pin router.

ROUTER JIG FOR GOOSENECK MOLDING

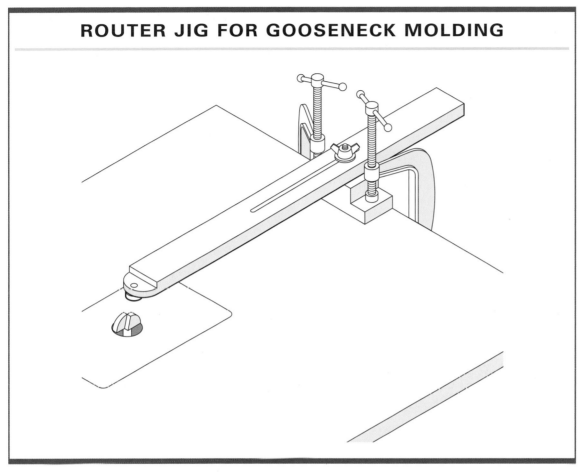

CREATING A GOOSENECK MOLDING
ON THE ROUTER TABLE

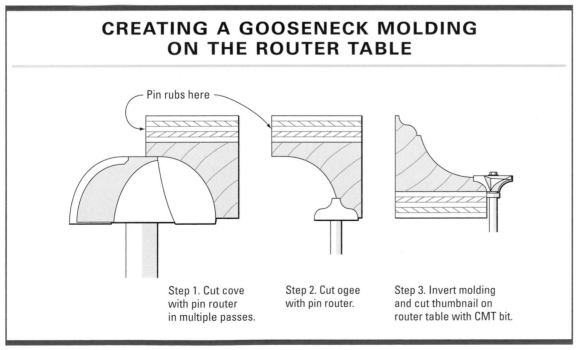

Pin rubs here

Step 1. Cut cove
with pin router
in multiple passes.

Step 2. Cut ogee
with pin router.

Step 3. Invert molding
and cut thumbnail on
router table with CMT bit.

The overhead arm holds a pin that guides the template. This technique requires skill. Take practice cuts in inexpensive stock first.

skill with the technique on some inexpensive stock first.

Moldings that follow an *elliptical curve* can be shaped easily with the router table and jig shown on p. 189. An elliptical template follows the bearing on the jig to shape the profile accurately.

Compound curves flow in two directions simultaneously. Moldings that follow compound curves are usually limited to simple profiles, such as a quirk bead along the edge of a chair back. By far the most practical method for shaping a molding profile on a compound curve is with a scratch stock. Depending on the sweep of the curve, it may be necessary to curve the face of the scratch stock.

▶ See *"Making a Scratch Stock"* on p. 146.

Mitering Gooseneck Moldings

It can seem puzzling—how do you miter the end of a molding with an S curve? It's actually quite easy. Here's how to do it. When building the template, extend it in a straight line beyond the point at which the molding will later be mitered. This creates a flat surface to register on the table of the miter saw. But you have only one chance to cut it, so it must be accurate. First position the molding on the pediment and mark the miter location. Next, make certain that the saw is cutting a precise 90-degree angle. Now position the molding on the saw and make the cut.

➤ MAKING A PATTERN FOR A GOOSENECK MOLDING

How do you draw two freeform curves that are absolutely parallel to each other? The answer is to use a disk to guide the pencil. The edge of the disk rolls along the edge of the first curve and guides the pencil for a parallel curve. You'll need to make the radius of the disk equal to the width of the molding. To ensure that the disk is a perfect circle, turn it on the lathe.

Begin by carefully sketching the freeform curve on thin plywood. Next, bandsaw the *negative* contour. Now tack the plywood over a second layer of plywood. Trace the negative pattern, then use the disk to draw a second line parallel to the first. The result is a perfect pattern.

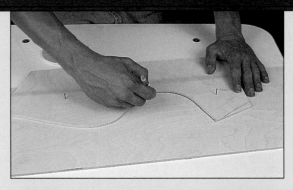

After bandsawing the *negative* pattern of the curve, transfer it to a second sheet of plywood.

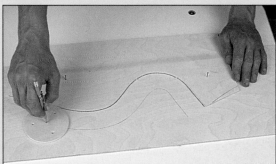

Use a disk equal in radius to the width of the molding to guide your pencil.

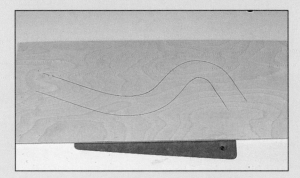

An accurate pattern results from cutting to the parallel line.

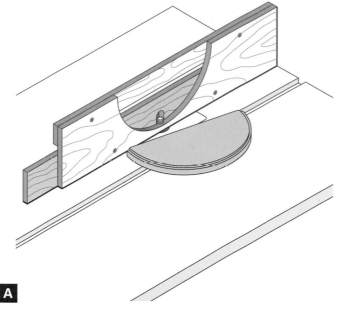

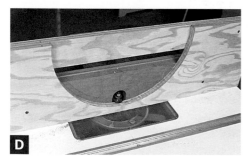

Arched Molding Face on the Router Table

This technique is useful anytime the profile has a quirk that can't be shaped from the edge. It involves making a curved jig, or cradle, in which the stock travels in an arc during shaping (**A**).

After milling the stock, strike the radius of the outside edge of the molding onto the face. Using the same compass setting, strike the radius onto a rectangle of plywood to serve as a cradle.

Now bandsaw the outside (convex) curve of the molding stock (**B**) and the inside (concave) curve of the cradle. Smooth the edge of the stock with a spokeshave (**C**) and fasten the cradle to the router table fence with screws (**D**). Now mount the bit and adjust the height to align with the edge of the stock—and you're ready to begin (**E**).

To shape the curve without spoiling the profile, it's necessary to keep the face of the stock against the fence and the edge of the stock against the cradle (**F**).

[**TIP**] **To get a feel for the technique, make a practice run without power.**

You may find it helpful to use a featherboard to maintain pressure against the fence. After cutting the bead, shape the cove using the same process (**G**). When you're finished, bandsaw the inside radius to complete the molding.

Arched Molding Edge on the Router Table

The process of shaping a curved strip molding is much like shaping a straight strip of molding. The difference is that you'll first have to bandsaw the curve into the stock (**A**). Then, when shaping, you'll guide the workpiece against a bearing instead of a fence (**B**).

After shaping, bandsaw the outside radius of the curved molding and smooth the edges (**C**).

> ⚠ **WARNING** Remember to use a starting pin as a fulcrum to enter the cut safely.

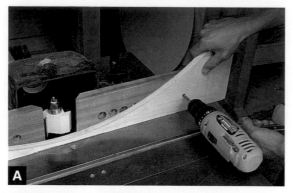

Arched Molding Face on the Shaper

The spindle of the shaper is much longer than the shank of a router bit. This allows you to shape arched moldings that are too wide for the router table. Examples of this type of molding are arched trim on a built-in bookcase and casing over an arched window.

Begin by striking the outside radius of the molding onto the stock. Using the same radius, strike an arc onto a plywood rectangle to serve as a cradle. Next, bandsaw the outside radius (convex) of the stock and the inside radius (concave) of the plywood. Now, fasten the cradle to the shaper fence with a couple of screws (**A**). Make certain that the lowest point of the cradle is located in front of the shaper spindle.

Begin by shaping the wide, flat section of the profile. Mount a tall, square cutter on the spindle (**B**) and position the fence for the required cutting depth. Next, clamp a featherboard to the shaper table to apply pressure as the stock is shaped (**C**). After checking the fence and spindle lock, you're ready to begin shaping (**D**). To avoid spoiling the stock, it's important that you keep it in contact with the cradle throughout the cut (**E**).

Now repeat the process with the remaining profiles to complete the molding design. After shaping, bandsaw the inside radius of the molding.

Gooseneck Molding on the Shaper

The shaper is the most efficient tool for shaping a gooseneck molding. By using a complex cutter and a template/jig to hold the stock, the profile can be shaped cleanly in just a few minutes.

Before shaping, you'll need to build a template/jig to hold the stock and guide the cutterhead in a curved path. Select a piece of ¾-in. plywood for the jig that's wide enough to position your hands a minimum of 8 in. from the cutterhead and long enough to extend several inches beyond the stock. After bandsawing the curve, attach a pair of toggle clamps to the jig to help hold the stock.

➤ See *"Making a Pattern for a Gooseneck Molding"* on p. 191.

Now select a wide piece of straight-grain stock for the molding and trace the inside curve directly from the pattern (**A**). Bandsaw the inside curve only (**B**) and fasten the stock to the jig with several screws. The screws, combined with the toggle clamps, keep the stock securely in the jig during shaping. Obviously, you'll need to locate the screws well out of the path of the cutterhead (**C**).

(Text continues on p. 196.)

> ⚠ **WARNING** Safety is always an issue with any machine. But it's a special concern with the shaper, especially when shaping curved stock. I strongly urge you to gain plenty of experience with the shaper before using this technique.

D

The cutterhead shown here is one I designed; it was custom manufactured by Freeborn Tool Company. It's important to shape the profile in multiple passes to reduce the feed resistance and increase safety. This is accomplished by switching to a smaller rub bearing after each successive pass. I used three bearing sizes with this cutterhead; the smallest bearing allows the cutterhead to shape the full profile. Also, notice that I'm using a disk guard that mounts above the cutterhead. This guard is available from Delta. Although I removed the guard so the photos would be clear, I don't recommend using this technique without it.

▶ See *"List of Suppliers"* on p. 285.

Once the construction of the jig is complete, set up the cutterhead assembly on the shaper spindle. Slip the largest bearing on the spindle first, then the cutterhead, and finally the guard. Then lock the assembly in place with the lockwasher and spindle nut. Now position the jig and workpiece next to the spindle to make the height adjustment; then lock the spindle height (**D**).

Now you're ready for the cut. Remember always to feed the stock against the spindle rotation. In this case, I'm feeding from right to left.

Turn on the shaper and position the extended portion of the jig against the rub bearing (**E**). Now begin feeding at a steady pace (**F**). As you feed the work, keep the jig resting on the table and the edge against the bearing. As the chips fly, you'll soon be at the end of the cut (**G**).

E

F

G

H

Pull the work away from the spindle and turn off the shaper. Now switch to a smaller bearing and repeat the procedure (**H**). Remember to shape the matching gooseneck each time. Finally, install the smallest bearing (**I**) and shape the complete profile (**J**). Now remove the molding from the jig and bandsaw the outside curve. Invert the molding and bandsaw from the back for an accurate cut (**K**). Next, place the molding into a second jig for flush trimming (**L**). This jig has a negative pattern that acts as an alignment strip (**M**).

When you're finished (**N**), place the fence around the cutterhead and shape the returns that miter to the ends of the gooseneck.

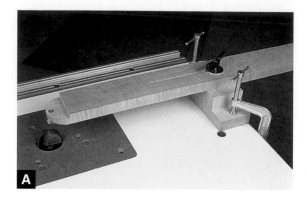

A

Gooseneck Molding on the Router Table with Pin Jig

Another method for shaping gooseneck and arched moldings is to use a pin router. A pin or bearing is suspended over the router, which is mounted in a table. A template, which is positioned over the stock, follows the guide pin. Because the pin can be positioned offset to the router bit, interior cuts can be made.

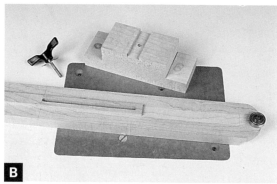

B

Although pin routers are expensive, the jig shown here clamps to the edge of your router table to convert it to a pin router. A bearing is fastened to the end of the arm to guide the template (**A**). The arm is held in position on the base with a bolt. A tongue under the arm slides within a groove in the base to prevent the arm from moving sideways (**B**).

After constructing the jig, make a full-size pattern of the gooseneck curve. Next, use the pattern to lay out the curve on both the template and the stock. Extend the line on the template beyond the curve of the molding. This way the template will contact the bearing before the router bit contacts the stock, eliminating potential grabbing at the entry of the cut.

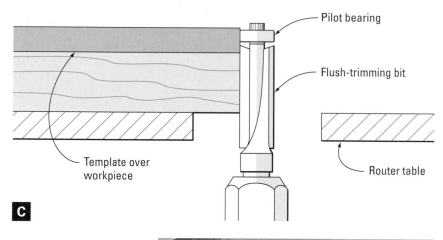

Pilot bearing

Flush-trimming bit

Template over workpiece

Router table

C

▶ See *"Making a Pattern for a Gooseneck Molding"* on p. 191.

Now fasten the workpiece to the template with several screws. Take care to keep them out of the path of the spinning bits. Allow the work to extend 1/16-in. beyond the template edge for flush

D

trimming. Next, fasten a large block of the same thickness toward the back of the template to stabilize it as you're shaping. Now you're ready to begin shaping.

Begin by flush trimming the work (**C**) with a flush-trimming router bit (**D**); you will not need the pin jig for this step. Next, begin shaping the cove. Because of the large size of the cove, it's necessary to make this cut in several passes. Mount the corebox bit in the router and clamp the jig to the table edge. Now slide the arm of the jig out and lock it in position for a light cut.

Before starting the cut, you must realize that it's necessary to keep the template edge in the same spot on the bearing throughout the cut; the location is a point tangent to the bearing at 90 degrees to the arm. This is necessary because the guide bearing and bit are not spinning on the same axis—they are offset. Performing this task is not difficult, but requires concentration. Also, realize that you'll gain experience as you go and keeping the template located properly is not extremely critical until the final pass.

Let's give it a try. Turn on the router, position the end of the template against the bearing, and begin feeding the stock (**E, F**). As the template curves, rotate it to maintain contact at the front of the bearing (**G, H, I**). Now turn off the router, retract the arm slightly, and repeat the process several times until the full profile of the cove has been shaped (**J**).

(Text continues on p. 200.)

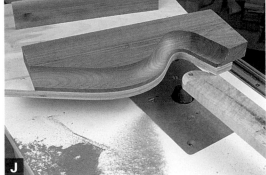

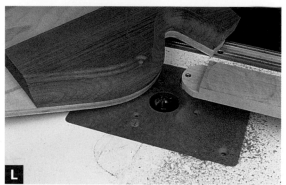

The next step is to shape the ogee at the top of the molding. If the router bit you're using has a bearing, you'll first need to remove it and grind off the stud (**K**). Now, mount the bit in the router and adjust the arm to position the bit correctly in relationship to the molding. Now make the cut (**L**).

The last step is to shape the thumbnail at the base of the molding (**M**). For this profile, you'll need a bit from CMT USA's crown-molding set. The inverted profile allows you to shape the thumbnail on the router table (**N**).

➤ See *"List of Suppliers"* on p. 285.

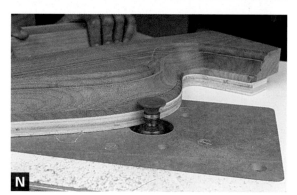

Quirk Bead on a Compound Curve

Remember that a compound curve is one that flows in two directions simultaneously. Some furniture components that have compound curves use simple profiles such as a quirk bead to provide additional detail and draw the eye to the flowing lines of the curve.

The easiest method for shaping a profile on compound curve is to use a scratch stock (**A**).

► See *"Making a Scratch Stock"* on p. 146.

After bandsawing and smoothing the curves, secure the workpiece in a vise. Using the scratch stock, gently scrape the quirk-bead profile onto the surface (**B**). As you work, keep the body of the scratch stock against the work and tilt it slightly in the direction of the cut (**C**).

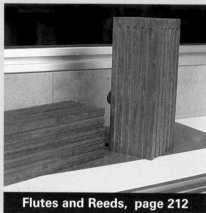

PART FOUR

Other Decorative Shapes

A S VERSATILE AS ROUTERS and shapers can be, there are times when some ingenuity is necessary to achieve a certain profile or shape. Cove cutting is a prime example. Large coves are often beyond the reach of all but the biggest shaper, and the profiles are limited to the cutters available. Fortunately, this shape can easily be cut on the table saw, producing coves of different sizes and arcs that are particularly useful in making crown molding.

Fluting and reeding have a special place in period furniture and architectural woodworking. Well-designed and proportioned flutes and reeds in a pilaster or column lend a formal, elegant look to a piece of furniture or a period room.

Although cove cutting, fluting, and reeding are decorative techniques, their utility cannot be underestimated. They can turn an ordinary piece of furniture into something distinctive.

Coves

Machine-Cut Coves

➤ Cove Cut on the Table Saw (p. 209)

➤ Cove Cut on the Router Table (p. 210)

Hand-Cut Coves

➤ Cove Cut with a Molding Plane (p. 211)

Coves have many applications, but perhaps their greatest use is in making moldings. Many large, complex moldings for furniture, casework, and architectural cornices use a cove as the main profile. The cove is usually flanked by smaller basic profiles, such as an ogee or thumbnail. The problem when making this type of molding is always how to cut a large, deep cove. Even the largest router bits cut a relatively small cove—and large shapers and molders are beyond the price range of most small shops. The table saw provides a viable solution.

Probably one of the most useful, yet unusual, table saw techniques is cove cutting. A strip of wood is clamped to the table at an angle to the blade to act as a fence. Then the stock is repeatedly passed over the top of the blade. For each successive pass, the blade is raised slightly, resulting in a deep cove throughout the length of the stock. Best of all, the shape and size of the cove can be varied tremendously with different fence angles and blade heights.

Coves are an important element in the design of crown moldings. This complex example uses two coves.

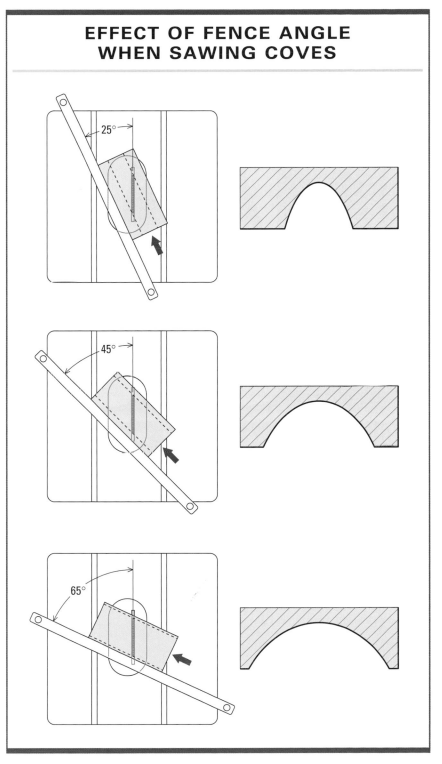

EFFECT OF FENCE ANGLE WHEN SAWING COVES

25°

45°

65°

The fence for cutting coves can be as simple as a sturdy piece of flat stock firmly clamped to the table of the table saw.

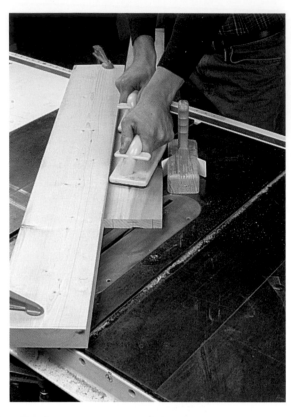

COVE SET-UP JIG

Width of cove

Hardwood strips

Wing nut

Fence angle

To visualize how this works, hold a circular sawblade at arm's length and pivot it slowly. As the viewing angle changes, the blade appears as a long, narrow ellipse. As you continue to pivot the blade the ellipse becomes broader until it appears as a full circle. Of course, you can't pivot the blade on the saw, so instead you attach an angled fence.

Making a Fence

The first step in using this technique is to mill a length of stock for use as a fence. The dimension of the stock isn't exact, but it must be of sufficient size to avoid flexing. A length of 2x4 works well once the edge has been trued on the jointer. Also, the stock must be longer than a standard fence to span the saw's table at various angles. An alternative to the single fence is a double fence through which the workpiece passes. Once you establish the angle, the fence must be securely clamped to the saw table using standard clamps or wooden handscrews.

Finding the Angle

Finding the correct angle may seem like somewhat of a mystery, but it's actually quite simple. In fact, there are a couple of methods from which you can choose.

For the first method, you'll need to build the parallelogram jig shown at left. The jig pivots at the corners and locks in place to hold a setting. Set the space between the bars for the width of the cove and raise the

COVES ON THE TABLE SAW

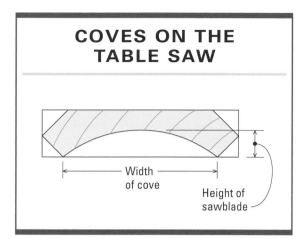

Width of cove

Height of sawblade

The best way to remove the saw marks from a table-sawn cove is to use a hand scraper with a curved profile.

sawblade to a height that equals the depth of the cove. Next, place the jig over the saw-blade and position it so that it contacts both the front and back of the blade. Now position the fence at the same angle and clamp it in place on the front and back rails of the table saw.

To find the angle using the second method, first mill the stock for the cove. Next, draw the cove on each end of the stock or simply mark layout lines to indicate the depth and width of the cove. Now raise the sawblade to equal the depth of the cove and position the fence so the blade enters the cove on one edge and exits on the oppo-site edge. Finally, clamp the fence securely on the table.

Making the Cut

It's essential for safety that you make the cove by taking multiple, light cuts. For the first cut, lower the blade to a height of $1/16$ in. Then raise the blade approximately $1/16$ in. for each successive pass. As you feed the stock over the blade, maintain contact with the fence and use push blocks to keep your hands a safe distance from the blade. On the final pass, the blade should contact the layout lines that mark the height and width of the cove.

Afterward, you'll need to smooth the sur-face and remove all traces of saw marks. A curved scraper makes this tedious process go much faster. After scraping, sand the surface lightly.

➤ SAFETY GUIDELINES FOR COVE CUTTING

Cove cutting is a great technique with broad applications; but as with most advanced methods, there are special safety concerns. Here's a list of guidelines.

- **Position the fence properly.** When you're cutting coves, you might wonder if the fence is positioned in front of the blade or behind it. There are two schools of thought on this question. Some woodworkers contend that the fence should be positioned in front of the blade to counteract blade force and limit the possibility of kickback. But using this position is awkward, because you're pushing the stock away from the fence as you feed it. Another option is to position the fence behind the blade. This setup feels positive because you can push the stock firmly against the fence as you feed it. Still another solution is to use two parallel fences and run the stock between them.

- **Clamp the fence securely.** Make certain that the fence will not move during the coving operation.

- **Take light cuts.** As with any woodworking machine, heavy cuts produce greater feed resistance and an invitation to kickback.

- **Use push blocks.** Keep your hands a safe distance from the sawblade at all times.

- **Use a guard.** If the guard that came with your table saw doesn't work, devise one of your own. An overarm guard, such as the Biesemeyer, works well with this technique.

Cove Cut on the Table Saw

The first woodworker to use this technique has been long forgotten. In fact, I suspect that cove cutting on the table saw is as old as the saw itself. It's a great technique that has a multitude of uses.

Begin by milling the stock and drawing the cove on each end. Next, adjust the blade height on the table saw to equal the depth of the cove (**A**). Now you're ready to set the fence angle.

Position the fence so that the blade enters the stock on one edge of the cove (**B**) and exits on the opposite edge (**C**), or use the jig on p. 206 to find the fence angle. Then clamp the fence securely to the table saw. Now check the fence once more. If necessary, make minor adjustments to the angle. Then lower the blade to 1/16 in., and you're ready to make the cut.

Use push blocks to safely distance your hands (**D**). As you push the stock over the top of the blade, maintain contact with the fence (**E**). Before each successive pass, raise the blade approximately 1/16 in. (**F**). For the final pass, take a very light cut and feed the workpiece slowly to achieve the smoothest surface possible (**G**).

Afterward, remove the saw marks with a curved scraper and sand the cove smooth (**H**). By tilting the blade, you can create asymmetrical coves (**I**).

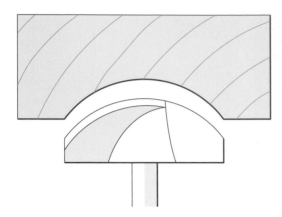

Even a large router bit can't shape a very large cove.

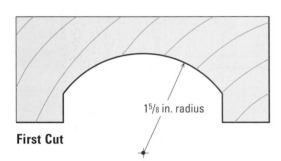

First Cut

$1^5/_8$ in. radius

Instead use two large router bits with different radii to create a large elliptical cove.

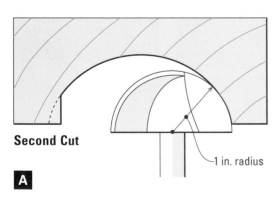

Second Cut

1 in. radius

A

B

C

D

Cove Cut on the Router Table

Even the largest router bits will not cut a very deep cove. But there's a practical way to increase the size of the cove. Use two bits of different radii and create an elliptical cove (**A**). This will greatly increase the depth and width of the cove and enable you to create a large molding profile. As an added benefit, an elliptical cove is more appealing than one with a constant radius.

Begin by making multiple light passes with the first bit (**B**). It's important to keep each cut light; heavy cuts are prone to kickback and tend to cause overheating of the router. Use featherboards to keep the workpiece in position.

After making the first portion of the cove, switch bits and complete the cut (**C**). Adjust the fence position and the bit height to blend the curves from each of the two router bits. The final cove should be a smooth, continuous curve (**D**).

Cove Cut with a Molding Plane

One of the most common molding planes is called a round. It's aptly named because of the semicircular, convex shape of its sole. Hollows, as the name implies, have a concave sole. Hollows and rounds were once produced together in matching pairs for making moldings—and they're still useful today.

► See *"Tools for Edge Treatments and Moldings"* on p. 18.

To make a cove with a wooden plane, begin by laying out the parameters of the cove on the stock (**A**). Next, cut a V groove down the length of the stock. This type of plane does not use a fence, so the V is required to keep it running in a straight path.

To cut the profile. make several passes down the V to establish a cove (**B**). Then widen and deepen the cove until the full profile is reached (**C**).

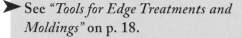

Flutes and Reeds

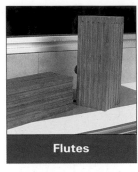

Flutes

Reeds

WITHOUT A DOUBT, proportions are the most critical element of any furniture design. This holds true for the overall proportions (such as height to width) as well as proportions of the details. Proportioning flutes is a good example, because there are several considerations to keep in mind if the final look is to be appealing. When making design decisions, it's always helpful to make full-scale drawings of the variations for side-by-side comparison.

Here's a list of guidelines to consider when adding flutes to a project:

■ **Keep the width of the flute proportional to the surface being shaped.** Often changes as small as $\frac{1}{16}$ in. can make a substantial difference in the final effect.

■ **Space the flutes closely.** The space between flutes should be smaller than the flutes themselves. The purpose of the flutes is to break up the flat surface and provide detail. To achieve this, don't skimp on the number of flutes.

■ **Decide if you want to use stop flutes or through flutes.** Flutes that run the entire length of the column or pilaster are attractive and are easier to cut, because you don't have to keeping the stopping point uniform. But stopped flutes certainly are more eye catching and provide additional detail. And besides, it requires only a few minutes more to set up stops if you're using a router table.

■ **Consider carved end details.** Want still more detail? Try carving a reverse arch at the base of each flute. Carving the arch is labor intensive, so you'll probably want to reserve this fine detail for your best work.

Carving a reversed arch at the base of a flute is an elegant detail for your best work.

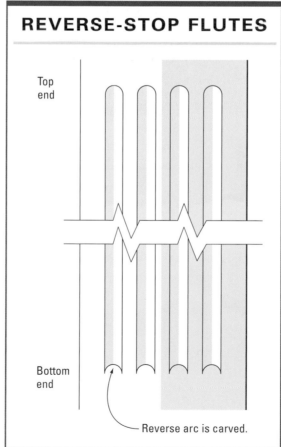

REVERSE-STOP FLUTES

Top end

Bottom end

Reverse arc is carved.

Large Pilaster Fluted with a Handheld Router

Fluting lengthy stock, such as this pilaster for a corner cabinet, can be awkward when passed across the short top of a router table. In situations such as this, it's much easier to pass the router over the stock. Before you begin, you'll need a guide accessory, which attaches to the base of your router. Or you can make a guide as I did here (**A**).

After attaching the guide, adjust the cutting depth of the bit (**B**). Next, mill the stock for the pilasters. If you mill it oversize in length, you'll have an area to lay out the flutes and check each router setting (**C**).

After layout, clamp a stop block at each end to keep the flutes uniform in length. Begin by routing the center flutes and work outward (**D**). Afterward, cut two flutes with each new setting (**E**). Each time you start a new flute, position the router base against the stop block (**F**).

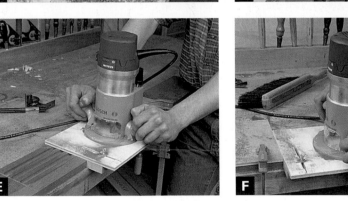

Small Stock Fluted on the Router Table

A router table will dramatically increase the versatility of your router. Here's a good example. This small fluted plinth is narrow, which makes it difficult to keep the router steady if it's handheld.

Begin with layout. You'll want to be accurate with the spacing, because it's used to set up the router. Also, mark the position of the end of the flute (**A**). Next, set the cutting depth of the bit and position the fence to cut the center flute. Finally, set stops at each fence to control the length of the flutes and keep them consistent. Now you're ready for shaping.

Position the workpiece against the infeed stop and lower it onto the spinning bit (**B**). Then push the stock to the next stop (**C**). Feed the stock slowly to avoid a fuzzy, torn surface; small-diameter bits have a relatively slow rim speed even at higher rotations per minute (rpms).

For each successive cut, move the fence closer to the bit (**D**). For each side of the center flute, each fence setting will make two flutes; simply turn the stock end for end.

Carved Reverse-Stop Flutes

Before carving stop flutes, you'll need to modify the edge of the gouge. Carving gouges are somewhat square when you buy them. Although this profile is effective for most types of carving, the outside corners of the gouge will dig in when incising a stop flute. Instead, the end of the gouge must be semicircular to follow the contour of the flute.

The most efficient way to change the tool shape is to use a grinder. Roll the tool from side to side on the grinding wheel to grind away the corners. As you grind, keep the tool moving to avoid dead spots in the curve. After grinding, sharpen the tool to a mirror surface with benchstones.

A reverse-stop flute is a neat detail at the lower end of a flute (see the drawing on p. 213). Rather than leave the flute end concave, as from the router, the end is carved to a convex profile. Like many details that add visual interest to a piece of furniture, reverse-stop flutes can't be created by machine. But for a special piece of furniture, the extra handwork is worth it.

Begin by routing stop flutes as shown on p. 215. Be certain to provide space for the carving. Next, lay out the stop flute. Use a combination square to extend the sides of the flute and a circle template to draw the arc (**A, B**).

Now select a carving gouge with a sweep that comes closest to the curve of the arc. Incise the curve by cutting vertically with the gouge (**C**). Then carve parallel to the flute to complete the profile (**D**).

Fluted Quarter Columns

Quarter columns, as the name implies, are one-quarter of a full circle. Typically fluted, the columns are inset within the front corners of casework such as desks, chest, and clocks. Like full-round columns and pilasters, quarter columns require a base and capital to complete them visually. Once complete, quarter columns provide a formal architectural look and additional detail.

To create quarter columns, you must glue four strips of wood together with heavy paper in the glue joints. After turning and fluting, the column is easily split into four segments, because the heavy paper in the joints allows the pieces to separate.

Begin by drawing a cross-section of the column full-scale (**A**). Columns typically have a 1¾ in. diameter, which yields a quarter column that's ⅞ in. across when viewed from the front of the case. Next, draw the flutes in place. The size and spacing of the flutes must look proportional to the column; spacing is determined by the index head on your lathe. More specifically, the number of flutes must divide equally into the number of divisions on the index head of your lathe.

The next step is to mill the stock for the columns. If you mill it slightly oversize, you'll easily be able to turn the column to the required diameter. After milling, you must glue the four sections together to create a full column. However, before you begin, remember that joint alignment is critical; the four seams must align perfectly. Otherwise the separate columns will not be exactly a quarter circle. Starting with the ends, align the joints with pressure from opposing clamps (**B**). You can check the alignment by examining the joint at the end of the assembly (**C**). After aligning

(Text continues on p. 218.)

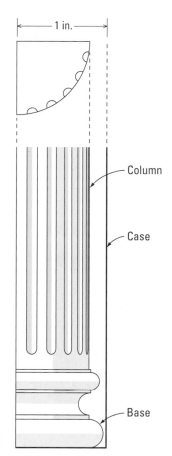

1 in.

Column

Case

Base

A

B

C

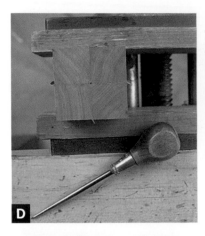

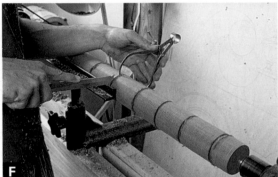

the ends, clamp the remainder of the work. For safety reasons, allow the glue to dry overnight before turning.

The next step is to turn the square to a uniform cylinder. Begin by squaring the ends of the turning blank. Then mark the centers for mounting in the lathe. Once again, alignment is critical. Mark the exact location with the point of an awl (**D**). Afterward, mount the blank securely in the lathe for turning.

Turning a straight, uniform cylinder isn't difficult if you follow a few easy steps. First, turn the blank round with a roughing gouge (**E**). Then carefully turn it to the required diameter. You can accomplish this by cutting to the diameter at several locations with a parting tool. As you lever the tool into the spinning stock with one hand, gauge the diameter with spring calipers in the other hand (**F**). Then turn the remaining portion of the cylinder to diameter with the roughing gouge. Afterward, smooth the cylinder with a block plane. Support the plane on the tool rest and push it slowly down the length of the slowly spinning stock (**G**). This is a great technique! The plane cleanly shears away the high spots to create a perfectly smooth, uniform surface (**H**).

➤ See *"Turning"* on p. 224.

The next step is to rout the flutes. But first you'll need to build a jig (**I**). The jig is actually a box that mounts to the bed of the lathe to support the router during the fluting process. Next, mount the box under the workpiece and, if necessary, attach a square base to your router to fit within the sides of the box (**J**). Finally, set the cutting depth of the bit and lock it in position.

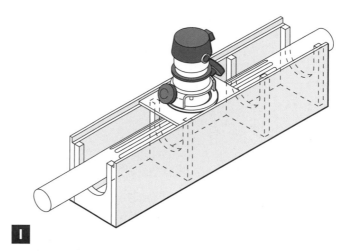

I

Before you begin routing, remember that the flutes must be spaced equally around each quarter column; the first and last flute on each quarter column should be adjacent to a glue joint. For this spacing to occur, it may be necessary to reposition the cylinder between the centers. Lock the cylinder in place with the pin on the index head (**K**); then make a very short test cut on one end of the cylinder. If the flute falls next to the glue joint, fine. If not, release the pressure slightly at the tailstock and rotate the column to bring the router bit into alignment. Now tighten the handwheel at the tailstock and make a second test cut.

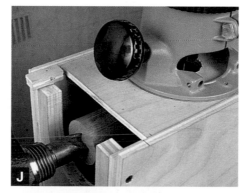

J

K

Once the column is aligned for the first flute, successive flutes will be correctly positioned in relation to the glue joints. Once the setup is complete, route the flutes (**L**). If you choose to stop the flutes, tack a wood block to the jig to act as a stop.

When fluting is complete, remove the column from the lathe and carefully split it into corners by placing a wide chisel at one end and tapping it gently (**M**).

L

M

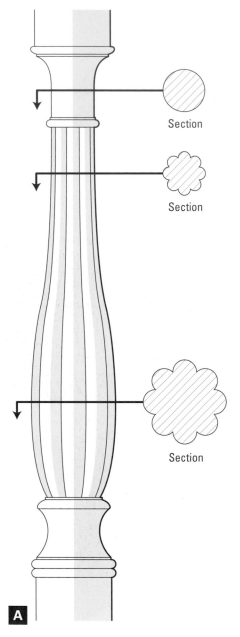

Section

Section

Section

A

B

C

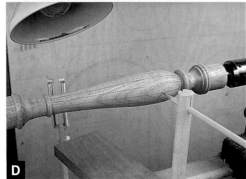

D

Reeded Surface

Reeding is a series of convex semicircular shapes, used as surface decoration (**A**). Although a router bit can be used for reeding, it's effective only when the surface to be reeded is straight. Surfaces that swell and taper, such as the example shown here, must be carved. Think about it this way: As the reeds flow down a tapered surface they must taper too (**B**). Furthermore, as they taper, the radius of each reed continually changes. Although a router guided by a tapered template will shape the reeds, it will not created a truly reeded surface—only a facsimile. This is because the radius of the router bit profile is constant.

Begin by turning the leg (**C**). Next, lay out the reeds equally around the circumference of the turning (**D**). This is easy to accomplish with the simple jig shown here (**E**). Use the index head on your lathe to keep the spacing accurate.

➤ See *"Turning"* on p. 224.

The next step is to outline each mark with a V gouge. First lock the turning in position with the pin on the index head. Then carefully follow each layout line with the gouge (**F**). Be sure to keep the lines running straight (**G**). Now round over the reeds with various sweeps of carving gouges (**H**). The wider portions of each reed will require gouges with a broader sweep; narrow areas require a gouge with a tighter sweep. Work carefully to keep each reed uniform as it tapers. Once you've carved each reed, inspect the surfaces for uniformity and make any necessary adjustments (**I**).

Complete the carving by sanding each reed lightly to smooth away any remaining facets from the gouges.

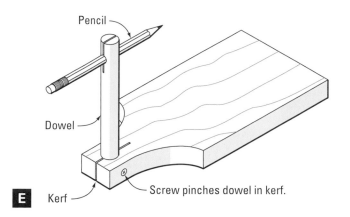

Pencil

Dowel

E Kerf

Screw pinches dowel in kerf.

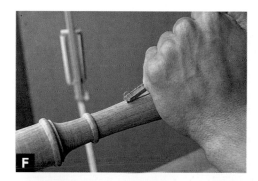

F

G

H

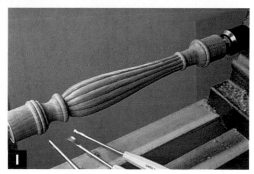

I

Turning, page 224

Carving, page 252

Bending, page 272

PART FIVE

Special Techniques

BEYOND THE MANY WAYS TO CUT SHAPES with familiar tools, there are specialized methods for shaping wood. Turned shapes are familiar in chair and table legs, bedposts, and other rounded symmetrical forms. In fact, turnings are essential to some period furniture styles. Carvings have enhanced furniture since time immemorial. One of the most artistic aspects of woodworking, carvings not only provide interesting detail but allow the maker a highly personal form of creative expression. Both turning and carving require a little more effort to learn, but the possibilities they offer the woodworker are well worth it. Finally, there's bending—the most distinctive technique in the repertoire of shaping methods, because it is the one way to shape wood that doesn't involve cutting. Instead it takes advantage of wood's natural flexibility and ability to be plasticized.

Turning

Turning Basic Shapes

Furniture Legs and Feet

Pedestal

Decorative Details

Complex Turnings

Rᴇᴅᴜᴄᴇᴅ ᴛᴏ ʙᴀʀᴇ ᴇssᴇɴᴛɪᴀʟs, turning is cutting the wood while it spins on a lathe. The final shape is always equidistant from the center. This enables symmetry while producing an amazing variety of curved shapes.

Try to imagine what furniture might look like if the lathe hadn't been invented. The beads, coves, and urns of the Jacobean table leg may not be to everyone's taste, but think how different the history of furniture design might be without turnings. Eighteenth-century furniture, which many consider a high point of furniture design, would look incomplete! Even a simple Shaker piece comes alive with the softer lincs of a turned leg.

Complex turnings are nothing more than combinations or modifications of simple shapes. A vase or urn shape starts out as a bead on one side and is cut like a tapered cove on the other. So even though turning may look challenging, once you learn to turn the basic shapes, you can combine them to create infinite permutations on these common themes. This section explains basic turning techniques so that you can add turnings to your designs.

Learn to Grind the Tools Properly

Sharp tools are essential to every kind of woodworking; but in turning, the shape of the edge is also critical. The bevel of a turning gouge or skew must be flat or hollow

This eighteenth-century-style gooseneck pediment is embellished with turned-and-carved rosettes and flame finials.

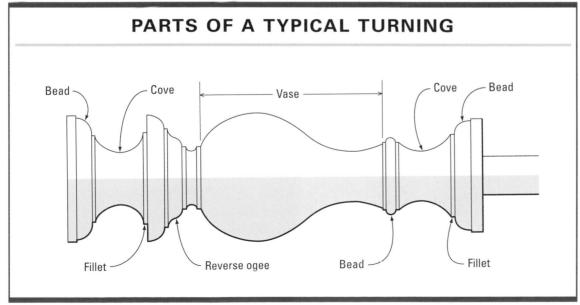

PARTS OF A TYPICAL TURNING

Bead — Cove ← Vase → Cove — Bead

Fillet — Reverse ogee — Bead — Fillet

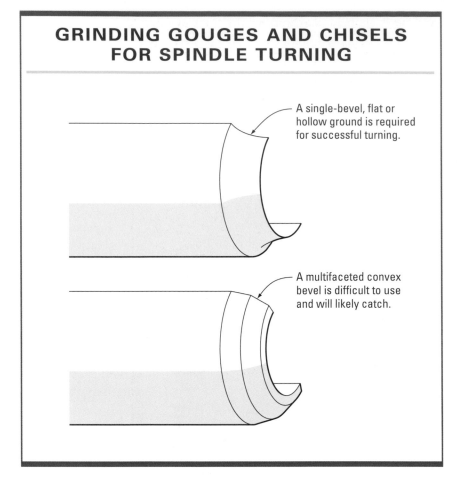

GRINDING GOUGES AND CHISELS FOR SPINDLE TURNING

A single-bevel, flat or hollow ground is required for successful turning.

A multifaceted convex bevel is difficult to use and will likely catch.

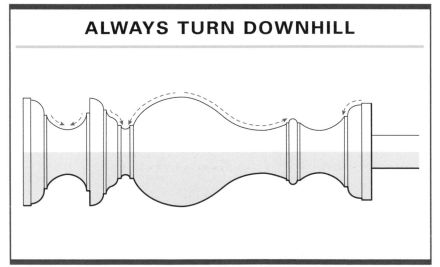

ALWAYS TURN DOWNHILL

ground. A tool with multiple facets will have a convex bevel. What's the difference? The bevel must continually rub the stock to support the edge while turning. A faceted, convex bevel won't accomplish this. Keep your tools sharp. You'll gain more control and experience fewer "catches" with a very sharp tool than with one that's only somewhat sharp. This is a universal principle that applies to all edge tools, from a bench chisel to a kitchen paring knife. Turning tools dull rather quickly because of the friction generated heat. Although high-speed steel (HSS) tools are more heat resistant than those of ordinary carbon steel, they still require frequent touching up with a slipstone.

Learning to Use the Basic Tools

Some turning tools are friendlier than others, and the spindle gouge is easily the beginning turner's best friend. You'll achieve success faster and most likely enjoy turning more if you begin by mastering the spindle gouge. Learn to sharpen it correctly and practice making the basic spindle shapes using this tool. Once you master the use of the spindle gouge, you'll have a foundation for the movements needed to use the other tools, including the notorious skew chisel. This tool is by far one of the most useful tools, but it's easier to catch the work. Once again, patience and practice will reward you.

Remember always to cut "downhill." To avoid a catch, it's crucial to cut from large diameters toward smaller ones. Woodturners call this cutting downhill.

Avoiding Chatter

Chatter is a woodworking term for "vibration." When turning, chatter creates a distinctive spiral pattern on the work, which can be difficult to remove. Chatter most often occurs when turning long, slender work. But even a heavy bedpost can sometimes be a problem because of its extended length. Fortunately, there are several solutions to the problem:

- **Try sharpening the tool.** A dull tool flexes the workpiece rather than cutting it cleanly.

- **Use a steady rest.** Position the rest firmly behind the stock close to the area that you're turning.

- **Steady the work with your hand.** This technique works extremely well, but use caution. Don't wear clothing or jewelry that can get caught by the spinning stock. Also, to avoid a nasty pinch, position your hand behind the work away from the rest.

- **Change the speed.** Adjusting the speed up or down slightly will often help put a stop to excessive vibration.

- **Turn the center of a long turning first.** Save the end portions for last to help reduce the occurrence of chatter.

- **Turn the smallest diameter last.** This will avoid weakening the turning, which causes it to flex and vibrate.

Special Cases

How do you turn something longer than the bed of your lathe? Divide it into two or more sections. This is an effective method for long, slender bedposts as well as shorter

> ## ► LET THE BEVEL RUB

A catch usually occurs when the bevel is lifted from the stock, leaving the unsupported edge to dig in. How can you be certain that the bevel is rubbing? Simply position the tool on the spinning stock so that the bevel rubs but the edge is not in contact. Then slowly lift the handle of the tool until shavings begin to fly. At this point, both the edge and the bevel are in contact. To limit dramatically the occurrence of catches, keep the bevel rubbing the stock as you turn.

POSITIONING THE GOUGE

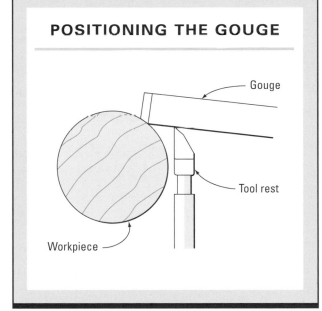

Gouge

Tool rest

Workpiece

turnings with small diameters. The finial shown on p. 242 is a good example. The narrow cove at the base of the flame makes this difficult to create as a one-piece turning. But by dividing it into two sections, the job's a snap. It also makes it easier to maneuver the gouges when carving the flame. As an

DIVIDING A TURNING INTO SECTIONS

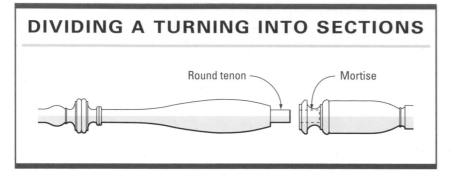

Round tenon —   — Mortise

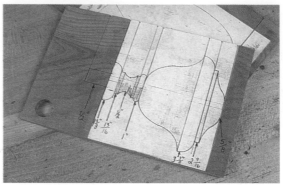

A story stick makes laying out a turning fast and easy. If you're turning multiples, it helps ensure consistent results.

added benefit, this method allows you to turn long posts on a short lathe.

When dividing a turning into sections, use a round mortise-and-tenon to join the sections afterward. Remember to plan ahead and position the joint adjacent to a bead where it will pass undetected.

Turning Multiples

Turning several pieces alike isn't nearly as difficult as it may seem if you do some planning ahead. The first thing you should do is design your turning and make a master. When you're turning its mates, you can position the master behind your lathe where you can view it while turning. It's much easier to duplicate something within view.

Use the master to create a *story stick*, which will allow you to lay out linear dimensions of a turning quickly and accurately. To make a story stick, glue a photocopy of your drawing onto ¼-in. plywood. Next, extend perpendicular lines from the plywood edge to the inside corner of each fillet. Finally, cut small V's along the edge of the stick as a rest for a pencil.

To use the story stick, place it on the tool rest against the spinning cylinder. Then mark the cylinder by placing a pencil in each notch or V. This method is much more

▶ DON'T EXPECT EXACT COPIES

It's both impossible and undesirable to create four perfectly identical turnings by hand. Even the best handcrafted turnings have minor variations. This is not only acceptable but the mark of handcrafted work. Mass-produced turnings are identical but they lack the crisp details and sensuous curves of good, handcrafted turnings.

accurate and efficient than measuring and marking each individual turning.

One way to dramatically increase your accuracy and efficiency when turning multiples is to use individual calipers for each diameter. This way you'll save time and avoid the inevitable errors associated with continually resetting a single caliper. You can find serviceable calipers of many sizes at flea markets and used-tool dealers.

Turning a Cylinder

Turning a cylinder involves removing the four corners of the stock to produce a smooth, uniform surface. It's typically the first step in producing a spindle turning, such as a leg or post. Because the stock contacts the tool only four times per revolution, the initial stage of this process is naturally rough. The best tool for the job is a massive, square-end gouge aptly called a roughing gouge.

Begin by securely mounting the work in the lathe. To begin the cut, start with the gouge handle low and gradually lift the handle until the cutting begins (**A**). Once the chips begin to fly, slide the gouge along the tool rest to shape the entire length of the stock (**B**). To keep the stock uniform in diameter, limit the cutting depth by bracing your fist against the tool rest.

[TIP] **When rounding square stock to form a cylinder, you can quickly and easily check for roundness by holding the middle of the gouge on the spinning stock. If it bounces lightly there's still a flat spot remaining.**

To shape the stock next to a pommel, rotate the gouge (**C**) and cut with the corner (**D**). As you approach a true cylinder, you can check the stock for roundness by placing the middle portion of the tool on top of the spinning work (**E**). This speeds the process by avoiding switching the lathe off and on again. The finished cylinder should be uniform and smooth, and its diameter should match the major diameter of the object you plan to turn.

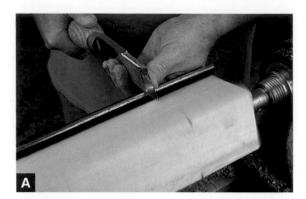

Turning a Pommel

A pommel is the square corner on a post or leg where a turned section intersects a square section. It's created by shearing a V into the square stock with a skew.

Begin by squaring the stock and milling it to size. Next, locate the center at each end of the stock by drawing diagonal lines. Mark the center with an awl to ensure accuracy. Then mount the work securely in the lathe.

Before turning, mark a layout line to indicate the location of the pommel. With the stock spinning relatively fast, nick the corners of the stock with the point of a skew. Next, make the cut deeper and wider by working the skew from the left and from the right (**A**). Each time you make a cut, lever the edge of the skew into the work (**B**). Use only the point of the skew to avoid catching the work and spoiling it. The pommel is complete when the cuts at each corner meet to surround the circumference of the work (**C**).

Bead Turned with a Spindle Gouge

A bead is a convex curve made up of one-quarter or one-half of a circle or ellipse.

Begin by establishing the size of the bead. First cut the fillets that flank the bead (**A**). Then cut the bead to the required diameter.

The next step is to shape the bead. Always work from the center toward the edges, or downhill. First, position the gouge so that the bevel rubs the spinning stock and then lift the handle until cutting begins. Now, roll the gouge to form one-half of the bead (**B**). As you roll the gouge, lift the handle and pivot the handle in the direction you are cutting (**C**). The three movements—roll, lift, and pivot—must be done simultaneously. It takes a bit of practice, but you'll soon begin to develop a feel for it. As you roll the bead, watch the top of the work so that you can view the bead as it is shaped.

After you've shaped half of the bead, start at the center once again and shape the second half (**D**).

If the gouge catches during the process, you've most likely pivoted the handle too far, lifting the bevel from the work. The result is that the unsupported edge digs in, an occurrence referred to as a *catch* by woodturners. If the cutting action stops before you've shaped the bead entirely, it's because you didn't pivot the handle far enough and consequently the edge is not making contact with the stock.

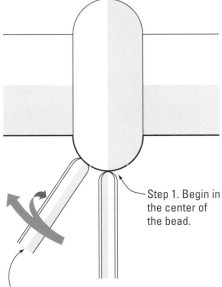

Step 1. Begin in the center of the bead.

Step 2. Roll, pivot, and lift the handle simultaneously.

Step 3. Repeat the process on the opposite side.

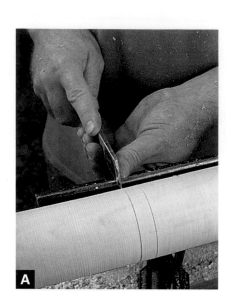

Bead Turned with a Skew

As you've probably heard, the skew is a difficult tool to master. It can catch easily and often. So why not shape a bead with a spindle gouge? Sometimes a bead is positioned adjacent to an ogee, pommel, or another bead. A gouge won't work in these tight situations; but the sharp, narrow point of a skew will.

[TIP] **Keep a block of paraffin at hand and periodically rub a coat on the tool rest. You will get more control, because the tools will slide much easier across the rest.**

There are some remedies for reducing the risk of a catch. First, keep the skew sharp. Sharp tools will always give you better control. Second, as you grind the skew, use a grinding method that keeps the bevel flat or hollow ground. A faceted, convex bevel will leave the edge unsupported, which will likely result in a catch.

To begin shaping a bead with a skew, first incise the width of the bead with the point (**A**). Next, cut V's at the incisions to remove the excess stock (**B**). Now, you're ready to shape the bead.

Using the heel of the skew, start off-center of the bead to take a light cut (**C**). Let the bevel rub, and lift the handle until the cutting begins. Then roll the skew, lift the handle, and pivot it. After the first light cut, start at the apex of the bead and repeat the process (**D**). The motions are very similar to those used with the spindle gouge (**E**). After shaping the first half, begin at the apex of the bead and shape the second half. The finished shape should be full and round (**F**).

Turning a Cove

The cove is a concave or hollow profile. The process of turning a cove is similar to turning a bead with a spindle gouge. The difference is that the profile and movements are reversed (**A**).

Begin by making two slight incisions with the point of a skew (**B**). These light cuts define the width of the cove and provide a notch to rest the gouge when starting the cut.

Next, remove some of the excess wood from the center of the cove with the spindle gouge. Let the bevel of the gouge rub (**C**) and lift the handle until the cutting begins; then cut a small hollow area (**D**).

Now you're ready to shape the cove. Position the gouge horizontally on the rest, with the gouge rolled to the side. Point the tip of the gouge toward the center of the work. Now, enter the stock (**E**). As you make the cut, simultaneously roll the gouge, pivot the handle, and lower the handle (**F**). To avoid a catch don't attempt to cut uphill; instead, end the cut at the bottom of the cove. Now repeat the process for the second side. As you shape the cove, view the top of the turning to watch the shape as you create it.

To enlarge the cove, repeat the process until the final width and depth are reached (**G**). Check the diameter at the bottom of the cove with a spring caliper.

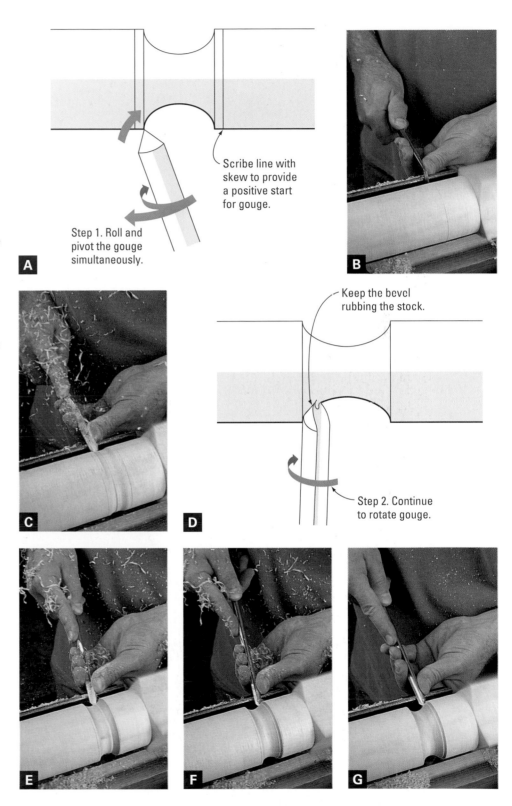

Scribe line with skew to provide a positive start for gouge.

Step 1. Roll and pivot the gouge simultaneously.

A

B

Keep the bevel rubbing the stock.

Step 2. Continue to rotate gouge.

C

D

E

F

G

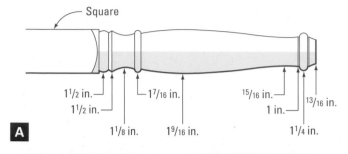

Square

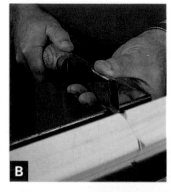

A

1½ in.
1½ in.
1⁷/₁₆ in.
1¹/₈ in.
1⁹/₁₆ in.
¹⁵/₁₆ in.
1 in.
¹³/₁₆ in.
1¼ in.

Turning a Tapered Leg

Because the leg used in this example has a square section for joinery, it's important to center the stock accurately in the lathe (**A**). Otherwise, the turned portion will be offset from the square portion.

Begin by turning the pommel with the point of a skew (**B**). First nick the corner; then cut from the right and the left. The pommel is complete when the cut from the skew runs the entire circumference (**C**).

Next, turn the leg round with a roughing gouge (**D**). Use the corner of the gouge to cut in the area adjacent to the pommel (**E**).

B

C

D

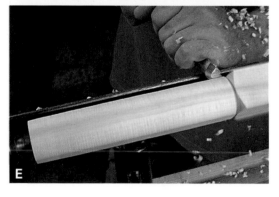

E

Once the leg is round, lay out the turning with a story stick (**F**). Next, shape the bead adjacent to the pommel. You'll need to use a skew to shape the bead in this tight spot.

The next step is to turn the cove and bead. Begin by cutting a fillet adjacent to the bead location (**G**). Then use a skew to remove the extra stock at the taper (**H**). Now, use a spindle gouge to shape the cove (**I**). Use a spring caliper to measure the final diameter of the cove. Most of the taper can be shaped with a gouge, but you'll need to use a skew to complete the taper as it approaches the bead. Finally, turn the bead and cove at the foot (**J**). Then sand the turning lightly to smooth it (**K**).

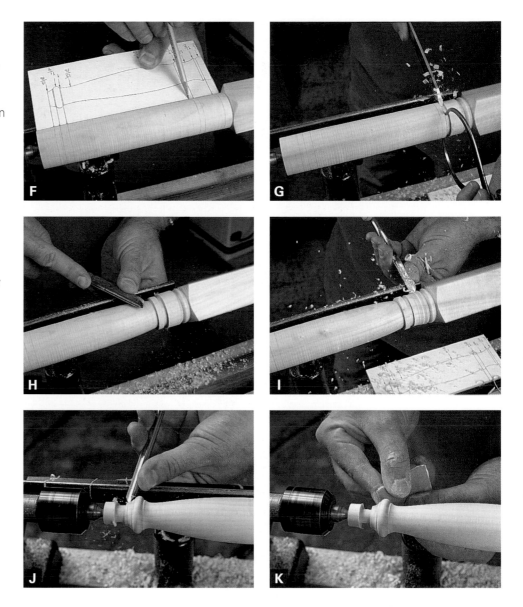

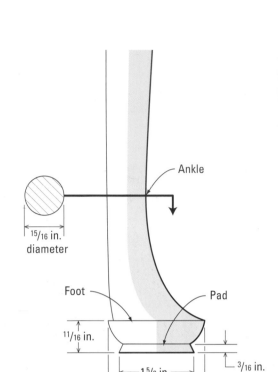

Ankle

$^{15}/_{16}$ in.
diameter

Foot

Pad

$^{11}/_{16}$ in.

$^{3}/_{16}$ in.

$1^{5}/_{8}$ in.

$2^{1}/_{4}$ in.

A Adjust dimensions to fit leg proportions.

B

C

D

E

F

G

H

Turning a Pad Foot

The pad foot was the most common form of foot used on eighteenth-century cabriole legs (**A**). It's quite easy to turn, and the entire process takes just a few minutes. You'll need to use a slow lathe speed, because the asymmetrical leg spins off balance.

Begin by bandsawing the leg. Next, locate the centers and mount the leg in the lathe with the foot at the tailstock. This avoids the possibility of the gouge coming in contact with the drive center. Now, turn the foot round with a spindle gouge (**B**); the roughing gouge is too large and awkward for this cut. As you round the foot, use care to avoid cutting the ankle, which would spoil the curve of the leg.

▶ See *"Bandsawing Broad, Sweeping Curves"* on p. 69.

As the work progresses, you can check for roundness by laying the shank of the gouge on top of the spinning foot (**C**). Once the foot is round, cut a small V at the top of the foot to indicate the height (**D**). Next, turn the pad to diameter with a parting tool and gauge it with a caliper (**E**).

The last step is to shape the foot. This step is identical to rolling a bead with a spindle gouge. For the first pass, start at the corner and round the foot to the pad (**F**). Remember, as you turn the foot, roll the gouge, lift the handle, and pivot the handle (**G**). To avoid chatter, it's a good idea to turn the foot in two or three passes. The final pass should be from the V to the pad to create a continuous curve (**H**).

Turning an Offset Leg

The simple, yet attractive, offset leg is most often used on small tables. Unlike a true cabriole leg, this leg is turned in entirety, which makes it quick to produce. To make the leg, first turn the pommel with the stock centered. Then offset the turning in the lathe to turn the ankle and the taper of the leg. Finally, return the leg to center and turn the foot. Because two sets of points are used, the turning will have two axes. For the leg to have the correct appearance the axes should converge at the pommel (**A**).

Begin by locating the true center of the stock on each end of the workpiece; then locate the center for the ankle (**B**). Next, mount the leg in the lathe with the foot at the tailstock. This will avoid the risk of striking the drive center as you turn the foot. Now, turn the pommel with the point of a skew. First nick the corner (**C**); then cut from the left (**D**) and the right (**E**) until the point of the skew scores the entire perimeter (**F**). Afterward, turn the leg round below the pommel with a roughing gouge (**G**). Then mark a line to indicate the top of the foot (**H**). Don't turn the foot yet; otherwise you will cut away the center needed for turning the ankle.

The next step is to offset the stock in the lathe (**I**). Most of the offset occurs at the foot end of the stock. However, it's important to slightly offset the opposite end as well. Check the offset for accuracy before turning. When offset correctly, the two separate axes will converge at the pommel. Turn on the lathe and watch the spinning "ghost" of the leg to see where the axes converge. If necessary, stop the lathe and reposition the leg at the top slightly. Don't adjust the center location at the foot—otherwise you'll change the diameter of the ankle.

(Text continues on p. 238.)

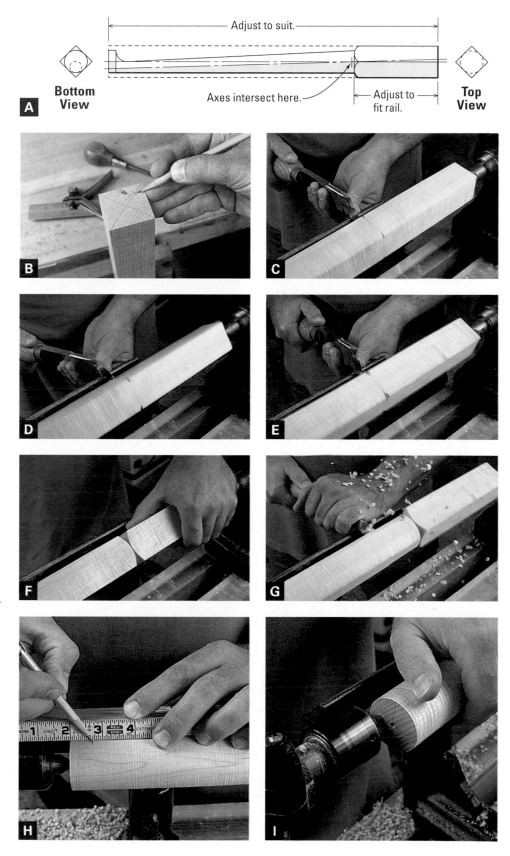

Adjust to suit.

A Bottom View

Axes intersect here.

Adjust to fit rail.

Top View

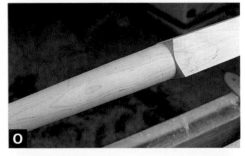

The next step is to turn the ankle. Before you begin, check the location of the tool rest. Position the rest as close as possible for the best support of the tool, but spin the work by hand to ensure that it clears the rest.

During the initial turning of the ankle, the gouge makes contact with the stock only once each revolution. Because of this, take light cuts to avoid having the stock grab the tool. Starting near the top of the foot, cut downward toward the ankle with a spindle gouge (**J**). Start with the gouge on edge, and roll it as you approach the bottom of the foot (**K**). Take several light cuts and then check the ankle size. When the cut encompasses the full perimeter, the ankle is complete.

Next, turn the tapered portion of the leg (**L**). If the leg vibrates, try wrapping one hand around it for support (**M**). The amount of stock to be removed diminishes as the taper ends at the pommel (**N**). Now, sand and smooth the taper before turning the foot (**O**).

To turn the foot, first reposition the turning on the true centers. Then turn the pad to diameter with a parting tool (**P**). Next, round the foot profile with a spindle gouge (**Q**). The technique is the same as that used when turning a bead. Sand the foot lightly to complete the turning (**R**).

! WARNING Supporting slender stock with your hand works extremely well, especially on a taper where it may be difficult to mount a steady rest. But avoid wearing jewelry or long sleeves, and keep your fingers away from the tool rest where they may be pinched.

Turning a Vase Pedestal

The pedestal shown here is typical of the form used on Shaker candle stands (**A**). Most such pedestals consist of a long, slender vase with a small number of beads and coves for simple embellishment.

Begin by mounting the stock and turning a cylinder to the largest diameter on the drawing (**B**). Now, lay out the measurements with a story stick (**C**); then cut each line to diameter with a parting tool (**D**). Next, turn the hub at the base of the turning and check it with a straightedge (**E**). Having the surface of the hub straight and parallel to the axis is important to the subsequent fit and stance of the legs.

(Text continues on p. 240.)

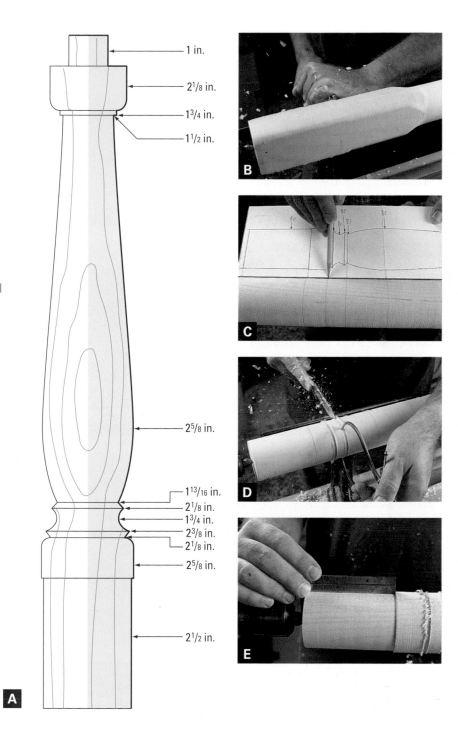

1 in.

2^{1}/$_{8}$ in.

1^{3}/$_{4}$ in.

1^{1}/$_{2}$ in.

2^{5}/$_{8}$ in.

1^{13}/$_{16}$ in.
2^{1}/$_{8}$ in.
1^{3}/$_{4}$ in.
2^{3}/$_{8}$ in.
2^{1}/$_{8}$ in.

2^{5}/$_{8}$ in.

2^{1}/$_{2}$ in.

A

B

C

D

E

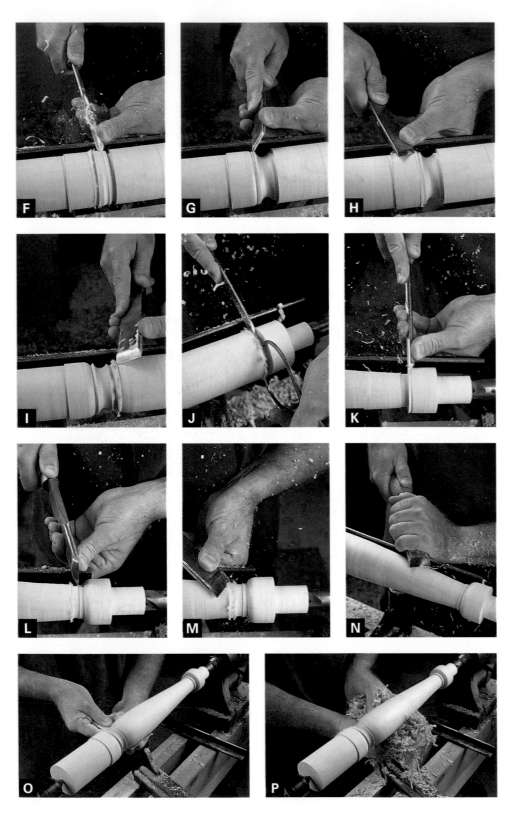

With the preliminary work completed, you're ready to create the shapes that define the turning. Begin by turning the cove at the base with a spindle gouge (**F**). Next, use a skew to turn the V's that flank the cove (**G**). While you're using the skew, turn the small rounded corner at the top of the hub (**H**). Then turn the bottom portion of the vase with a skew (**I**). Now roll the bead at the top of the pedestal. Cut the fillet first with a parting tool to clear the excess stock (**J**). Then shape the bead (**K**).

The last step is to shape the vase. Begin by incising the stock next to the fillet (**L**). Then use a large, sharp skew and remove light, slender shavings (**M**). Watch the top of the turning to view the shape as it's created and gradually remove stock until you're satisfied with the profile (**N**). Then sand the turning lightly and avoid softening the crisp details (**O**). Finally, burnish the turning with a handful of shavings (**P**).

Turning a Rosette

This rosette is a simple faceplate turning (**A**). To avoid scarring the work with a screw it's first glued to a scrap of plywood with heavy paper in the joint. Then the plywood is fastened to the faceplate with screws. After the turning and carving are completed, the glue joint is separated.

Begin by gluing the stock to a scrap of plywood; ¾-in.-thick plywood is sufficient to screw the faceplate. After the glue has dried, bandsaw an oversize circle out of the stock and mount it on the lathe.

Before turning, mark the dimensions of the rosette (**B**). Next, turn the rosette to diameter with a parting tool (**C**). Now you're ready to turn the beveled shape on the face of the rosette.

Position the scraper on the tool rest with the edge slightly lowered. This will cause the burr on the scraper to cut clean shavings from the face of the disk. Now simply pivot the tool side to side to create the desired shape (**D, E**). It's that easy!

Don't sand the turning; otherwise the fine abrasive grit will lodge in the pores of the wood and dull your carving tools. A sharp scraper will leave the surface relatively smooth; and besides, much of the surface is carved away.

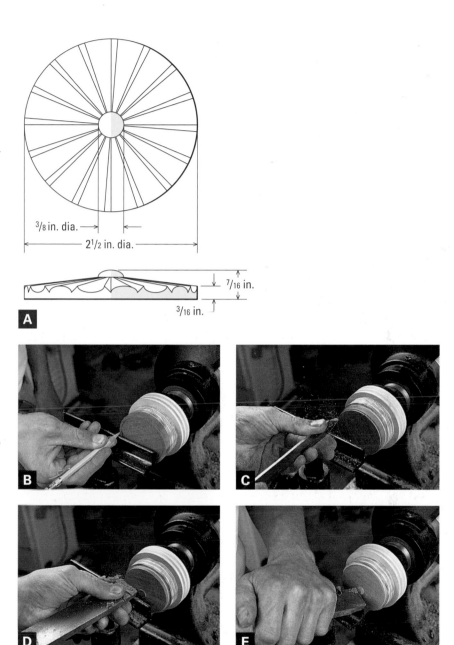

³/₈ in. dia.
2¹/₂ in. dia.
⁷/₁₆ in.
³/₁₆ in.

A
B
C
D
E

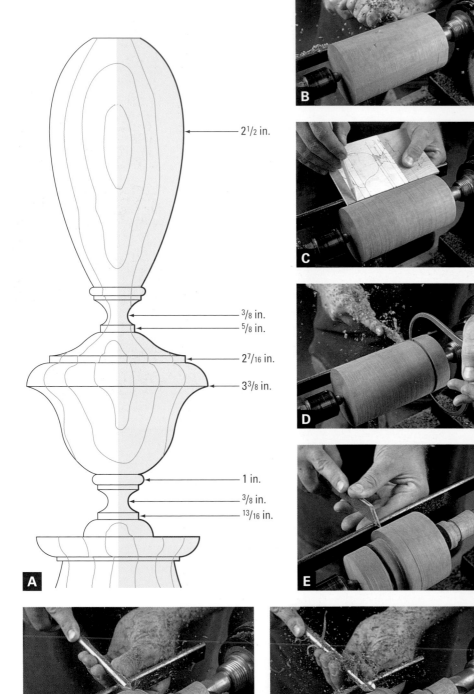

A

- 2½ in.
- ³⁄₈ in.
- ⁵⁄₈ in.
- 2⁷⁄₁₆ in.
- 3³⁄₈ in.
- 1 in.
- ³⁄₈ in.
- ¹³⁄₁₆ in.

B

C

D

E

F

G

Turning a Flame Finial

Finials are typically used as embellishment on casework such as clocks, desks, and chests. After turning the upper portion of the finial, the flame is carved.

➤ See *"Carving"* on p. 252.

This large finial (**A**) is easiest to turn as two pieces. Otherwise the narrow section at the base of the flame is quite fragile and causes considerable vibration and difficulty during turning. After turning and carving the urn and flame, the two are joined together with a round mortise-and-tenon joint.

Begin the urn by turning the blank round with a roughing gouge to the largest diameter (**B**). For accuracy, gauge the diameter with a spring caliper. Next, lay out the linear measurements with a story stick (**C**). With a parting tool, cut each of the diameters as indicated on the story stick (**D**). With the sizing complete, you're ready to turn the various shapes.

First turn the reverse ogee. Scribe a shallow line with the point of a skew at the start of the ogee (**E**). This incision will give you a positive start when shaping the profile. Begin turning by shaping the bottom of the ogee as a bead (**F**). Then turn the top portion as a cove (**G**) and blend the two to create a fluid cyma curve (**H**). Next, turn the bead at the top, which is adjacent to the fillet (**I**). Afterward, remove the extra stock to provide room to maneuver (**J**). Then cut the ogee at the top of the turning (**K**). If necessary, clean up the fillet to make the surface smooth and the corner crisp (**L, M**).

Now shape the bead at the base of the turning (**N**). Then direct your attention to the tiny bead at the base of the ogee. Shaping the bead requires a delicate touch with the heel of a small skew. You can gauge the width of this bead with a small set of dividers. The last profile is the small cove. Use a small spindle gouge and a light touch as you shape each side of the cove toward the bottom (**O**). If necessary, sharpen the fillets that flank the cove with a small skew.

(Text continues on p. 244.)

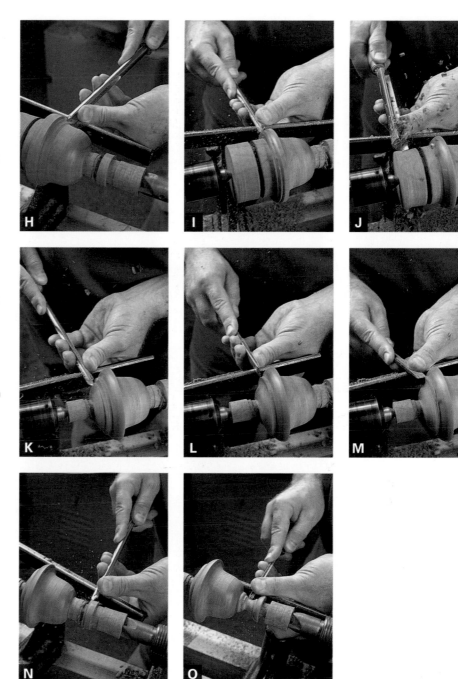

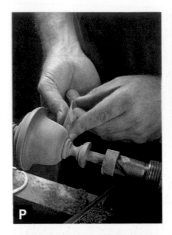

Now lightly sand the turning (**P**) and burnish it with a handful of shavings (**Q**); then cut the top off with a parting tool. As you cut the top off you'll need to support the turning with one hand while controlling the tool with the other (**R**).

The next step is to bore the mortise that accepts the tenon on the flame. First mount a chuck equipped with a ⅜-in. bit into the tailstock. Next, center the bit on the turning and advance it into the spinning work with the handwheel on the tailstock (**S**).

To turn the flame, first remove the corners of the stock with a roughing gouge to the major diameter. Next, lay out the linear measurements with a story stick (**T**) and cut into the final diameters with a parting tool (**U**).

The next step is to turn the top of the flame. Simply approach this convex curve as a bead and roll it over with a spindle gouge (**V**). Next, shape the tapered lower portion of the flame with a skew or large spindle gouge (**W**). Then incise the width of the bead with the point of a skew (**X**); then use the skew to turn the base of the flame further (**Y**). Next, roll the bead to the left and right until it is full and round (**Z**). The last shape is the small cove under the bead (**AA**).

After the turning is complete (**BB**), cut the round tenon for a snug fit within the mortise. To check the tenon for accuracy, make a gauge by boring a hole in a scrap of thin plywood (**CC**).

Don't sand the flame turning. If you do, abrasive grit will lodge in the pores and quickly dull your carving tools later on. Use a parting tool to cut the remaining stock from the end of the tenon and fit it into the mortise in the base (**DD**).

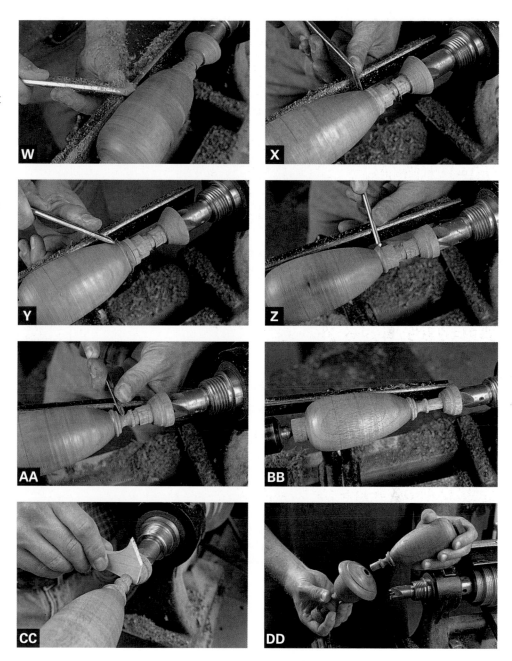

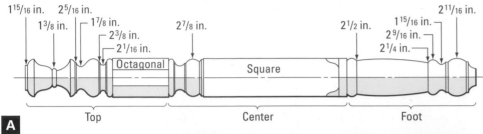

1$^{15}/_{16}$ in. 2$^5/_{16}$ in.
1$^3/_8$ in. 1$^7/_8$ in.
2$^3/_8$ in.
2$^1/_{16}$ in.
2$^7/_8$ in.
2$^1/_2$ in.
1$^{15}/_{16}$ in.
2$^{11}/_{16}$ in.
2$^9/_{16}$ in.
2$^1/_4$ in.

Octagonal
Square

A Top Center Foot

A Complex Turning

The bedpost design in this example is from the nineteenth century. It's a challenging post to turn because it has several shapes that require use of a skew (**A**). To gain the most control of the skew and avoid catching the stock, keep it sharp. In fact, it's a good idea to stop periodically and hone the edges of the skew with a very fine slip-stone. Also, for each cut that requires a skew, use the largest skew in your arsenal. The wide edge and extra mass of a large skew will add to your control of the tool on a large turning such as this bedpost.

In addition to the square section of the post, which accommodates the rail joinery, this post also has a decorative octagonal section between the turnings. The octagon is cut on the table saw before turning.

After cutting the octagon, carefully locate the centers of the stock and mount the stock securely in the lathe. Next, mark the separate sections of turnings, square, and octagon.

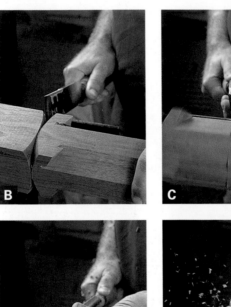

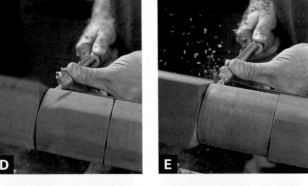

Turn the center of the post first. Beginning with the center turning, score the corners at each end of the turned section to create the pommels. Then turn the square (**B**) and octagon pommels (**C**) with the point of a large skew. Use care at the octagon; it's easy to cut too deep. Next, turn the stock round with a roughing gouge (**D**). Use the corner of the gouge to turn carefully next to the pommels (**E**). Then use a story stick to lay out the linear dimensions (**F**). Before turning the shapes, cut the diameters with a parting tool; lever the tool into the spinning work using the tool rest as a fulcrum (**G**).

Now you're ready to cut the shapes. The V cuts cleanly with a skew. Hold the skew at an angle corresponding to the angle of the V, and lever the tool's edge into the work (**H**). Next, use the skew to cut the half of the bead adjacent to the V (**I**). Before shaping the second half of the bead, remove the excess stock adjacent to the bead to provide room to maneuver the tool (**J**). You can also complete the other half of the bead with a skew or, if you prefer, use a spindle gouge, which is less likely to catch (**K**). Finally, turn the large bead (**L**) and complete this section by turning the cove (**M**). Because of its long length, even a massive turning such as this bedpost may vibrate. This is especially true when turning in the center, far from the support of the headstock and tailstock. If this occurs, it's helpful to add a steady rest (**N**).

To make the top of the post, begin by incising the octagon with a skew and turning the top of the post cylindrical. Lay out the dimensions and cut the diameters with a parting tool.

[**TIP**] **When turning the shapes, start at the base and work upward toward the top of the bedpost.**

(Text continues on p. 248.)

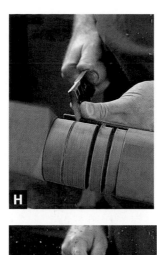

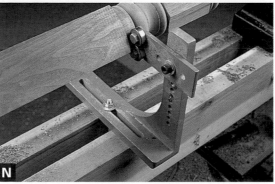

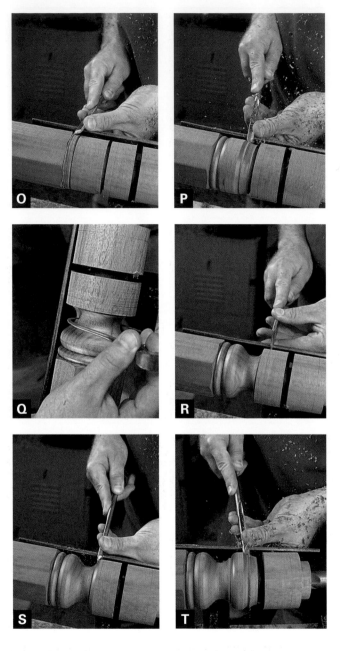

Next, incise the bead; then roll the edges (**O**). After turning the bead, concentrate on the short vase. This elegant shape, or a variation of it, is quite common on the turned elements from the eighteenth and nineteenth centuries. It's really nothing more than a combined bead and cove. Begin by hollowing out the cove to remove some of the excess stock (**P**). Then, starting at the apex of the bead, roll the bead and continue the curve downward to the bottom of the cove. Watch the top of the turning and concentrate on shaping a fluid cyma curve. Afterward, gauge the cove with calipers to keep all four bedposts identical (**Q**). Next, incise the edge of the bead (**R**) and shape it to the fillet (**S**).

The next section of the post is unusual and requires careful sequencing of the cuts. The required shapes consist of a large cove and a reverse ogee separated by a small, round bead. Begin by shaping the cove using a spindle gouge (**T**); then incise next to the bead (**U**) and deepen the cove further (**V**). After removing the extra stock, start at the large diameter (**W**) and shape a fluid ogee, which ends adjacent to the bead (**X**). Take several passes with the gouge until you reach the diameter of the small bead. Next, turn the reverse ogee.

Now turn the small bead. Because it's flanked by a large cove on one side and a reverse ogee on the other, you'll need to shape the bead with a skew. Use a small (½-in.) skew, because it's easy to maneuver in this tight, narrow location. Begin with the skew nearly parallel to the axis (**Y**). Next, use the heel of the skew to roll the bead to the left and the right until you've achieved a full, round profile (**Z**). Then use the spindle gouge to shape the final contour on the cove where it joins the bead (**AA**). Finally, turn the bead at the top of the post (**BB**).

(Text continues on p. 250.)

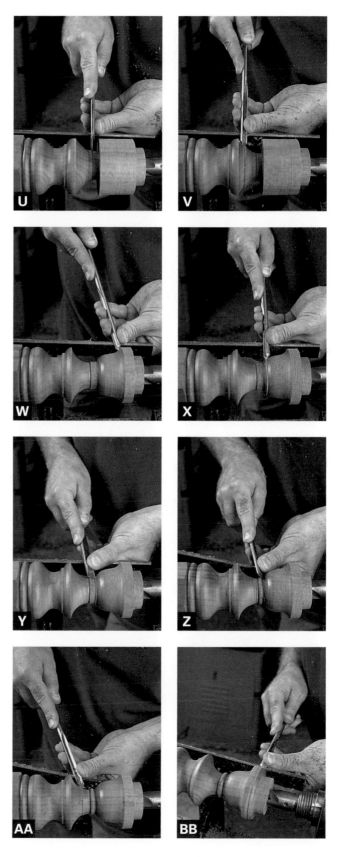

CC

When the top of the bedpost is complete (**CC**), it's time to turn the details at the foot.

The foot is turned by beginning with the pommel, which is turned with a large skew (**DD**) and then removing the corners of the stock with a roughing gouge (**EE**). You can quickly check for roundness by placing the gouge on top of the work as it spins (**FF**).

Next, lay out the linear measurements with a story stick and turn the diameters with a parting tool. The order in which you shape the elements of the foot is not as critical as it is for other turnings. You can begin by turning the ogee (**GG**) and then turning the large bead (**HH**). Next, shape the cove at the base of the post (**II**). Use a spindle gouge and turn the cove to the required diameter.

DD

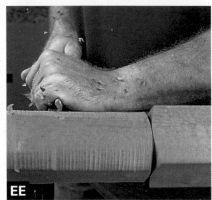

EE

FF

GG

HH

II

Now incise the width of the bead (**JJ**) and roll the bead with a skew (**KK**). Finally, turn the taper with a large skew (**LL**). Use the skew to take delicate shavings and work the taper into the corner.

To complete the bedpost, first smooth the octagonal and square sections with a bench plane to remove the saw marks left from the table saw (**MM**). Next, sand the turning lightly. First curl the sandpaper to fit the contours of the turning, which prevents removing the crisp details of the design (**NN**). Afterward, sand the taper with the grain (**OO**). Finally, burnish the work with handfuls of shavings (**PP**).

JJ

KK

LL

MM

NN

OO

PP

Carving

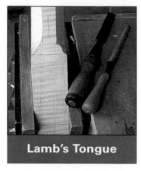

Lamb's Tongue

➤ Carving a Lamb's Tongue (p. 256)

Shell

➤ Carving a Shell (p. 257)

Volute

➤ Carving a Volute (p. 261)

Rosette

➤ Carving a Rosette (p. 262)

Flame Finial

➤ Carving a Flame Finial (p. 263)

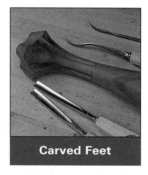

Carved Feet

➤ Carving a Trifid Foot (p. 267)

➤ Carving a Ball-and-Claw Foot (p. 269)

CARVED ELEMENTS HAVE BEEN USED since the beginning of time as furniture embellishment. Despite the seeming complexity of the carvings, anyone with hand-tool skills can learn to carve simple shells, fans, and rosettes—all of which can add interest to a piece of furniture.

Why add carving to your repertoire of woodworking skills? Obviously, if your goal is making reproduction furniture of certain periods, especially the eighteenth century, you know that carvings are an essential element in many pieces. But there's another reason. Carving allows you a way to express yourself as few other aspects of woodworking. Even if you're attempting to reproduce a historical carving, yours will never be exactly the same as the original. A carving is made one patient cut at a time. And each cut is made by the individual maker's hand. Why not yours?

Designing Carvings

Successful carving begins with a good design. You don't have to be an artist to design carvings. Beautifully designed carvings have been used to decorate furniture for centuries. Get some good books that show carved details and study them for inspiration. Remember that it's important to blend the carving with the furniture design on which it will be used. An ornate eighteenth-century motif will look out of place on a modern piece.

Proportion is also essential. If the carved ornament is disproportionate with the scale of the overall piece, it will distract rather than add to the piece.

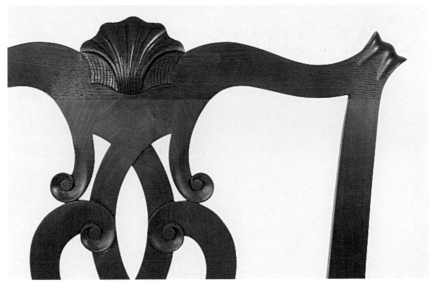

This chair back features a carved shell and carved volutes.

Once you've chosen the motif you want to carve and determined its proportions, the next step is to create a drawing. It's difficult to overemphasize the importance of the drawing; it provides an essential road map for carving. Create the drawing full size and add the details. This means not simply the outlines of the carving and its highest points. Because carving is three-dimensional, you'll need to consider the play of light on the parts. Indicate the highs and lows with shading. Once you're satisfied with your sketch, transfer it to your workpiece to use as a guide when you begin to cut.

Secure the Work

If the carved surface is not secure you run the risk of two things: ruining your carving or, worse, cutting yourself. The way you secure your carving is determined by the work itself. Directly carved work may be secured by clamping the part on which it is carved. However, many carvings are glued or fastened to a backup board. Feet, such as the trifid and ball and claw, can be secured in a pipe clamp. Sometimes, as in the case of the flame finial, it's necessary to devise a special jig to clamp the work without damaging it. Applied carvings, such as the shell, can be glued to a backup board for carving. Make sure to clamp the backup board to a sturdy surface such as a workbench.

Keep the Tools Sharp

Your best work begins with sharp tools. There's nothing more frustrating than having a gouge slip because it's not sharp enough to bite into the wood. Invest in a set of good slipstones for honing the many shapes of carving tools. A small number of

tapered slipstones can service many shapes. Keep a leather strop nearby for quick touch up, and hone the tools often, especially when carving fine details.

Go with the Grain

Always cut with the grain or across it, never against it. When you cut against the grain, you risk splintering and tearing out the wood instead of cutting it. Sometimes it's hard to determine the grain direction, especially in multilayered, complex carvings. Try taking a light cut. If the tool is digging in instead of cutting cleanly, turn around. Cutting across the grain is a good method for initial shaping and quickly removing excess stock. When possible, the final surface should be created by cutting with the grain.

Use the Tools to Your Advantage

Gouges come in various widths and sweeps (curvature) to create the curves. Although many carvings can be accomplished with a dozen or so tools, it's necessary to have a good assortment. Don't cramp your style by attempting to carve complex designs with two or three gouges. On the other hand don't go out a buy a set of tools just to have a selection. Start with a few basic shapes and learn to use each well. You can always add individual carving tools for a given project. Before you begin to cut, study the project to determine which tools you'll need to accomplish the carving.

Use clamps mounted in a vise to hold complex-shaped carvings.

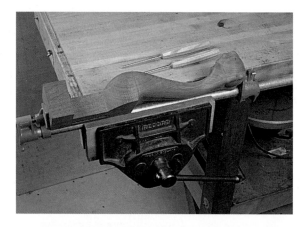

An assortment of slipstones in various shapes is useful for keeping your carving tools sharp.

CUT WITH OR ACROSS THE GRAIN

Grain
direction

Cutting with the grain leaves the surface smooth.

Grain
direction

Cutting against the grain leaves the surface torn and rough.

Furniture carvings can be created with just a small assortment of tools.

➤ THE HAZARDS OF SANDPAPER

When carving, use sandpaper as little as possible. If you sand between stages, the abrasive grit will lodge in the pores of the wood, quickly dulling your tools later in the carving process. Think twice about sanding the finished product. It's easy to quickly and inadvertently sand away the crisp details that you created with the carving tools. If you must sand, be careful and use a fine abrasive (240 grit) a minimal amount.

Keep the Details Crisp

The best carvings show the clean definition achieved by cutting the wood rather than abrading it. A rasp may help remove large amounts of material, but when you come to the final surface, pick up your carving tools. Avoid excessive sanding. Use light sanding to smooth the carving, not shape it. Coarse abrasive and excessive sanding only spoil the crisp edges and details that you worked so hard to create. And don't try to remove all of the tool marks; they're the true sign of hand-carved work.

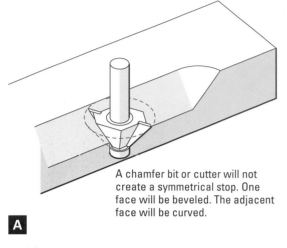

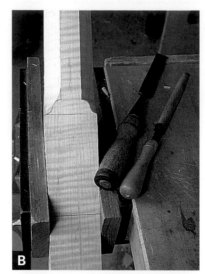

Carving a Lamb's Tongue

When creating an octagonal taper with a router or shaper, the cutter will leave the end asymmetrical (**A**). Because the tool cuts in a spinning motion, one face will be an arc, the other a bevel.

To create visual unity, you'll probably prefer to finish the detail by hand. One option is simply to make both surfaces either curved or beveled. Either choice is attractive, and each creates a more contemporary look.

A chamfer bit or cutter will not create a symmetrical stop. One face will be beveled. The adjacent face will be curved.

Another more traditional approach is to carve an ogee at the end of the taper (**B**). This detail is, obviously, a bit more time consuming. But the unique effect is worth the effort because of the distinction it adds to the piece.

To carve a lamb's tongue on a post, begin by drawing the design along the edge of thin plywood to make a pattern (**C**). After bandsawing and smoothing the curves with a file, trace the pattern onto the post (**D**).

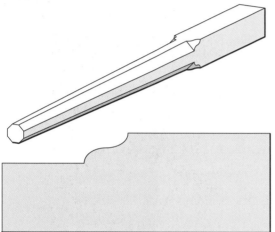

Before carving, make a pattern for tracing the lamb's tongue onto the post.

Start shaping the lamb's tongue by removing the excess stock with a chisel, bevel down, and then bevel up (**E**). The convex segment of the lamb's tongue intersects the post at a crisp inside corner (**F**). If the grain is running in a reverse direction, cut across the grain to prevent tearout (**G**). To finish the detail, smooth it with a file (**H**).

Carving a Shell

The first step is to draw and proportion the shell that you would like to carve. All carvings, including shells, can be varied in size and proportion to fit with the design of the furniture to which they're applied. The shell shown here (**A**) is a five-lobe example that I designed for a Pennsylvania armchair (**B**).

When you're satisfied with the drawing, make several photocopies of it. Next, glue a copy of the drawing to the stock for the shell (**C**). After carving, this shell will be glued to the front seat rail of the chair; it's important that the grain in the shell runs from side to side to coincide with the grain in the seat rail.

The next step is to select the gouges for carving. The sweep, or curvature, of the gouge should closely follow the outline that you sketched earlier. For the lobes on this shell, use a 14mm no. 7 gouge (**D**). For the area around the hinge, use a 25mm no. 5 gouge. Although the narrow gouge could be used for both, the wide gouge is more efficient and easily yields smooth, uninterrupted curves around the hinge.

The next step is to bandsaw the outline of the shell to remove the excess stock. It's important to saw approximately 1⁄16 in. from the line (**E**) because the final outline of the shell is created with carving tools.

Next, begin incising the perimeter of the shell with gouges (**F**). Be aware that the grain at the top center lobe has a tendency to split off. To avoid this problem, position the corner of the gouge beyond the stock when incising the concave areas that flank the center lobe (**G**). This will prevent the center lobe from

(*Text continues on p. 258.*)

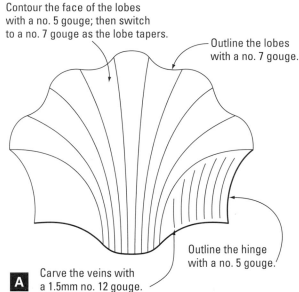

Contour the face of the lobes with a no. 5 gouge; then switch to a no. 7 gouge as the lobe tapers.

Outline the lobes with a no. 7 gouge.

Outline the hinge with a no. 5 gouge.

Carve the veins with a 1.5mm no. 12 gouge.

A

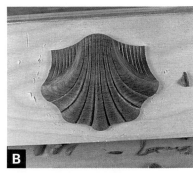

B

C

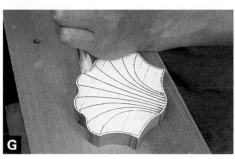

D

E

G

F

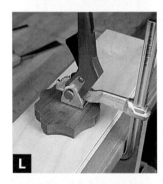

splitting (**H**). The entire outline will later be inverted to become the base of the shell, so it's not necessary to incise beyond ³⁄₁₆ in. deep (**I**).

When incising the outline of the shell, it's important to keep the cuts vertical. To achieve this, you'll need to angle the gouge away from the work for the concave cuts. This will compensate for the bevel on the edge of the tool. Also, concentrate on keeping the cuts interconnected and flowing uninterrupted around the shell.

When you're satisfied with the outline of the shell (**J**), you're ready to move on. The next step is to glue it face down to a short length of inexpensive stock. Afterward, the clamps are positioned on the scrap stock to give you full access to the shell for carving. Don't use a lot of glue; the shell must be pried up after carving. Besides, a small amount of glue is all that's necessary to hold it firmly (**K**). Clamp the shell to the board and allow the glue to thoroughly dry (**L**).

The next stage of the process is to contour the face of the shell. But first mark the high point of the contour. The point is centered left to right and slightly below center from top to bottom (**M**). Now select a 25mm no. 2 gouge for shaping the contour. The goal of this process is to produce sweeping curves from left to right and top to bottom (**N**). After paring the face of the shell, the only original surface remaining will be the high point that you marked earlier. Watch the grain direction and cut with the grain or across; you'll want to produce clean shavings, not splinters. Carve the surface down to the ³⁄₁₆-in. perimeter that you incised in the first step.

After carving the contour, you can remove any remaining facets with a smooth file (**O**). Avoid using sandpaper though—the abrasive grit will settle in the pores of the wood and quickly dull your tools later in the process.

The next step is to draw the lobes as a guide for carving. Using your original drawing as a guide, locate the points of the lobes with dividers (**P**). Then divide the base of the shell into equal spaces (**Q**). Next, connect the points by sketching smooth, flowing curves (**R**). To achieve visual balance in the carving, spacing is important. Examine the curves closely and, if necessary, redraw any that need improvement.

Now you're ready for the next stage of carving. The first step in this stage is to incise the hinge area. Hold a 25mm no. 5 gouge nearly vertical to create a steep wall (**S**) and carve this area gradually until you reach the layout line (**T**). Finish the inside corner with a 6mm no. 7 gouge. Take long, sweeping cuts to blend the wall with the hinge area (**U**).

The next step is to outline the curves on the face of the shell with a V gouge. For greatest control, take several light cuts and progressively deepen the V. Also, as you carve the V's, watch the spacing and flow of the curves; if necessary, make corrections as you deepen the cuts (**V**).

Next, carve the convex lobes. Start by contouring the ends of the lobes with a 12mm no. 5 gouge (**W**). As the lobe tapers back, the curvature becomes tighter, so you'll need to switch to a 10mm no. 7 gouge; then a 6mm no. 7 gouge. Gradually, as the lobe reaches the apex of the shell, switch to a 4mm no. 7 gouge. Finally, the curve on the face of the lobe diminishes.

(Text continues on p. 260.)

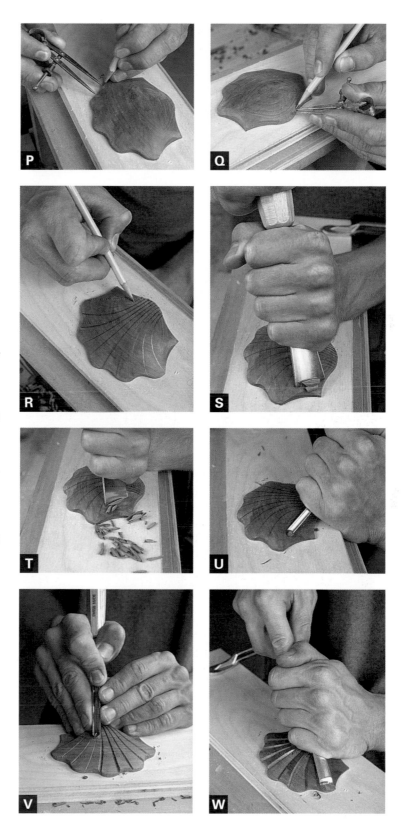

X

Y

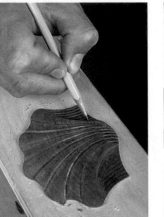

Z

AA

BB

Next, carve the concave rays between the lobes (**X**). Beginning with a 10mm no. 7 gouge, work back gradually; then switch to a 6mm no. 7 and, finally, a 4mm no. 7 gouge. As you carve the rays and lobes, use the gouges to blend the curves (**Y**). During the entire process, stop periodically and hone the gouges; sharpness is the key to accuracy and control.

The final step is to carve the veins into the surface of the hinge. These tiny U-shaped grooves break up the flat surface to add more interesting detail.

Starting at the outer edge, sketch each vein with a pencil (**Z**). Keep the spacing uniform and follow the curve at the edge of the hinge. Next, use a 1.5mm no. 11 gouge to carve the veins (**AA**).

The completed carving should be crisp, flowing, and full of visual details (**BB**). You can smooth the carving lightly with 240-grit sandpaper to blend the facets. But be careful not to spoil the sharp details.

Carving a Volute

A volute is a spiral (**A**). It's used as embellishment on the ends of arms and the back of chairs—among other areas—to create the appearance of a scroll. As the volute unwinds, the curve naturally broadens. This beautiful effect is easily created by using a series of gouges.

Begin by drawing the volute. Although it would be easy if the volute fit within a mathematical framework, it seldom does. Instead, the volute must fit within the area of the workpiece on which it will be carved. For this example, I've connected volutes of two sizes to create a sample carving block.

Whether found on furniture or architecture, volutes are typically carved in pairs. As you might imagine, drawing accurate pairs of volutes can be time consuming. So for ease of duplication, I prefer to make a plastic template. First draw the design on paper; then position a transparent plastic sheet over the drawing and incise the outline to form a template (**B**). Next, trace the template onto the stock (**C**) and begin carving (**D**).

Beginning with the center hub, incise the outline of the volute with the same series of gouges that you used to incise the template (**E**). As the curves become broader, use wider gouges with less sweep (**F**). A typical series of cuts would begin with a no. 7, progress to a no. 5, and end with a no. 3 gouge. Incise the volute to a depth of ⅛ in.

Next, make a second series of cuts that intersect the first cut at a shallow angle (**G**). Each time you make a cut, a small chip of wood should be released. This will have the effect of creating a raised spiral ridge (**H**). After this procedure is followed around the entire spiral, a series of facets will remain. Use a no. 3 gouge and take sweeping cuts around the volute to remove the facets (**I**).

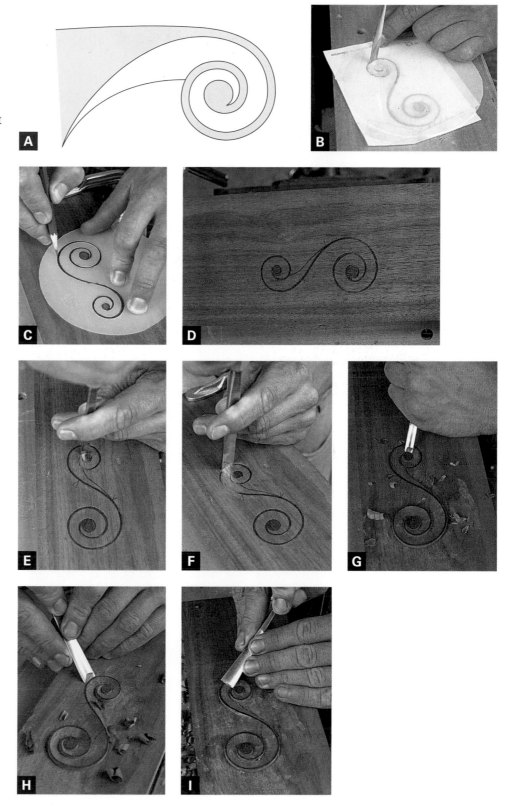

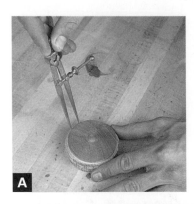

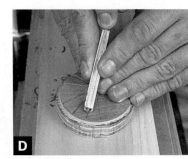

Carving a Rosette

A rosette is an ornamental terminus for a goose-neck molding on a pediment. The variations of this design are numerous. The example shown here is a small, simple design that is used on a clock.

Begin by turning the rosette on a lathe to the required shape. Next, step off an even number of spaces around the perimeter (**A**) with dividers and make a mark at each division (**B**). With the aid of a center head, draw a line from each division mark to the hub (**C**).

► See *"Turning"* on p. 224.

With the layout complete, you can turn your attention to carving. Begin by outlining each layout line with a V gouge (**D**). The depth of each V should be greatest at the perimeter and gradually diminish in size as it reaches the hub (**E**).

Next, use a ¼-in. no. 5 gouge to carve the rays and lobes (**F**). Begin carving at the perimeter and work back toward the hub. As you approach the hub, it will be necessary to carve from the opposite direction (**G**).

You can sand the carving lightly with 240-grit sandpaper to blend the facets from the gouge. Use care to avoid sanding away the crisp ridges on the V's.

Carving a Flame Finial

Finials are a turned and carved decoration most commonly used on the pediments of casework. The stylized flame finial shown here was a popular ornament on Pennsylvania furniture during the eighteenth century. Although smaller finials are crafted from one piece of stock, large finials, such as this example, are easier to turn in two pieces.

▶ See *"Turning a Flame Finial"* on p. 242.

After turning, the next step is to sketch the design. Good layout allows you to work through the design details and proportions before you begin to carve (**A**). It also provides an essential road map to give you direction as you're working. Although seemingly complex, the layout for this finial is relatively easy. It involves repeatedly sketching cyma curves around the perimeter of the turning. Spacing the curves is important, too, but it's easily accomplished with dividers.

Begin layout by sketching the first curve. It becomes a ridge that rises from the base and spirals one-quarter of the circle as it reaches the top. Use the lathe dividing wheel to mark the beginning (**B**) and end (**C**) of the curve. It's most important that the curve is pleasing to the eye, especially because all the other ridges will be modeled according to the first one. You'll find it easier to sketch the curve if you pivot the pencil from your wrist or the knuckle of your little finger (**D**). Just below the midpoint of the turning is the transition point at which the curve changes direction. You'll probably find it easier to invert the turning to draw the upper portion of the curve.

(Text continues on p. 264.)

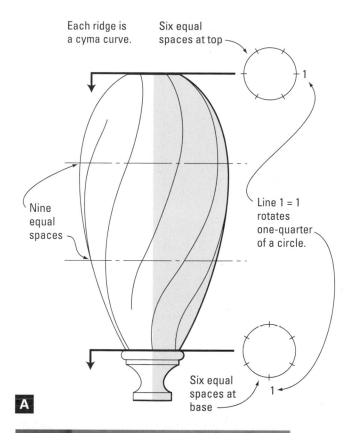

Each ridge is a cyma curve.

Six equal spaces at top

Line 1 = 1 rotates one-quarter of a circle.

Nine equal spaces

Six equal spaces at base

A

B

C

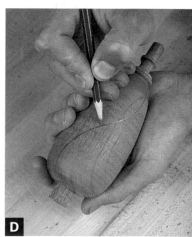

D

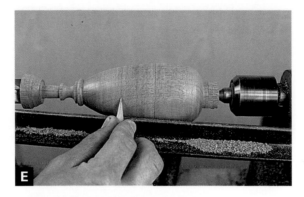

E

F

G

When you're satisfied with the first curve, the next step is to repeat the sketch around the perimeter of the turning. To make the spacing somewhat even, it's necessary to divide the turning into equal segments. But first, notice the pattern in the carving. The first ridge starts at the base and rises to the top. The second ridge begins at the base but it ends before reaching the top. The third ridge starts at the top and ends before reaching the base. Then the pattern repeats itself two more times for a total of nine ridges.

Before sketching the rest of the ridges, put the turning back in the lathe and divide the height of the flame into thirds. Next, draw a line around the circumference at the point of each division (**E**). Now you're ready to divide the turning into separate ridges—nine around the middle and six at the top and the base.

Beginning with the base, position one leg of the dividers on the first ridge and step off six spaces (**F**). Next, step off six spaces at the top starting with the ridge you've already drawn. Finally, divide the turning into nine equal spaces at each of the circumference lines, starting each time at the ridge (**G**). Now you're ready to sketch in the rest of the ridges.

Starting to the right of the first ridge, sketch in the adjacent ridge. It begins at the base and flows upward, ending before it reaches the top. Use the division points as guidelines, but remember that they are there as only a guide; it's not necessary to follow them precisely. It's most important to draw a smooth, flowing curve (**H**). The third ridge starts at the top and ends before reaching the base. Then the pattern is repeated twice more. When the layout is complete, you should have a total of nine ridges, yet only six points at the top and six at the base. Before carving, study your layout and check for spacing and irregularities in the curves. The layout doesn't require mechanical precision, but instead the lines should flow gracefully as they spiral toward the top. Spacing should look somewhat uniform; but it doesn't need to be, or should be, perfect. The idea is to create a carving that is well proportioned with pleasing curves.

Before you begin carving, take a few minutes to build the jig shown in photo I (at right) and photo M (on p. 266). It's essentially a V block with a build-in clamp for securing the work.

A sectional view of the carving reveals a series of ridges and V's. Each of the cyma curves that you sketched earlier becomes a ridge; the area between a pair of ridges forms a V. Carving is now simply a matter of removing the area between the ridges. And if you keep a couple of key points in mind as you carve, success is virtually ensured. First, keep the tools sharp; sharpness is critical to control of the tool. I keep a leather strop on my bench and hone the edges periodically. Second, always carve with or across the grain, not against it. If you attempt to work against the grain the wood will splinter and tear.

Begin by carving across the grain toward the bottom of each V (**I**). Alternate the cuts from either side of the V so that the wood between the cuts is removed cleanly (**J**). Work from the center of the V outward toward the ridges and from the base of the flame to the tip. Cutting across the grain will leave the surface slightly coarse; but the technique removes wood quickly, and you'll smooth and refine the surface later by carving with the grain.

As you carve, remember that each layout line becomes a ridge. Also, it's important that the line formed by the bottom of the V is smooth and flows in harmony with the ridges. As you deepen each V adjust the line, if necessary, to cause it to flow smoothly.

(Text continues on p. 266.)

Avoid carving too deep at first. Once you've carved the entire circumference of the turning you'll have a better feel for the look you're trying to achieve, and you can deepen the cuts, if necessary. Unlike many other areas of woodworking, carving isn't a process of cutting to a set of precise dimensions. Instead, it's a matter of creating balanced, flowing lines. Often the lines can't be gauged or measured but are judged by a critical eye. In this case, each line should spiral along its length in a flowing, uninterrupted cyma curve.

As the carving progresses, the only remaining portion of the original turned surface will be each ridge. Be careful to leave the ridges intact—otherwise the flow of the curve that you created on the lathe will be spoiled. The only exception is the ridges that stop before reaching the base or the tip. Carve these ridges downward at the ends so that their lines flow smoothly toward the center of the work (**K**).

When you're satisfied with the initial carving, the next step is to refine the work. With a 12mm no. 2 gouge, smooth the surface of each curve by cutting with the grain (**L**). Sever the end grain at the base between the flames with the point of a skew.

The final touch is to carve the tiny veins on the surfaces of the flame. These shallow grooves break up the otherwise flat surface to give the carving greater detail and visual interest. But first, sketch them in with a pencil.

Depending on the width of the surface, each has three to five veins. Using your middle finger as a gauge, draw each vein beginning with the ones at the outer edges (**M**). The veins toward the inside may not flow entirely from top to bottom but may fade out as the surface narrows. Then with a steady hand, carve each vein with a 1.5mm no. 11 gouge (**N**).

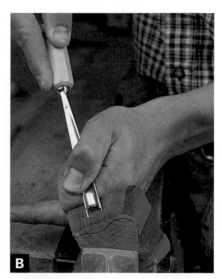

Carving a Trifid Foot

The trifid, or three-toe, foot is a simple, yet elegant carved foot commonly found on period furniture from Pennsylvania and the Delaware Valley. Begin by bandsawing and shaping the leg.

➤ See *"Complex Shapes"* on p. 78.

Next, make a pattern for the bottom of the foot to serve as a guide while carving. Heavy cardboard works well for the pattern; simply incise the outline with gouges that match the curves. Then position the pattern on the base of the foot and trace the outline (**A**).

To begin carving, secure the leg in a pipe clamp that is mounted in a vise. For consistency, use the same gouges for carving that you used for incising the pattern. Carve the profile of the toes starting at the top of the foot and working toward the base (**B**). As you carve, maintain the angles on the edge of the foot that were established earlier when bandsawing. Invert the gouge to carve the convex area (**C, D**). Afterward, smooth and blend the areas with a small file (**E**).

The next step is to carve the stocking. Begin with layout. First locate the height of the stocking with a compass (**F**). Used as a divider, the compass ensures that this measurement is consistent from one foot to the next.

(Text continues on p. 268.)

A

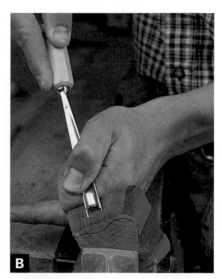

C

B

D

E

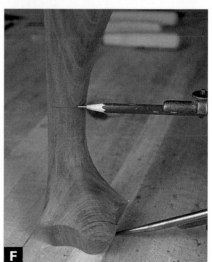

F

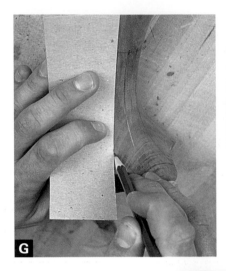

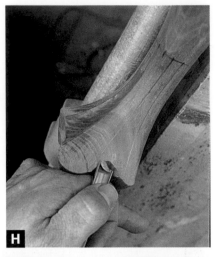

To outline the concave areas that form the stocking, flex a straightedge into the curve and trace it from toe to ankle (**G**). Now you're ready for the next stage of carving.

Beginning at the toe, scoop out the wood between the toes with a no. 5 gouge (**H**). As you near the sharp curve at the ankle the gouge will have a natural tendency to dig in (**I**). At this point, switch to a narrow spoon gouge and carve a little farther until the gouge begins to lift the grain. This is a sign that the grain direction has changed; switch directions and carve from the top of the stocking to this transition point and blend the two areas where they meet (**J**).

After carving the stockings, they will be somewhat faceted from the gouges. But sanding this area will spoil the sharp ridges that outline the stocking. Instead, use a small bent file, otherwise known as a riffler (**K**). This unique tool will allow you to preserve the details as you smooth the surface.

Carving a Ball-and-Claw Foot

The ball-and-claw foot is a classic design that has become an icon of Colonial American furniture. It first emerged during the mid-eighteenth century and quickly became popular as a sign of wealth and status. The foot shown here (**A**) is modeled after Pennsylvania examples. It features tense, powerful claws gripping a slightly flattened ball.

Begin by bandsawing the leg and shaping the contours with a rasp and file. Shaping the leg first ensures that the contours of the leg and foot blend together.

▶ See *"Complex Shapes"* on p. 78.

The next step is layout. Start by marking diagonal lines from the corners to locate the center of the foot. Next, draw a circle with a compass to serve as a guide when carving the ball (**B**). To outline the claws, draw a pair of parallel lines ⁵⁄₁₆ in. from each centerline (**C**). Then extend each line upward to the ankle where the lines converge (**D**). Finally, mark the apex of the ball on each of the four faces.

With the layout complete (**E**), you're ready to begin carving. The first stage involves roughing in the contours of the ball. As the ball is shaped, the corners of the block are further exposed to be later formed into the claws. My favorite tool for carving the ball is an old ⅜-in. socket firmer chisel about 12 in. long. The extended length of this tool provides leverage beyond that of a standard carving gouge for quick removal of stock. Later on, after the contours of the ball are roughed in, further refine the ball and remove the facets with a no. 2 gouge.

(Text continues on p. 270.)

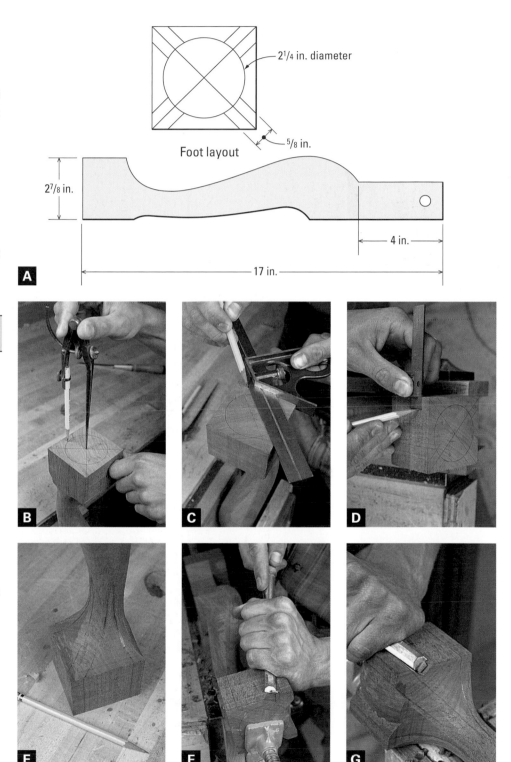

Foot layout

2¼ in. diameter

⅝ in.

2⅞ in.

4 in.

17 in.

A

B

C

D

E

F

G

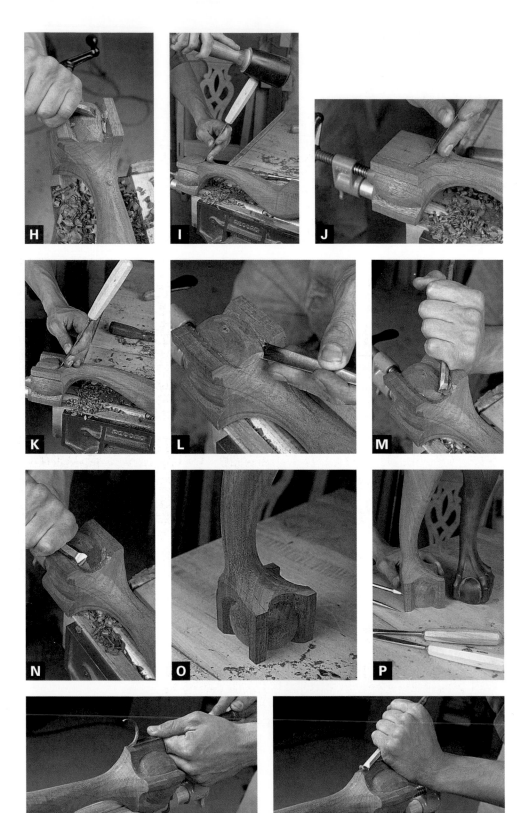

Start by carving from the apex of the ball downward toward the circle on the underside of the foot (**F**). Next, change directions and carve from the apex toward the top (**G**). Compare the curvature of the top to that at the bottom and keep the two alike. Add additional curvature to the ball by carving across the grain from the apex toward the claw (**H**).

At the back of the foot, begin carving by outlining the curve at the top of the ball with a no. 5 gouge. Aim the gouge toward the ball's center and tap it lightly with a mallet (**I**). Repeat the process several times to form an arc. Afterward, carve the face of the ball downward toward the arc (**J**). Just as on the front, carve from the apex of the ball in every direction, and the ball will begin to emerge from the block (**K**).

Next, turn your attention to the front. Outline the web with a no. 5 gouge (**L**). Then use the corner of the chisel to remove stock at this area (**M**). With each cut, the ball will further emerge and the web will begin to form. Also, the height of the ball will shorten as it becomes round and fully formed (**N**).

Once all four surfaces of the ball begin to take shape, it becomes easier to visualize the overall form. Work your way around the ball once more and refine it so that the four surfaces become one sphere (**O**). Then you're ready to begin roughing in the claws.

Before carving the claws, use compass as a divider to lay out the location of each knuckle (**P**). Next, begin roughing in the claws by first removing the corners (**Q**). Then carve the excess block away so that the claws bend at the knuckles to follow the contours of the ball (**R**). Afterward, check the knuckle spacing with dividers and make any necessary adjustments (**S**).

With the claws contoured to follow the ball, the next step is to refine them (**T**). Using a no. 5 gouge, cut across the grain to hollow the space between each knuckle. This gives the knuckles a more lifelike appearance.

Next, use a no. 7 gouge to remove the excess stock at the web (**U**). This area is tough end grain, so keep the gouge sharp for greatest control. As you pare the excess stock away at the web, the claws at the top of the ball will begin to form (**V**). Continue to contour the web until you reach the ankle. At this point, the web diminishes as it blends into the curves of the ankle.

At the sides the claws flex inward at the second knuckle to follow the contour of the ball. Remove stock at the back of the claw to yield this effect (**W**).

Now carve the talons. Curve the surfaces of the talon with a no. 5 gouge and taper them to a blunt point (**X**). Next, add further refinement to the web by hollowing the corners adjacent to each claw with a no. 7 gouge (**Y**). Finally, smooth all of the surfaces. A no. 2 gouge will remove facets on the surface of the ball left by the chisel (**Z**). Afterward, smooth the ball with a file (**AA**). A short bent file known as a riffler is useful for smoothing the concave surface of the web (**BB**). Final smoothing is done with 240-grit sandpaper.

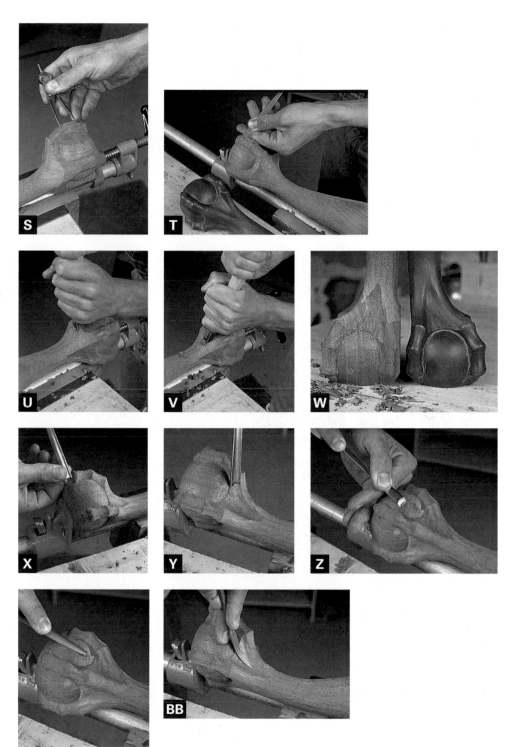

Bending

Steam Bending

➤ Steam Bending
(p. 276)

➤ Bending
Lightweight Stock
(p. 277)

➤ Bending Heavy
Stock (p. 277)

Bent Lamination

➤ Bent Lamination
with a Two-Part
Form (p. 278)

➤ Bent Lamination
with a Vacuum
Press (p. 279)

➤ Bent Lamination
with Flexible
Plywood (p. 280)

Kerf Bending

➤ Kerf Bending
(p. 281)

BENDING IS ONE OF THOSE TECHNIQUES that seems exotic but is really simple. Bending opens many design options to the furniture maker, especially when a large curve is required and cutting the wood will leave too much short grain, weakening the curved part. This section covers bending techniques that can be applied to making furniture.

The furniture maker has basically two practical strategies for bending wood: laminating and plasticizing the wood using heat. The most practical heat method is steam bending, which is widely used in boatbuilding and other types of woodworking where long bends are required. A specialized method called hot pipe bending also employs heat but is limited to bending very thin parts for musical instruments. Another specialized method, called kerf bending, has some utility in making mirror and picture frames as well as in high-end architectural woodwork, where it is sometimes used to bend trim. Because the kerfs are visible in the finished work, this method has obvious shortcomings.

Bent Lamination

Laminated bends are made by bending thin layers of glue-coated stock around a curved form. The layers are held in position with clamps or a vacuum press until the glue sets.

This rocking chair contains several steam-bent parts.

The steam-bent rungs of this chair back provide not only an interesting design element but also comfort.

In bent lamination, the layers, or *laminae,* are visible once the edges are jointed flush.

Afterward, the excess glue is scraped and removed and the edges are trimmed flush.

Bent laminations are very strong, and the method is extremely versatile. Narrow laminations are used for legs of tables and chairs; wide laminations are used as the sides for casework. Laminations are also widely used in architectural woodwork from beams in churches to stringers in circular and geometric stairs.

The only downside to bent laminations are the layers themselves, which can sometimes be distracting. To overcome this problem, it's helpful to mill the lamina from one piece of stock, keeping track of the layers and gluing them together in the original order. Still, some of the stock is lost in the kerf during milling, so the grain in the lamination won't be a perfect match. Tapers should be cut before laminating. Otherwise the taper will cut through the individual layers, adding to the visual distraction.

Steam Bending

Steam bending is a process of softening the wood fibers with a combination of heat and moisture until they are sufficiently pliable to bend. The hot, wet sticks are pulled from a steam box and quickly wrapped around a

curved form. Depending on the size of the stock, pressure for the bend can be supplied by physical force or supplemented with clamps. After the bend, the part is held in position until it has cooled and sufficiently dried to maintain its new shape.

Wood that is steam bent undergoes extreme stress. The cell structure on the convex side of the bend is stretched while that on the concave side is simultaneously compressed. The fact that wood can be bent this way is remarkable in itself.

Although steam-bent parts lack the strength of bent laminations, they are still remarkably strong. And they are obviously much stronger than bandsawn stock, which has been weakened by short grain.

Also, steam-bent stock lacks the distracting layer lines present in laminations. Instead, the grain runs naturally and continually throughout the curves of the stock. Steam-bent stock can be carved, too; whereas the glue and constant grain changes of bent laminations make carving impractical.

Bending Forms

Bending forms should be stiff and strong to resist the forces of bending. Most important, the curve of the form should be smooth and consistent. The best material for forms is plywood. Solid wood tends to have weak areas resulting from short grain; particle board is harsh and quickly dulls tools. However, plywood doesn't have these shortcomings. It's easily worked and doesn't move drastically with humidity changes.

To create a thick form, stack the plywood in layers and use glue and screws to fasten the layers together. Make certain that the screws are located away from the path of the eventual curve.

Steam-bending forms require a system for holding the parts in position until they have cooled and dried sufficiently to retain their new shape. This can be a simple arrangement of pins and wedges or a more complex system of steel rods and bolts driven with a pneumatic (impact) wrench. The decision often rests on the thickness of the stock and the severity of the bend.

Bent lamination forms to be used in a vacuum bag require softening along edges and corners. Otherwise, a sharp corner may puncture the bag.

Kerf Bending

Kerf bending involves sawing a series of deep kerfs across the grain to weaken the stock. After kerfing, the thin upper layer that remains is flexible, which allows a bend to be made. After bending, the stock is quite fragile and must be supported.

As you have probably concluded, kerf bending is impractical. The kerfs are quite distracting; and, even if hidden, they telegraph through the face of the bend. Also, the stock is severely weakened and has absolutely no structural integrity unless the kerfs are later filled with wood or epoxy. Even so, this simply adds to the visual distraction.

If you need to create a wide curved panel without the time and fuss of laminations and the inherent weaknesses of kerf bending, a better solution is bendable plywood.

▶ See *"Tools for Bending"* on p. 26.

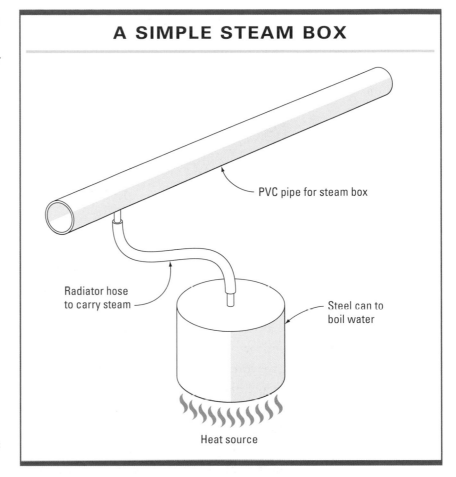

A SIMPLE STEAM BOX

PVC pipe for steam box

Radiator hose to carry steam

Steel can to boil water

Heat source

A form for bent lamination needs to be strong. Plywood provides more strength than solid wood when making forms.

Steam Bending

To find the examples given in this section on steam bending, I visited Brian Boggs at his shop in Berea, Kentucky. A long-time chairmaker, Brian has taken steam bending to a science. He uses a pressure cooker to supply the steam, and his steam box is stainless steel. The steel steam box is fitted within a well-insulated wooden box. His forms are sophisticated, too. Built up of layers of plywood, the forms have stainless-steel straps that fit over the outer portion of the bend to prevent failure from the extreme stresses that occur when bending.

Begin by selecting the stock and working it to rough size. It's important that the grain is straight and runs in the same direction as the stock. The stock can be rived (split) or sawn, as long as the grain direction is parallel with the edge and face (**A**). After rough sizing, mill the stock to final size.

The next step is to steam the parts. A rule of thumb is to steam the parts 1 hour for each inch of thickness. Make certain that the steam box is hot before loading the parts (**B**).

Take advantage of the time while the parts are steaming to make preparations for bending. Make certain your form is in place and that you have the necessary clamps at hand. Once the parts are sufficiently pliable to bend around the form, remove them from the steam box.

> ⚠ **WARNING Wooden parts coming out of a steam box are very hot! Protect your hands with a pair of leather work gloves.**

Bending Lightweight Stock

Brian prebends the thin slats for his ladder-back chairs over a plywood form. The tight, smooth curve of the prebending form ensures a smooth, fair curve on the stock. A stainless-steel strap supports the bend on the convex face to prevent failure from tension stress. Brian centers the stock over the form (**A**) and applies force from his upper body (**B**). After holding the stock over the form for approximately 1 minute, he places it into a drying rack (**C**). Brian's rack is designed to hold a complete set of slats for one chair (**D**).

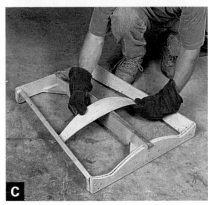

Bending Heavy Stock

Bending thick, heavy stock requires greater force in addition to the longer steaming time (**A**). To bend the rear legs for his chairs, Brian slides the end of the leg into a jig (**B**). He makes the first bend by tightening a U-bolt with an impact wrench (**C**). Then he bends the top of the leg using the leverage from a length of steel bar (**D**). The top of the leg is held in position for drying with a steel pin and a wedge. While holding the leg against the form, Brian slips the pin through a pair of holes and slides the wedge under the pin. A couple of taps with a mallet tightens the wedge firmly against the leg (**E**).

Bent Lamination with a Two-Part Form

Begin by resawing stock for the laminae (**A**). Experiment to find a thickness that easily conforms to the curve of the plywood form. After sawing, scrape or sand the surfaces to smooth away the saw marks. If you choose to sand, it's a good idea to remove the fine dust from the pores of the wood with compressed air.

The next step is to prepare for glue-up. If you use plastic resin glue, you'll need measuring cups and a stirring stick. A small foam paint roller works well for glue application. I like to have the clamps I'll be using ready and waiting (**B**). These simple steps make the gluing process proceed smoothly and without fuss.

After spreading the glue, stack the layers and position them within the form. Then apply clamp pressure from the center and work toward each end (**C**).

A

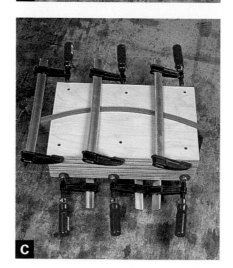

B

C

> ⚠ **WARNING** Plastic resin and other two-part adhesives cure by chemical reaction as the two parts are mixed. During this process, toxic chemical fumes are often released. Protect yourself by having good cross-ventilation.

Bent Lamination with a Vacuum Press

A vacuum press makes the lamination process easy and convenient. There's no need for clamps or a mating half to the form. Just make certain that you've softened all the sharp edges on both the work and the form; otherwise you risk puncturing the vacuum bag.

Begin by resawing stock for the laminae. Experiment to find a thickness that flexes easily to the curves of the form. After resawing, smooth away the bandsaw marks by scraping or sanding. If you sand the laminae use a burst of compressed air to blow the dust from the pores.

The next step is to prepare for glue-up (**A**). If you're using plastic resin glue you'll need measuring cups and a stirring stick. A small foam paint roller makes it easy to spread an even application of glue.

After mixing thoroughly (**B**), spread an even coat of glue on each layer (**C**). Then stack the layers and bind them with masking tape to keep them aligned (**D**). Position the stack over the form, seal the bag, and turn on the pump (**E**).

Afterward, scrape away the excess glue and use a jointer or handplane to true the edges.

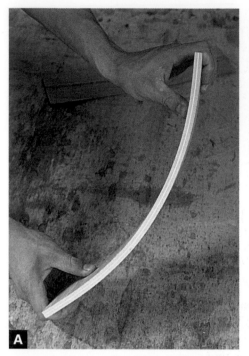

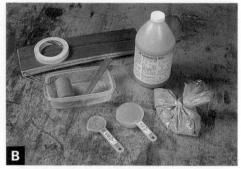

Bent Lamination with Flexible Plywood

Flexible plywood provides a fast, convenient method for creating curved panels, especially wide panels for casework (**A**). By gluing two layers of plywood and covering them with veneer, a strong, attractive panel is easily produced.

Begin by cutting two sections of flexible plywood to the required dimension. Next, cut two sheets of veneer to cover the outer layers of the plywood. To keep the moisture in equilibrium in the finished panel, it's always best to veneer both faces.

The next step is to prepare for glue-up (**B**). Gather the tools for measuring and mixing the adhesive. After mixing the two parts of the adhesive (**C**), spread an even coat on each member of the lamination (**D**). Stack the layers and bind them with tape to keep them in alignment (**E**). Now position the stack over the form; seal the bag and turn on the pump (**F**).

Afterward, scrape away the dried adhesive from the edges of the panel.

Kerf Bending

Kerf bending is an old method that has been mostly replaced by newer materials and methods that yield better results, such as flexible plywood. However, kerf bending may still be occasionally useful when strength and appearance are not extremely important.

To kerf bend a plywood panel, rip a series of tightly spaced kerfs on the table saw (**A**). The depth of the kerf should be nearly the entire stock thickness; spacing the kerfs closely will help avoid a faceted appearance on the face of the curved panel. Now simply flex the stock to the desired curve.

There are several methods for reinforcing the weakened panel. One way is to attach it to curved ribs (**B**). Other methods include filling the kerfs with wood strips or epoxy.

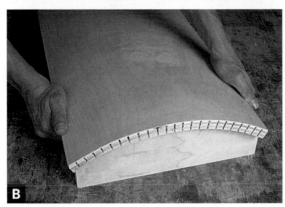

Appendix: Shaping Small Parts

Template Shaping Small Parts

These tiny blocks (**A**) measure approximately ½ in. by ⅞ in. by 3 in. and require a thumbnail profile along one edge and both ends. Because the entire edge is shaped, the setup requires either a fence or a template to limit the cutting depth. After shaping, the blocks will be mitered on the ends and carefully fit into a notch in the seat board.

Begin by milling the stock to the final thickness, but leave it oversize in width and length. Next, glue the stock to a piece of ¼-in.-thick plywood with heavy paper in the joint (**B**). The plywood will provide a template for the router bearing during the shaping process. After shaping, the paper will allow you to separate the plywood easily from the workpiece.

After the glue has dried, joint the edge of the assembly with a bench plane or jointer (**C**). Then rip the stock to final width and crosscut it to final length (**D**).

The next step is to shape the profile. There are a couple of keys to shaping such a small piece: add mass to reduce chatter and provide a method to grasp the part safely for shaping. One solution is to grip the part within the jaws of a wooden handscrew. The heavy wooden clamp effectively adds mass and positions hands a safe distance from the spinning router bit. Also, if the bit inadvertently contacts the jaws of the clamp, there's no dangerous metal-to-metal contact.

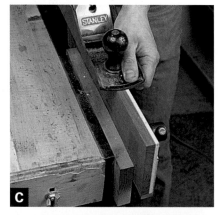

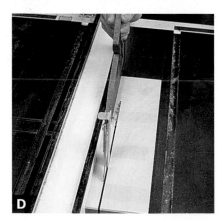

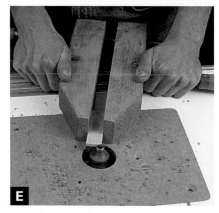

Begin by shaping the ends. Tighten the jaws of the clamp firmly around the stock. Next, feed the work into the spinning bit until the plywood template makes contact with the bearing (**E**). After shaping the ends, shape the edge using the same procedure (**F**).

After the shaping is complete, gently pry the plywood from the workpiece by placing a chisel into the seam along the back edge (**G**).

F

G

Shaping Small Parts with a Jig

Here's a second method for shaping the entire edge of a small part. It involves a simple jig that is designed for shaping multiple parts, such as the candle-slide front for a desk. The jig is a piece of ¾-in.-thick plywood with pockets for holding the work (**A**). A rabbet holds the first workpiece as it is shaped along the edge; the second workpiece is held within a groove as the end is shaped. The fit of the workpiece within the groove must be snug; a finger hole in the top of the jig provides a way to push the work free from the jig after shaping.

Furthermore, the rabbet that secures the work for shaping the edge must be slightly less in dimension than the stock being shaped. This way pressure is applied to the stock as it is shaped, preventing chatter.

After making the jig, mill the stock for a snug fit within the groove of the jig (**B**). Next, shape the ends of the stock. Then place it into the rabbet for shaping an edge. If you are shaping multiple pieces, you can also position a second piece into the jig for end shaping (**C**). As you use the jig, maintain firm pressure against the router table and fence (**D**).

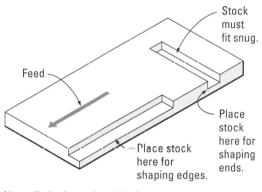

Stock must fit snug.

Feed

Place stock here for shaping edges.

Place stock here for shaping ends.

Note: Jig is pictured upside down.

A

B

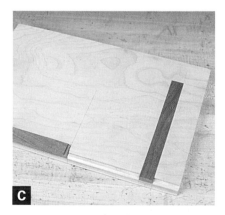

C

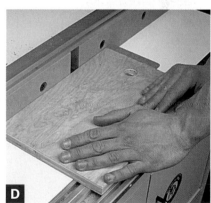

D

A

Shaping Small Parts with a Miter Gauge

This small-part setup uses a miter gauge in conjunction with a backup board, which is fastened to the head of the gauge with a pair of screws. The router table fence is first secured parallel to the miter gauge slot; the small workpiece is then clamped to the backup board for safe shaping.

The parts being shaped in this example are the base and capital for a pilaster, or flat column. After shaping, the complete pilaster is added to the interior of a desk.

➤ See *"Fluted Quarter Columns"* on p. 217.

The first stage in this process involves shaping a strip of molding.

After shaping, short blocks of the molding are cut from the strip for use as the base and capital (**A**). But first, the ends of the blocks must be shaped, or "returned," with the same profiles used on the face of the block. This setup allows safe and accurate shaping of very small workpieces such as these.

For each profile, orient the stock on the edge (**B**) or end (**C**) and firmly clamp it to the backup board on the miter gauge.

B

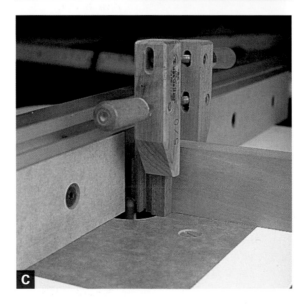

C

List of Suppliers

I wish to gratefully acknowledge the following companies for providing tools for photos in this book.

Stationary Power Tools

Laguna Tools
800-234-1976
lagunatools.com

Jet Equipment & Tools
800-274-6848
jettools.com

Portable Power Tools

Porter-Cable
800-487-8665
porter-cable.com

Makita
800-4MAKITA
makitatools.com

Bosch
877-267-2499
boschtools.com

DeWalt
800-4DEWALT
dewalt.com

Shaper Cutters

Freeborn Tool Company, Inc.
800-523-8988
freeborntool.com

Table Saw Molding Head

LRH Enterprises, Inc.
800-423-2544
lrhent.com

Hand Tools

Lie-Nielson Tool Works, Inc.
800-327-2520
lie-nielson.com

Woodcraft
800-542-9115
woodcraft.com

Stubai
800-326-5316
diefenbacher.com

Bandsaw Blades

American Saw & Manufacturing Co.
800-628-3030
lenoxsaw.com

Clamps

American Clamping Corporation
800-828-1004
americanclamping.com

Router Tables

Bench-Dog
800-786-8902
benchdog.com

Router Bits

CMT USA, Inc.
888-268-2487
cmtusa.com

Vacuum Presses

Vacuum Pressing Systems
207-725-0935
vacupress.com

Antique Tools

The Tool Merchant
740-373-9973

Further Reading

CABINET MAKING

Joyce, Ernest. *Encyclopedia of Furniture Making.* Sterling Publishing.

Krenov, James. *The Fine Art of Cabinetmaking.* Sterling Publishing.

Tolpin, Jim. *Building Traditional Kitchen Cabinets.* The Taunton Press.

WOOD TECHNOLOGY

Forest Products Laboratory. *Wood Handbook: Wood as an Engineering Material.* Forest Products Laboratory.

Hoadley, R. Bruce. *Identifying Wood.* The Taunton Press.

———*Understanding Wood.* The Taunton Press.

DESIGN

Aronson, Joseph. *The Encyclopedia of Furniture.* Crown Publishing.

Editors of *Fine Woodworking. Practical Design.* The Taunton Press.

Graves, Garth. *The Woodworker's Guide to Furniture Design.* Popular Woodworking Books.

Morley, John. *The History of Furniture: Twenty-Five Centuries of Style and Design in the Western Tradition.* Bulfinch Press.

Pye, David. *The Nature and Aesthetics.* Cambium Press.

TOOLS AND MACHINERY

Bird, Lonnie. *The Bandsaw Book.* The Taunton Press.

———*The Shaper Book.* The Taunton Press.

Duginske, Mark. *Mastering Woodworking Machines.* The Taunton Press.

Hack, Garrett. *Classic Hand Tools.* The Taunton Press.

———*The Handplane Book.* The Taunton Press.

Lee, Leonard. *The Complete Guide to Sharpening.* The Taunton Press.

Mehler, Kelly. *The Table Saw Book.* The Taunton Press.

Nagyszalanczy, Sandor. *The Art of Fine Tools.* The Taunton Press.

———*Woodshop Jigs and Fixtures.* The Taunton Press.

WOODSHOPS

Landis, Scott. *The Workbench Book.* The Taunton Press.

———*The Workshop Book.* The Taunton Press.

Nagyszalanczy, Sandor. *Setting Up Shop.* The Taunton Press.

———*Woodshop Dust Control.* The Taunton Press.

Tolpin, Jim. *The Toolbox Book.* The Taunton Press.

WOOD FINISHING

Charron, Andy. *Water-Based Finishes.* The Taunton Press.

Dresdner, Michael. *The New Wood Finishing Book.* The Taunton Press.

Jewitt, Jeff. *Great Wood Finishes.* The Taunton Press.

———*Hand-Applied Finishes.* The Taunton Press.

Index

S